The Partisans Handbook

By Sorcha Faal (English Translation)

Essential Survival Guide For Resisting
Foreign Military Occupation, Escape And
Evasion Techniques, Surviving
Interrogation, Facing Execution,
Wilderness Survival

© 2006
ISBN: 0-9753228-5-0

Long Trail Acres Publishing
22 Mattheson Road
Antrim, New Hampshire 03440

Introduction

"The art of war is simple enough. Find out where your enemy is. Get at him as soon as you can. Strike him as hard as you can, and keep moving."
Ulysses S. Grant

The purpose of this book is to provide you with the basic information you will need to know in order to survive an invasion and occupation of your country.

In what you are facing you are far from alone, and in fact by becoming a Partisan you join countless millions of your fellow human beings who down through the ages have likewise become fighters for their freedoms.

There is one 'common thread' that connects all Partisans, the knowledge and certitude that their lives are forfeit to a cause much larger than themselves.

And by you becoming a Partisan, your life will also cease to be your own and become instead a part of the much larger struggle in which you have become engaged in.

It is therefore your most essential task to reconcile within yourself what your life truly means, what are your goals, and do you have it within yourself to face both the barbarities of war and your own death, for above all else, the life of a Partisan is a life of death.

1

The many shapes and forms of death surround every waking and sleeping moment of the Partisan, from not just having to take a human life, but to also contemplating your own.

Therefore, the first skill that must be mastered by the Partisan is the ability to form a state of mind that puts aside all thoughts of the individual and at the same time bring forward all thoughts of accomplishing whatever task there may be for you to accomplish your ultimate goal, the retention of your freedom.

The very moment that a Partisan puts their life before either their mission, or of others, is the worst death one can imagine, for the life of a coward and traitor benefits no one, least of all the Partisan.

If the battle to which, as a Partisan, you are committing yourself to is not one sufficient enough for you to give your life for than this is not a journey you should even begin to make.

For walking with the Partisan every moment of their fighting lives are Fear, Terror, Suspicion, Deception and Death.

Of all of these the Partisan becomes both familiar with and an expert on, or if failing to becomes their victim.

There are also no 'half measures' in being a Partisan, you either are committed to your actions with everything you possess, or you are dead.

In becoming a Partisan your decision should be based upon either to be a slave to those who have invaded your country, or those powers within your country that have usurped your freedoms and liberties, or to die as a free human being, and on your own terms.

With this knowledge in mind it is equally important for you to realize that neither this book, nor any book, can equip you with the full knowledge of all that you will need to know in order for you to survive as a Partisan.

What this book does contain however is the nexus of the knowledge that you will need in order to build and refine those skills needed to ensure your best chances of survival.

The presentations of facts presented in this book are based not only on the perspective of the Partisan, but also upon those that are the Partisans enemies. This is done for the reason of your not only having to know what your own skills and knowledge will have to be in order for you to survive, but also those skills and knowledge that your enemies will bring to bear against you.

The knowledge presented in this book will be worthless to you without your commitment to both familiarize and practice the skill sets as outlined. It is one thing to read about these things, but it is an entirely different thing to put them into practice.

Without your training, and putting into practice the basic guidelines we are presenting here, you can fully expect that you will not survive, that is the most basic truth about this book you need to fully understand and accept.

And what you are holding in your hands, right at this exact moment, is the beginning step towards your becoming a survivor, and not a war statistic.

Sorcha Faal
December, 2005
St. Petersburg, Russia

Chapter 1 Belarus, A Case History Of Partisans

"Liberty means responsibility. That is why most men dread it."
George Bernard Shaw

The dictionary definition of Partisan is: A member of an organized body of fighters who attack or harass an enemy, especially within occupied territory.

Other names given to Partisans include: Rebel, Guerilla and Terrorist.

Partisan resistance is the term used to describe quasi-military individual and small-group covert activities. The practice is common in countries occupied by a victorious military force.

Unable to retaliate with equal force, patriotic citizens often band together secretly to fight their oppressor. On the other hand, collaborators are citizens of an occupied country who, out of fear or resentment of their own government, cooperate with the enemy.

Partisan resistance movements have existed long before recorded history. In the Western tradition, Greek historian Herodotus referred to partisans in his histories.

The difference in the names that a Partisan could be labeled depends upon whom they are fighting. In the first case example for you here are the events that occurred in the European country of Belarus during World War II.

World War II wrought death and destruction across Europe. But few countries suffered as much as Belarus. Up to one-third of the country's population perished during a three-year Nazi occupation.

Virtually all of its Jewish population was exterminated. In the process, the war and decades of Soviet rule dashed the tiny country's hopes for fully independent nationhood.

In but one example, Freida Raisin was 8 years old when invading Nazis hanged her mother in central Minsk, leaving her body dangling in public for more than a week.

As the Germans went about exterminating most of the Belarusian capital's Jews, Raisin also saw a group of teenage girls dragged from their homes, beaten, and shot in the head. The sight of their blood spilling into the street is one of many memories that sill haunt Raisin, now 70.

"There were several things that we were always thinking about -- to be always on the alert, because death was around the corner at any moment, and hunger, constant hunger, where to find food," she says.

It was not just that Belarus, then divided between Poland and the Soviet Union, was thoroughly devastated. As the famous Belarusian writer Vasil Bykau noted shortly before his death in 2003, the conflict also killed the hopes of Belarusians for independent nationhood. Belarus was swiftly reincorporated into the Soviet Union, then led by brutal dictator Josef Stalin.

"I think that the victory was really taken away both from the Belarusians and the Russians, and not only from them. This happened right after the victory. It was taken by the great idol of these nations -- the 'Great Stalin,'" Bykau said.

Proportionately, Belarus lost three times more of its population -- up to 30 percent, or 3 million people -- than any other nation. About a third constituted nearly its entire Jewish population.

Canadian Franklin J. Swartz directs the Eastern European Jewish Revival Project, a Minsk-based organization engaged in recovering the region's Jewish heritage. He says the country's wartime devastation is still felt today.

"Up to 30 percent of the population were killed on the territory of Belarus, and 80 percent of the towns and villages were destroyed," Swartz says. "Of the towns and villages destroyed, approximately 470 of them were intentionally destroyed by Germans, along with their inhabitants.

The inhabitants were usually locked into a barn and the barn was burnt down along with the rest of the village. About 180 of those villages never came back to life. So that gives you an idea of the extent of the destruction and the nature of the very personal experience that many people had here in relation to the war. It's very much still a living memory."

And a complicated memory.

Belarus arguably was invaded by two different powers. After Germany invaded Poland on 1 September 1939, the Soviet Union grabbed the Belarusian half of Poland.

Under the secret Molotov-Ribbentrop Pact, Stalin and Adolf Hitler had agreed to divide Poland, which included parts of present-day Ukraine and Belarus.

Among the war's first victims in Belarus were 20,000 Polish officers and professionals taken prisoner by the Soviets in western Belarus in 1940. They were slaughtered, many in the Katyn Forest near Smolensk, in a crime blamed on the Nazis -- and not acknowledged by Moscow until 1990.

Hitler turned on Stalin on 22 June 1941. In Operation Barbarossa, Germany attacked the Soviet Union -- and within a week, Minsk had fallen to the Nazis.

As the front moved eastward into Russia, the largely anti-Nazi population of Belarus waged an all-out partisan war on the occupiers. Belarus counted nearly 400,000 partisan fighters, including Jews who had dodged the Holocaust by fleeing to the forests to join the resistance.

The partisan history is the stuff of legend. Bykau's whole opus is centered on the experience. It often involved entire families, as a woman from the town of Rudabielsk recently recalled in an interview with RFE/RL's Belarusian Service: "We took families, children, and ran to the forest. We were in a guerrilla unit.

There was nothing to eat, we were hungry. We would go to the village and ask for some food. When we managed to get some potatoes, we would grate them, put them in water together with skins, boil, and eat once a day. We wanted to eat, so we sang to reduce the hunger."

The partisans were hailed as vital to the Allied victory. But they also helped facilitate the country's destruction. The Nazis flattened towns and villages and liquidated inhabitants in retaliation for attacks by partisans and collaboration with them.

In more detail:

Throughout history, Belarus has been the scene of many destructive wars. But the most extensive and particularly ferocious was the Soviet-German War

1941-1945, an important part of the Second World War 1939-1945.

On 22 June 1941, the army troops of Germany and her allies began an attack on the Soviet Union. This war was supposed to be over in a matter of months, but it lasted for four years until 9 May 1945, and grew into the largest and most costly conflict in all history. In Belarus, combat operations were conducted from 22 June 1941 until 28 July 1944.

The Nazi leadership purposed to liquidate the Soviet Union, to germanise the European territory of the USSR, and either to exterminate or to oust the major part of its population. According to Barbarossa Plan, Germany and its allies put 190 divisions and four air fleets against the Soviet Union.

In all, they had 5.5 million manpower, 47,200 guns and mortars, about 4,300 tanks and assault guns, and 4,980 battle aircraft. The Soviet side had 170 divisions and two brigades (2,9 million manpower), 37,500 guns and mortars, 1,800 heavy and medium tanks including 1,475 tanks of new design, 1,540 battle planes of new design, and a considerable number of light tanks and battle planes of older designs.

Belarus had to withstand one of the strongest groups of Hitler's armies - Army Group Centre, which designed the main thrust in the direction of Moscow.

The German forces had 50 divisions and two motorized brigades supported by 1,680 battle planes; within the first week of the war their strength increased to 60 divisions. Against the Army Group Centre were 44 Soviet divisions of the Western Special Military District located mainly in Belarus. German divisions ranged from 14,000 to 16,000 men, while the Soviet divisions had 8,000 men or less each.

The enemy had considerable dominance in artillery and manpower, and also prevailed in tanks, aircraft, and artillery of new type. In several directions of the offensive, German troops prevailed five times in manpower, almost three times in tanks, and more than three times in artillery.

At the moment of Nazi invasion, many troops of the Western Special Military District were not prepared for battle - some troops stayed in summer camps, some part were in the state of reformation and rearmament, weapons and equipment were as a rule conserved in parks.

On the first day of the war the Soviet troops located in Belarus lost 738 planes, 47% their strength, and for long remained without air protection. The command of the Western Front, created from the Western Special Military District, lost control over the army and could not stop the enemy in the frontier area.

In the early days of the war Belarus was the location of ferocious battles. No frontier post surrendered to the enemy nor left their position without senior commands. The garrison of Brest Fortress fought over one month, the city of Mogilev defended over three weeks, and the Soviet soldiers gave severe resistance to the enemy near the Belarusian capital Minsk.

In the summer of 1941 the Soviet troops fought not only defensive battles but also conducted offensive operations. Several towns were liberated from the Nazis as a result of the Lepel and Rogachev-Zhlobin counterattacks.

The towns of Rogachev and Zhlobin were recaptured by the Germans only one month later. On 14 July 1941, the famous Katyusha rockets were first used against the Germans near the town of Orsha. The severe resistance of the Soviet troops in Belarus ruined the German plans for Blitzkrieg and the quick breakthrough to Moscow.

But despite markedly heroic resistance, they could not stop the enemy; and by the beginning of September the whole territory of Belarus had been occupied by Nazi forces.

The Nazi Plan Ost for Eastern Europe designed to germanise and use as forced labourers 25% of the Belarusians, and either to annihilate or to oust the remaining 75%.

On the occupied territory the Nazis established so-called New Order, a system of political, military, and economic measures aimed at liquidating the Soviet state and society. About eight million residents and 900,000 Soviet prisoners of war found themselves under the German occupation which lasted almost three years.

The German military and civilian administration exercised control over the occupied territory of Belarus. With the assistance of the SS, SD, and SA troops, and the criminal and security police, they established the Occupation regime in Belarus. A certain role in the German occupation policy was played by the local collaborators.

To superimpose the New Order in Belarus, Nazis used the policy of genocide, terror and mass executions. Concentration camps, prisons and ghettos existed in almost each administrative district.

In all, there were 260 death camps and over 170 ghettos in Belarus. 206,500 people were killed in the village of Trostenets near Minsk, where one of the biggest death camps was located. And unlike Auschwitz, Majdanek, and Treblinka, Trostenets held mainly local people as prisoners.

In Belarus, the occupiers carried out over 140 punitive expeditions aimed to suppress the Partisan movement, to enslave the civilians, and to plunder their property.

During the punitive expeditions, they destroyed about 5,500 localities. The village of Khatyn, burned to the ground with its residents, became a terrifying symbol of Nazi crime on Belarusian soil. Khatyn's fate was shared by other 630 rural localities, 186 of which have never been restored.

Belarus became the location of an extensive struggle against the Occupation. The Partisan movement involved 374,000 people and played a major role in undermining the Nazi regime.

Representatives from various Soviet nationalities and anti-Nazi fighters from Poland, Czechoslovakia, Yugoslavia, Germany, France, and other countries participated in this movement. In addition, approximately 400,000 local people supported the partisans in the struggle against Nazis.

In Belarus there were over 20 partisan-controlled zones which the Germans failed to occupy. By the end of 1943, partisans controlled over 108,000 sq km (59%) of the occupied territory, of which 37,000 sq km were completely cleared from the enemy.

Partisans inflicted heavy damage to the enemy - they detonated over 11,000 trains, raided 948 headquarters and garrisons, blew up 1,355 tanks and armored personnel vehicles, annihilated hundreds of thousands of Hitlerites.

Particularly extensive was the Partisan operation "Rail War" aimed at a large-scale destruction of the enemy's railway communications in the occupied territory. In the first half of 1944, Hitler's command used 18 divisions against Belarusian partisans.

An estimated 70,000 people fought in the urban underground organizations. They collected intelligence on the enemy, disseminated anti-Nazi propaganda, and carried out acts of sabotage. Minsk underground fighters with the assistance of partisans killed the General Commissar of Belarus, gauleiter Wilhelm Kube.

In September 1943, the Soviet troops liberated south-eastern Belarus. The extensive Belarusian Offensive Bagration (June 23 - August 29, 1944) completed the liberation of Belarus from the Nazi troops.

During the operation the Red Army forces together with the partisans defeated the German Army Group Centre. The Soviets had 2.4 million men, over 36,000 guns and mortars, 5,200 tanks and self-propelled artillery guns, and about 5,300 aircraft.

Against the Soviets were 1.2 million German soldiers and officers, 9,500 guns and mortars, 900 tanks and assault guns, and 1,350 aircraft. The Red Army completely annihilated 17 Hitler's divisions and three brigades, and 50 German divisions lost over half their strength.

A group of armies of 105,000 men was annihilated in the Minsk pocket, and a group of 40,000 men was destroyed in the Bobruisk pocket. Operation Bagration resulted in the liberation of Belarus, the major part of Lithuania, part of Latvia, and eastern parts of Poland. The Red Army came to the border of East Prussia.

In the estimation of many historians and scholars, Belarus suffered more in this war than any other European country. Belarus lost more than half of its national wealth. 209 towns and 9,200 villages were destroyed or burned down. But the most painful and huge loss was the loss of life.

In the current estimation, between 2.5 to 3 million people - almost every third resident of Belarus - perished during WWII.

Over 1.3 million Belarusian's and natives of Belarus fought at WWII fronts; 446 of them were honored with the highest Soviet award of the Hero of the Soviet Union, four people received this title twice. About 400,000 Belarusian soldiers were awarded the combat orders and medals.

Over 400 Belarusian's were promoted to generals and admirals during the war. Many Belarusian's participated in the European Resistance. Belarusian partisan M. Egorov was one of the first who raised the Victory Banner over the defeated Reichstag in Berlin.

In recognition of their heroic struggle against the invaders, 12 cities of the former Soviet Union, Belarusian capital Minsk among them, received the honorary title of the Hero-City.

The Brest fortress received the title of the hero-fortress. In Belarus there are about 6,000 monuments, obelisks, memorial complexes, and Mounds of Glory which testify the people's heroism and bravery in WWII.

The example of Belarus for any Partisan is important because it shows that determined and sustained efforts against a more powerful and organized military force is indeed possible.

But also to be remembered, this type of resistance is not only devastating to the invading armies, but also to the Partisans themselves.

Keep this lesson in mind.

Chapter 2 Resistance during World War II

Resistance during World War II occurred in every occupied country by a variety of means, ranging from non-cooperation, disinformation and propaganda to hiding crashed pilots and even to outright warfare and the recapturing of towns. Resistance movements are sometimes also referred to as "the underground".

Among the most notable resistance movements were the French Maquis, the Polish Home Army, and the Yugoslav Partisans. The Communist resistance was among the fiercest since they were already organized and militant even before the war and their ideology was in many respects directly opposite of that of the Nazis.

Many countries had resistance movements dedicated to fighting the Axis invaders, and Germany itself also had an anti-Nazi movement. Although mainland Britain did not suffer invasion in World War II, the British made preparations for a British resistance movement, called the Auxiliary Units, in the event of a German invasion.

Various organizations were also formed to establish foreign resistance cells or support existing resistance movements, like the British SOE and the American OSS (the forerunner of the CIA).

After the first shock after the Blitzkrieg, people slowly started to get organized, both locally and on a larger scale, especially when Jews and other groups were starting to be deported and used for the Arbeitseinsatz (working for the Germans).

Organization was dangerous; so much of the resistance efforts of the Partisans were done by individuals. The possibilities depended much on the terrain; where there were large tracts of uninhabited land, especially hills and forests, resistance could more easily get organized undetected.

This favored in particular the Partisans in Eastern Europe. But also in the much more densely populated Netherlands, the Biesbosch wilderness could be used to go into hiding.

There were many different types of groups, ranging in activity from humanitarian aid to armed resistance, and sometimes cooperating to a varying degree.

Resistance usually arose spontaneously, but was encouraged and helped mainly from London, the "capital of the European resistance" (also helping communist resistance groups) and Moscow (helping the partisans).

Various forms of resistance were:

Sabotage - the Arbeitseinsatz ("Work Contribution") forced locals to work for the Germans, but work was often done slowly or bad

Strikes and manifestations

Based on existing organizations, such as the churches, students, communists and doctors (professional resistance)

Armed raids on distribution offices to get food coupons or various documents such as Ausweise or on birth registry offices to get rid of information about Jews

Temporary liberation of areas, such as in Yugoslavia and Northern Italy, occasionally in cooperation with the Allied forces

Uprisings such as in Warsaw in 1943 and 1944

Continuing battle and guerrilla warfare, such as the partisans in the USSR and Yugoslavia and the Maquis in France

Espionage, including sending reports of military importance (e.g. troop movements, weather reports etc.)

Illegal press to counter the Nazi propaganda

Political resistance to prepare for the reorganization after the war. For instance, the Dutch resistance took part in forming the new government in the Netherlands after the war.

Helping people to go into hiding (e.g. to escape the Arbeitseinsatz or deportation) - this was one of the main activities in the Netherlands, due to the large number of Jews and the high level of administration, which made it easy for the Germans to identify Jews

Forgery of documents

Some Famous Resistance Operations:

An intricate series of resistance operations were launched in France prior to, and during, Operation Overlord.

On June 5 1944, the BBC broadcasted a group of unusual sentences, which the Germans knew were code words—possibly for the invasion of Normandy. The BBC would regularly transmit hundreds of personal messages, of which only a few were really significant.

A few days before D-Day, the commanding officers of the Resistance heard the first line of Verlaine's poem , Chanson d'Automne, "Les sanglots longs des violons de l'automne" (Long sobs of autumn violins) which meant that the "day" was imminent.

When the second line "Blessent mon coeur d'une langueur monotone" (wound my heart with a montonous langour) was heard, the Resistance knew that the invasion would take place within the next 48 hours. They then knew it was time to go about their respective pre-assigned missions.

All over France resistance groups had been coordinated, and various groups throughout the country increased their sabotage. Communications were cut, trains derailed, roads, water towers and ammunition depots destroyed and German garrisons were attacked.

Some relayed info about German defensive positions on the beaches of Normandy to American and British commanders by radio, just prior to 6 June.

Victory did not come easily; in June and July, in the Vercors plateau a newly reinforced Maquis group fought 15,000 Waffen SS soldiers under General Karl Pflaum and was defeated with 600 casualties. On June 10 Major Otto Dickmann's troops wiped out the village of Oradour-sur-Glane in retaliation. The resistance also assisted later Allied invasions in south of France in Operations Dragoon and Anvil.

Other famous resistance operations were the Norwegian sabotages of the German nuclear program (see Norwegian heavy water sabotage).

Operation Anthropoid was another famous resistance move during the WWII. It was the assassination of Reinhard Heydrich in 1941, the Nazi "Protector of Protectorate of Bohemia and Moravia" and the chief of Nazi's final solution, by the Czech resistance in Prague.

Over fifteen thousand Czechs were killed in reprisals, with the most infamous incidents being the complete destruction of the towns of Lidice and Ležáky.

Some of the Partisan Resistance movements during World War II were:

Auxiliary Units (planned British resistance movement against German invaders)

Albanian resistance movement

Burmese resistance movement (AFPFL - Anti-Fascist People's Freedom League)

Lithuanian, Latvian and Estonian anti-Soviet resistance movements ("Forest Brothers")

Czech Resistance movement

Danish resistance movement

Dutch resistance movement

Valkenburg resistance

French resistance movement, including the Maquis

German resistance movements:
The White Rose
The Red Orchestra
The Edelweiss Pirates

Greek resistance movement

Hong Kong resistance movements

Gangjiu dadui (Hong Kong-Kowloon big army)

Dongjiang Guerillas (East River Guerillas, Southern China and Hong Kong organization)

Italian resistance movement

Norwegian resistance movement

Philippine resistance movement

Polish resistance movements:
Armia Krajowa (the Home Army)
Armia Ludowa (the Peoples' Army)
Gwardia Ludowa (the Peoples' Guard)

Zydowska Organizacja Bojowa (ZOB, the Jewish Fighting Organisation)

Zydowski Zwiazek Walki (ZZW, the Jewish Fighting Union)

Romanian resistance movement

Slovak resistance movement
Soviet resistance movement

Ukrainian Insurgent Army

Yugoslav resistance movements:
People's Liberation Army – the partisans (Communist)
Yugoslav Royal Army in the Fatherland aka Chetniks (Royalist)

Chapter 3 Partisan Organizations of World War II

Germany: White Rose

The White Rose Society (German, Die Weiße Rose) was a World War II-era resistance movement in Germany calling for nonviolent resistance against the Nazi regime.

The group of Munich students released six leaflets from June 1942 to February 1943. A seventh leaflet, which may have been prepared, was never released because the group was captured by the Gestapo.

The White Rose consisted of five students, all in their early twenties, at Munich University. Hans Scholl and his sister Sophie led the rest of the group, including Christoph Probst, Alexander Schmorell and Willi Graf. They were joined by a professor, Kurt Huber, who drafted the final two leaflets.

The men of White Rose were war veterans, who had fought on the French and Russian fronts. They were influenced by the German Youth Movement, of which Hans Scholl and Christoph Probst were members.

They had witnessed the German atrocities, both on the battlefield and during the Holocaust, and sensed that the reversal of fortunes that the Wehrmacht suffered at Stalingrad would eventually lead to

Germany's defeat. They rejected the fascism and militarism of Adolf Hitler's Germany and believed in a federated Europe that adhered to Christian principles of tolerance and justice.

Quoting extensively from the Bible, Lao Zi, Aristotle and Novalis, as well as Goethe and Schiller, they appealed to what they considered the German intelligentsia, believing that they would be intrinsically opposed to Nazism.

At first, the leaflets were sent out in mass mailings from different cities in Bavaria and Austria, since the members believed that southern Germany would be more receptive to their anti-militarist message.

Following an extended lull in activities after mid-July 1942, the White Rose took a more vigorous stance against Hitler in February 1943, issuing the final two leaflets and painting anti-Nazi slogans throughout Munich, most notably on the gates of the university.

The shift in their position is obvious from the heading of their new leaflets, which now read, "The Resistance Movement in Germany". The sixth leaflet was distributed in the university on February 18, 1943 to coincide with students leaving their lectures.

With almost all of the leaflets distributed in prominent places, Sophie Scholl made the headstrong decision of climbing the stairs to the top of the atrium and dropping the final leaflets onto the students below.

She was spotted by a caretaker, who was a member of the Nazi party, and arrested together with her brother. The other active members were soon rounded up and the group and everyone associated with them were brought in for questioning.

The Scholls and Probst were the first to stand trial, on February 22, 1943. They were found guilty of treason. Roland Freisler (the Supreme Judge of the People's Court of Germany) sentenced them to be executed by guillotine that same day.

The other key members of the group were also beheaded later that summer. Friends and colleagues of the White Rose, who helped in the preparation and distribution of leaflets and in collecting money for the widow and young children of Probst, were sentenced to prison terms ranging from six months to ten years.

The monument to the "Weiße Rose" is in front of the university in Munich. With the fall of Nazi Germany, the White Rose came to represent opposition to tyranny in the German psyche, seen to have been without interest in personal power or self-aggrandizement.

Their story became so well-known that the composer Carl Orff claimed (by some accounts falsely) to his Allied interrogators that he was a founding member of the White Rose and was released. While he was personally acquainted with Huber, there is a lack of other evidence (other than Orff's word) that Orff was involved in the movement, and he may well have made his claim to escape imprisonment.

The square where the central hall of Munich University is located has been named "Geschwister-Scholl-Platz" after Hans and Sophie Scholl, the square next to it "Professor-Huber-Platz." Many schools, streets and places all over Germany were named in memory of the members of the White Rose.

Germany: Red Orchestra

German counterintelligence used the name "Red Orchestra" to denote a group engaged in pure resistance to the Nazi regime.

This group was a friendship network centred around Harro Schulze-Boysen an intelligence officer for the German Air Ministry and Arvid Harnack in the German Ministry of Economics. Running the gamut of German society, it contained Communists and political conservatives, Jews, Catholics and atheists united in to fight the Nazis and their human rights violations.

Unusual for that time and unique within the forms of German resistance, this group contained 40%

women, working equally alongside the men. The oldest person arrested was 86, the youngest 16.

Among the arrested were theatre producer Adam Kuckhoff and his wife Greta Kuckhoff, Horst Heilmann codebreaker in the Wehrmacht communications division, Günther Weisenborn German author, the journalist John Graudenz who had previously been expelled from the Soviet Union for reporting negatively about their famine, the potter Cato Bontjes van Beek, the pianist Helmut Roloff and others.

The main activity of the Schulze-Boysen group was collecting information about Nazi atrocities and distributing leaflets against Hitler rather than espionage. Part of their information campaign included the communication of Nazi secrets to foreign countries, specifically through personal contacts with the US embassy and a less direct connection to the Soviet government.

A problem arose when, in addition to Kent, Soviet agents were parachuted into Germany to contact the resisters. Their arrival was observed and interspersed by the Getsapo. Before the German invasion of the Soviet Union, Schulze-Boysen had made contact with the Soviet Embassy. However, when the Soviets tried to enlist the resistance group in their service, the resisters refused. They wanted to maintain their political independence and were wary of Stalin.

German intelligence chose to label the Schulze-Boysen group as the Red Orchestra, in order to justify their persecution of anti-Nazi Germans.

Many different people were arrested and listed under that name. Rudolf von Scheliha, who was in charge of countering foreign press reports about Nazi atrocities at the German Foreign Office, had irritated Gestapo officials by requesting details about actual atrocities, and became a target for annihilation because of his activities.

The Gestapo claimed to have intercepted a message about NKVD agents coming to help von Scheliha and arrested him. Von Scheliha was sentenced to death and executed by hanging on December 22, 1942 together with resistance fighters of the group around Harnack and Schulze-Boysen. Hilde Coppi's execution was delayed until her son was weaned, and she was executed immediately thereafter.

After the war, Helmut Roeder, the Prosecutor in the trial against the Red Orchestra, was charged because of his role in that trial, and as a defense, invented the story of the Red Orchestra as an important Soviet espionage ring. Roeder became an informant for the CIC.

France: French Resistance

The French Resistance is the name used for resistance movements that fought military occupation of France by Nazi Germany and the

Vichy France undemocratic regime during World War II after the government and the high command of France surrendered in 1940. Resistance groups included groups of armed men (usually referred to as the Maquis), publishers of underground newspapers or even cinematography and escape networks that helped allied soldiers.

French Resistance cooperated with Allied secret services, especially in providing intelligence on the Atlantic Wall and coordinating sabotages and other actions to contribute to the success of Operation Overlord.

The French resistance could claim its origin externally in Charles de Gaulle's Appeal of 18 June (1940) on the BBC where he proclaimed that the war was not over. Marshal Philippe Pétain had already signed the armistice treaty and the formation of Vichy France government had begun.

De Gaulle also became a de facto leader of Free France. Internally the Resistance began in the Alpilles and Vaucluse areas in Provence. The first acts of resistance were organized by secondary school students on 14 July and 11 November 1940.

Also, sabotage actions started, as well as occupation strikes by workers - for instance, miners in Nord and Pas-de-Calais went on strike from 27 May 1941 to 8 June 1941. Students protested during meetings with followers of Pétain.

In the opinion of some French historians, armed resistance began on 21 August 1941 when two members of youthful battalions, Pierre Georges and Gilbert Brustlein, killed a German seaman named Alfons Moser.

Resistance groups such as the PAT Line established by George Rodocanachi and his wife Fanny Vlasto-Rodocanachi helped Allied pilots who had been shot down to get back to Britain. They minimized the threat of discovery by adopting a cell structure.

Poland: Armia Krajowa (AK)

The AK originated from the Sluzba Zwyciestwu Polski (Polish Victory Service), set up on 27 September 1939 by General Micha• Karaszewicz-Tokarzewski. On 17 November 1939 General Wladyslaw Sikorski replaced this organization with the Zwiazek Walki Zbrojnej (Union for Armed Struggle), which after joining with the Polski Zwiazek Powstanczy (Polish Union of Resistance) became the AK on 14 February 1942.

Stefan Rowecki (known as Grot, or "arrowhead"), served as the AK's first commander until his arrest in 1943; Tadeusz Bór-Komorowski commanded from July 1943 until his capture in September 1944. Leopold Okulicki, known as Niedzwiadek ("bear cub") led the organisation in its final days.

The executive branch of the AK was the operational command, composed of many units. Estimates of the AK membership in the first half of 1944 range from 250,000 to 350,000, with more than 10,000 officers.

Most of the other Polish underground armies became incorporated into the AK, including:

The Konfederacja Narodu (Confederation of the People) (1943).
The Bataliony Chlopskie (Peasants' Battalions).
A large military organization of the Stronnictwo Ludowe (People's Party).
The Socjalistyczna Organizacja Bojowa (Socialist Fighting Organization), established by the Polska Partia Socjalistyczna (Polish Socialist Party).
The Narodowa Organizacja Wojskowa (National Army), established by the Stronnictwo Narodowe (National Party).
From March 1944, part of the extreme right-wing organization, the Narodowe Sily Zbrojne (National Armed Forces).

The AK divided itself organizationally in Poland into sixteen regional branches, subdivided in turn into eighty-nine inspectorates, which further comprised 278 districts.

The supreme command defined the main tasks of the AK as preparation for action and, after the termination of the German occupation, general armed revolt until victory.

At that stage plans envisaged the seizure of power in Poland by the delegatura establishment, the representatives of the London-based Polish government in exile; and by the government-in-exile itself, which would return to Poland.

As a clandestine army operating in a country occupied by the enemy, separated by over a thousand kilometers from any friendly territory, the AK faced unique challenges in acquiring arms and equipment.

In a tremendous achievement, the AK was able to overcome these difficulties to some extent and put tens of thousands of armed soldiers into the field. Nevertheless, the difficult conditions meant that only infantry forces armed with light weapons could be fielded.

Any use of artillery, armor or aviation was obviously out of the question (except for a few instances during the Warsaw Uprising). Even these light infantry units were as a rule armed with a mixture of weapons of various types, usually in quantities sufficient to arm only a fraction of the unit's soldiers.

In contrast their opponents, the German armed forces and their allies, were almost universally supplied with plenty of arms and ammunition, and could count on a full array of support forces. Unit for unit, its German opponents enjoyed a crushing material superiority over the AK and this severely restricted the kind of operations that it could successfully undertake.

The arms and equipment for Armia Krajowa mostly came from four sources: arms buried by the Polish armies on the battlefields after the September Campaign in 1939, arms purchased or captured from the Germans and their allies, arms clandestinely manufactured by Armia Krajowa itself, and arms received from Allied air drops.

From the arms caches hidden in 1939, the AK obtained: 614 heavy machine guns, 1,193 light machine guns, 33,052 rifles, 6,732 pistols, 28 antitank light field guns, 25 antitank rifles and 43,154 hand grenades. However, because of inadequate conservation which had to be improvised in the chaos of the September campaign, most of these guns were in poor condition. Of those that were hidden in the ground and dug up in 1944 during preparation for Operation Tempest, only 30% were usable.

Arms purchases from German soldiers were conducted on a "grass roots" level. Purchases were made by individual units and sometimes by individual soldiers. As Germany's prospects for victory diminished and the morale in German units dropped, the number of soldiers willing to sell their weapons correspondingly increased and thus made this source more important.

All such purchases were highly risky, as the Gestapo was well aware of this black market in arms and tried to check it by setting up sting operations. For the most part this trade was limited to personal weapons, but occasionally light and heavy machine guns could also be purchased.

It was much easier to trade with Italian and Hungarian units stationed in Poland, which willingly sold their arms to the Polish underground as long as they could conceal this trade from the Germans.

The efforts to capture weapons from Germans also proved highly successful. Raids were conducted on trains carrying equipment to the front, as well as guardhouses and gendarmerie posts. Sometimes weapons were taken from individual German soldiers accosted in the street. During the Warsaw Uprising, the AK even managed to capture a few German armored vehicles.

Arms were clandestinely manufactured by the AK in its own secret workshops, and also by its members working in German armament factories. In this way the AK was able to procure submachine guns (copies of British Sten and indigenous B•yskawica), pistols (Vis), flamethrowers, bombs, road mines and hand grenades. Hundreds of people were involved in this manufacturing effort.

The final source of supply were Allied air drops. This was the only way to obtain more exotic but highly useful equipment such as plastic explosives or antitank weapons (PIAT).

During the war 485 Allied planes made air drops destined for the AK, delivering 600.9 tons of supplies. During these operations, 70 planes and 62 crews (of which 28 were Polish) were lost.

Besides equipment, the planes also parachuted highly qualified instructors (the Cichociemni), of whom 346 were inserted into Poland during the war.

Due to the large distance from bases in Britain and the Mediterranean, and lukewarm political support, the airdrops were only a fraction of those carried out in support of French or Yugoslavian resistance movements.

While the AK did not engender a general revolt, its forces did carry out intensive economic and armed sabotage. In 1944 it acted on a broad scale, notably in initiating the Warsaw Uprising, which broke out on 1 August 1944. It had the aim of liberating Warsaw before the arrival of the Soviet Red Army.

While the insurgents released a few hundred prisoners from the Gesia St. concentration camp and carried out fierce street-fighting, the Germans eventually defeated the rebels and burned the city, finally quelling the Uprising only on 2 October 1944.

AK units carried out thousands of armed raids and daring intelligence operations, bombed hundreds of railway shipments, and participated in many partisan clashes and battles with the German police and Wehrmacht units.

The AK officially disbanded on 19 January 1945 to avoid armed conflict with the Soviets and a civil war. However, many units decided to continue their struggle under new circumstances.

Chapter 4 Escape and Evasion While Driving

One of the keys to avoiding a confrontation is recognizing when you are under surveillance. In most planned arrests you can assume that you have been under surveillance for a period of time prior to the confrontation. The observation period may range from one day to even several months prior.

In order to stop a confrontation before it takes place you must develop surveillance awareness. To develop this ability you must be constantly alert to suspicious people in the vicinity of you home and at work. This especially goes for those who live in an area where houses are spread greatly apart.

In stalking their victims, police and military forces have posed as laborers, hookers, derelicts, and used numerous other ruses. Always keep in the back of your mind that someone's eyes might be watching you.

The easiest type of surveillance to detect is when you are being followed by a single surveillant. The loner must stay close enough to keep you in sight, yet far enough away to avoid detection -- no easy feat. In residential areas, he can remain a few cars back because of the density of traffic. Also he has the option of following the victim on a parallel street. In rural areas, about all he can do is remain well back and hope for the best.

The single tail may employ certain tricks of the trade to make his job easier. At night, he may break a taillight or place a small luminous sticker on the rear of the victim's vehicle to make it more distinguishable. To decrease the possibility of detection, he may change his seating position or use various types of disguise.

If you suspect you are being followed by a single tail, try things like speeding through some areas and going slow through others. The signal lights can be used to your advantage if you come up to an intersection; try signaling right and wait until your suspects signal comes on - just drive straight through with your signal on and see what happens.

Professional investigators, whether governmental or private, rarely conduct a surveillance using a single unit. The risk of their being spotted is just too great.

PARALLEL SURVEILLANCE

This type of surveillance is conducted by two or more vehicles. One vehicle tails the victim at a reasonable distance. His comrades follow on parallel streets ready to take up close surveillance should the victim turn. (See figure 1). Obviously, this method will not work in areas without parallel roads.

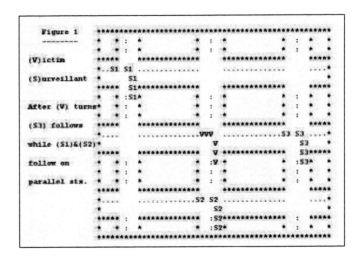

LEAP FROG SURVEILLANCE

(V)ictim
(S)urveillant
(C)ivilian

```
        *   ..  *
          *  ..S *
   Road -> *C ..    *
          *   ..  C*
         *    ..    *
   Figure 2  *C ..V *
          *     ..  *
           *   ..C *
   (V)ictim      *    ..S *
   (S)urveillant * C..    *
   (C)ivilian       *  ..   *
```

In this method the tailing and lead vehicles must be in radio contact for this it to be effective.

BUMPER BEEPERS

The most effective means of tailing a vehicle is with a bumper beeper. An electronic tailing device, the bumper beeper attaches to the underside of the victims car.

The device sends beeping signals to a receiver in the tailing vehicle. The closer the tailing vehicle gets to the target vehicle, the louder the beeps become. The more sophisticated beepers are equipped with a null switch, whereby a different

43

tone in the beep is produced if the victim turns right or left.

Bumper beepers have an effective range of 2 to 12 km (1 to 5 miles). They are usually attached to the vehicle with powerful magnets, although heavy metal clamps are sometimes used. Beepers can be either battery powered or attached directly to the target vehicle's own electrical system.

DETECTION OF BUMPER BEEPERS

To determine if you are the victim of these dreaded devices, first make a complete visual inspection of the underside of your vehicle. What you are looking for is a small metal box with one or two skinny antennas sticking out of it.

If your search turns up nothing, go out and buy a field strength meter. These devices detect all radio transmissions. With meter in hand and car ignition on, check in, on, and especially under your car. If you are a victim of a bumper beeper you will find it.

ELUDING A TAIL

(1) After running a red light or driving the wrong way on a one way street, watch to see if anyone follows.

(2) While traveling on a freeway at high speed, suddenly cut across 4 lanes of traffic and make an exit.

44

(3) After rounding a blind curve, make a bootlegger's turn and take off in the opposite direction.

(4) After turning a corner, pull over and park. Take note of all vehicles passing by.

(5) Go through alleys, dirt roads, or even cut across people's lawns.

(6) While driving over a long undivided bridge, suddenly make a bootlegger's turn.

(7) Have a friend follow you to detect any surveillance.

CORNERING

It is a commonly held belief that the best way to handle corners is to blast through them as quickly as possible. This is completely wrong. The speed at which you exit a corner is much more important than the speed at which you take the corner itself. Assuming identical cars, the car which exits the corner at the greater speed will be going faster on any straight stretch of road that follows.

PROPER APEX

The apex of any turn is that POINT IN WHICH YOUR WHEELS ARE CLOSEST TO THE INSIDE EDGE OF THE CORNER. By choosing a relatively late apex, the driver can exit a corner at a greater speed than if he had chosen an early one.

THE 90-DEGREE TURN

Figure 3 shows how to handle a 90-degree turn. This is the most common type of turn, particularly in urban areas.

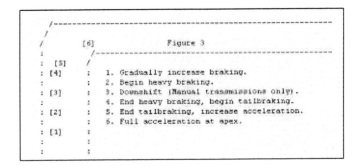

This turn is begun as far to the outside as possible. Obviously, if there is a lot of traffic on the road, you are going to have to adjust your turn. In that case, drive as far to the outside as you can within the confines of your lane.

Approaching the corner, gradually increase braking pressure to heavy braking. Be careful not to lock the brakes, as all this does is prevent you from steering. If you feel any of the brakes locking up, let off for an instant, then reapply braking.

After downshifting (manual transmissions only), start trailing off the brakes into the first third of the

46

turn. Then gradually increase the throttle to full acceleration coming out of the turn.

An S type turn is a series of turns in which the road winds with small degree on alternating sides (A giant S). Actually, this need not be a turn at all, as you can go straight through it. Remember to set yourself up to take full advantage of any straight that might follow.

CONSTANT RADIUS TURNS

Figure 4 shows how to handle a constant radius, or "hairpin" turn. The illustration is pretty much self-explanatory. Don't go too fast on these turns, as you can easily end up off the road.

```
     Figure 4
  /------------------\
 /                    \    1. Gradually increase braking.
 /      [4]   [5]       \   2. Begin heavy braking.
/                        \  3. Downshift (manual transmissions only).
:          /-----\ [6]    : 4. End heavy braking, begin tailbraking.
: [3]    :       :        : 5. End tailbraking, increase acceleration.
:        :       :        : 6. Full acceleration at apex.
:[2]     :       :     [7]: 7. Keep on going.
:        :       :        :
:[1]     :       :        :
:        :       :        :
```

These cornering techniques are those taught in anti-terrorist driving schools throughout the world. The instructors at these schools are first-rate and among the best drivers in the world. However, I believe they make a serious mistake when they spend 70% of the course time teaching cornering techniques.

My reasons for saying this are:

1) If you are involved in a chase situation (with you being the one pursued) it is very possible that you will be unfamiliar with the area you are driving in. If you don't know what kind of turn or corner is ahead, how can you set yourself up to take it properly? Obviously, you can't. Also, with traffic coming in all directions and pedestrians on the road, proper cornering technique goes out the window.

2) As mentioned previously, by taking a late apex, you can exit a corner at greater speed than if you had taken an earlier one. However, if your pursuer takes an early apex while you take a late one, there is a chance (albeit a small one) that he can catch you in a turn. This is because he actually gets through the corner quicker than you. After the turn if he hasn't quite caught up you'll take off much faster than he will.

What does all this mean? If you are in a superior car to that of your pursuer and you have a big enough lead on him (say a couple of car lengths) it is probably worthwhile to take turns with a late apex. However, if you are in an inferior car or a pursuer is right on your tail, it is extremely important not to let him pull up alongside you. By taking an early apex, you effectively prevent him from doing so.

These examples of corners are representative of what you face in everyday driving. By mastering them, you should be able to handle any turn you might encounter.

The only way to become skilled at cornering is to practice, practice and then practice some more. The best places to practice are on back country roads at while it is dark.

THE BOOTLEGGER'S TURN

Legend has it that the bootlegger's turn was invented by hillbilly moonshiners for the purpose of eluding revenue agents.

The maneuver enables you to change your direction 180 degrees, without stopping, within the width of a two lane road. It has been used to get away from roadblocks and also to elude pursuers.

The bootlegger's turn is easiest to perform in cars having an automatic transmission and a hand emergency brake. See figure 5.

```
      Figure 5           *
 *          :        *
 *          :        *    1. Speed at around 45-50  km  (25-30 m.p.h.)
 * [RB]  : [RB]  *         2. Get off the gas and  crank  the  steering
 *          :        *        wheel 1/4 to 1/2  of a full turn.  At the
 *  [4]  :         *           EXACT same time, pull or hit the E. Brake
 *       [3b]      *           hard.  Those  of  you  with  a  manual
 *          :        *           transmission will  have  to  depress  the
 *  [5]  : [3]  *              clutch as well.
 *          :        *    3. When your vehicle is at  approximately 90
 *       : [2]     *           degrees,  release  the  emergency  brake,
 *          :        *           step on the gas, and straighten  out  the
 *       : [1]     *           steering wheel.  If  you  have  a  manual
 *          :        *           transmission, you  will  have  to let  the
                                 clutch out as you are hitting the  gas.
                            4-5. Get  out  of  the  area  in  a  hurry.
```

Angle of car during steps: 1 - 90 degrees 2 - 110 degrees
3 - 195 degrees 3b- 260 degrees
4 - 270 degrees (have turned 180)

The bootlegger's turn will cause incredible wear and tear on your front tires. For this reason, it is recommended that you learn how to do this maneuver on rental cars. You should be able to find something similar to what you now drive.

MOONSHINERS TURN

The moonshiners turn is another maneuver pioneered by the mountain people of the Southern United States. Looking like a bootlegger turn in reverse, the moonshiners turn allows you to change your direction 180 degrees within the confines of a two lane road, while going backwards. See figure 6.

```
    Figure 6
  :             :
: [RB] :  [RB]  :      1. Accelerate in reverse 40-50 km (20-30 mi.
:      :        :      2. Get off the gas and crank the steering
:      :  [1]   :         wheel all the way to the left as fast as
:      :        :         possible.
:      :  [2]   :      3. When the car had turned 90 degrees, shift
:      :        :         into low gear, hit the gas, and straighten
:        [3]    :         out the steering wheel.
:       [3B]    :      4. Get out of the area fast.
:        :      :
: [4]  :        :
:      :        :
```

This maneuver is particularly effective against roadblocks at night. Often the attackers manning the roadblock will use high intensity lights to blind the victim as he approaches. By using the moonshiners turn, the victim's vision is directed away from the lights.

THE TIME FOR EXOTIC TURNS

When being pursued and are approaching a roadblock there are many paths to choose; you can perform an exotic turn, you can jump a curb and go around or ram the roadblock.

It is up to you and the situation to decide which to follow. Obviously if a 6 foot ditch lies on either side of the road you can't go curb jumping, but otherwise this can be a very good solution.

If you are being very closely followed by another vehicle and they recognize you're pulling a bootlegger turn it's possible that they could ram you (hitting the driver's door) possibly killing you or at least doing excessive damage to the vehicle.

Even if a following vehicle is too far back to ram, it's possible that the driver will pull a 90 degree turn placing his car in the middle of the road. It's true that exotic turns may help but don't forget that their probably not the last evasive maneuver you'll make in a chase/roadblock situation.

By the way, if a following vehicle does happen to skid 90 degrees and block your new path while he is still in the car - ram the driver door if you've got time and it won't happen again.

RAMMING

The most common type of vehicle ambush is the stationary roadblock. In this type of attack, on or two vehicles are lined up across the road. The attackers will usually be standing alongside the blockade vehicles with high intensity lights and lots of firepower (automatic weapons and high powered rifles).

When the unwary and untrained victim sees the roadblock, he will stop, whereupon the attackers will rush the vehicle and drag him away. Faced with the above situation you might decide to ram.

To those of you who have experienced it only through television shows, ramming may seem like a suicidal stunt reserved for daredevil types. Actually, as long as you wear a seat belt, ramming is almost completely safe. The true danger of ramming is that your vehicle may become inoperable after the collision. For this reason, ramming is usually a method of last resort. If at all possible, go around rather than ram a roadblock.

SINGLE VEHICLE BLOCKADES

(1) Slow down almost to a complete stop and put the car in low gear. This will give your attackers the impression that you are going to stop.

(2) Suddenly hit the gas hard and pick a ramming point (below).

(3) Hit the target at an angle and keep the accelerator fully depressed through the collision. Your speed at impact should be between 30 and 50 km (15 - 30 mph).

(4) After breaking through, get out of the area fast. Even if your car is badly damaged, keep going.

The ramming points on the blockade vehicle listed in order of preference are: (1) the rear wheel and rear fender area; (2) the front wheel and front fender area. If either end of the vehicle is up against a curb or wall, you will have to ram through the other end. A car can't drive with a bent out of shape axel.

DOUBLE VEHICLE BLOCKADE

Follow procedure as described in the ramming of a single vehicle blockade except the preferred ramming point is right in the middle of the two cars. If any of the attackers are so foolish as to get in front of you -- run them over.

To practice ramming, go to your local auto junkyard and buy three running wrecks. Move all three to an unused parking lot or abandoned area and practice per the directions above. For safety's sake, wear a helmet and seatbelt. You might also want to smash out all the glass ahead of time. Work with the three cars until not one will even so much as start.

VEHICLE ATTACK

If you are the attacker and are able to catch up with the victim, or you are the victim and are fortunate enough to get behind your attacker's car, you can easily knock him off the road.

The most effective means of doing so is to ram his bumper on the left hand side, with the right hand side of yours... as if you were going to pass but didn't pull left far enough. You should be going 15 to 35 km (10 to 20 mph) faster than he is as you must HIT, not PUSH.

After impact, his vehicle will be facing slightly right and go sliding sideways down the road until his tires regain traction. When this happens, his car will go in the direction it is pointing -- off the road.

A secondary effective method is one in which you would pull alongside the rear of the enemy vehicle, very quickly turn to the right enough to turn a corner and slam into his rear section -- you will actually be facing the edge of the road. This will cause him to spin out and go off the road. Immediately after impact, hit the brakes and counter-steer to break contact.

If you don't want to hit the other vehicle hard, or it is much larger and heavier than yours follow this procedure; Pull up alongside the enemy vehicle and position yourself so as the center of your vehicle is in line with the other vehicles front tires. Now crank slightly to the left and press the center of your car against the front of his -- now steer him off the road and keep going.

ASSASSINATIONS

A very common method of assassination is for an attacking vehicle to pull alongside the victim's car and simply blast away at everyone inside. If the driver is hit their all as good as dead.

The best defense against this type of attack is to slam on the brakes, causing the attacker to overshoot your vehicle. A bootlegger's turn could also be employed (if the shoulder of the road is wide enough), or you could make a quick turn off the road.

Keep in mind that after you slam on the brakes, a moonshiners turn may be the only escape -- pray for no on-coming traffic. If you are faced with an attack from a motorcycle, ram him as hard as possible, thereby ending the threat.

CHASE SITUATIONS

The most important thing to remember in any chase situation is not to crash. Even if you should somehow make it through an accident in one piece, you would be a sitting duck for any pursuer.

Because the probability of an accident is so great, high speeds are not recommended in chase situations. By keeping your speed relatively low, say under 100 km (60 mph), you will have greater vehicle control and evasive maneuvers will be easier to accomplish. Of course, if you have a superior car to that of your pursuer, you can just flat outrun him on open roads.

GENERAL SUMMARY

The Overtaking Vehicle -- Never let anyone pull up alongside you.

If he does manage to position himself there, he is either going to shoot, or try and run you off the road. If an attempt is made to overtake you, it will probably be on your left side. To make this more difficult, drive as far to the left as you possibly can. Should he try to overtake you anyway, swerve in front of him or attempt to run him off.

Special Devices -- Special devices such as smokescreens, oil slicks, and spotlights should be employed just before turns. If your pursuer is blinded or goes into a skid just before a turn, he will very likely crash.

Going Off the Road -- It may be necessary to go of the road to lose a pursuer. Be sure not to get stuck in a ditch or drive into a dead end, however. It is surprising how far off the road an ordinary car will actually go, if you drive it carefully.

Jumping Curbs -- Jumping a curb is a good way to avoid a road- block as mentioned earlier. A curb can be easily jumped as long as you remember to hit it at and angle of approximately 45 deg. and at a speed under 70 km (45 mph).

Shooting -- Any passages that you intend to have shooting should be seated in the back. This allows them to shoot in any direction without interfering with the driver.

Targets of choice are the driver and front tires. For best results, try to score a direct hit on the sidewall. Following are the results of various tests done on junk cars with various calibers;

(1) No pistol round can be counted on to penetrate the vehicle body or glass or tires. Pistol rounds will crack the glass and deflect away. While the rounds used (.46 and 9mm) did penetrate the tires, it took about 20 minutes for them to go completely flat.

(2) Rifle rounds of .223 and .308 caliber will definitely penetrate any unarmored vehicle. The .308 flattened tires much faster than the .223.

(3) Shotgun loads with the exception of slugs are useless for stopping any vehicle. They won't penetrate the glass, body, or tires. Slugs, however, will blast huge holes through the vehicle and almost instantly flatten a tire.

If you absolutely cannot get away from your pursuers, you have tried turning left in front of on-coming cars at intersections, gone up one ways, etc. drive your car into a wooded area. When your car won't go any further, get out and get behind cover. If your pursuers are still intent on coming after you, they are going to have to exit their vehicle. When they do, you can ambush them.

SUGGESTED TRAINING SCHEDUAL

(1) Read this chapter thoroughly and know in your mind how to do the maneuvers.

(2) Learn to do the bootlegger's turn first. This maneuver is relatively easy to do and once learned is a real confidence booster. I have found it takes twenty tries at the bootlegger's turn for the average person to get it down pat. If you are learning on a standard, it will take twice as long to become proficient. Remember to use a rental car for this maneuver.

(3) Learn the moonshiners turn. It takes about the same time as the bootlegger's turn. Again, use a rental car.

(4) Buy or steal some junk cars in running condition from an auto wrecker and practice ramming and vehicle attack.

(5) Practice the cornering techniques with your own car. You should also practice the exotic turns once

or twice to get the feel of them (AFTER PROFICIENCY IS ATTAINED).

(6) Practice driving fast on highways. Having driven very fast (200 km or 140 mph) makes you feel comfortable at lower speeds.

You can learn to do all the maneuvers in this text in a few days and you won't have to pay the $3000 or so it costs to learn them in an anti-terrorist driving school. After you have learned these maneuvers, you will be a better driver than 95% of the people on the road.

Chapter 5   Surveillance

Surveillance, Undercover, and Task Force Operations

PREPARATIONS

If you are selected for surveillance, get all the background you can on the subject. If he is not known to you, have him pointed out to let you make your own observation. Learn the subject's habits. Learn his contacts, friends, and places he frequents. Try to get a picture or an accurate, detailed description of the subject and his automobile.

If the subject of your surveillance is a place, locate entrances, exits, and vantage points. You may find more surveillants are needed. And check the character of the neighborhood. You will learn where to watch from and how to dress to blend in with the environment.

Make sure your attire is like that worn by others in the area. That way, if the subject sees you, you will not draw attention. On a military base you might wear an appropriate uniform. But avoid wearing unauthorized rank or insignia. It could bring unwanted attention from an innocent third party.

Concern with your appearance should not stop with clothes. Do not wear rings or other jewelry that denote status or club membership. If you usually wear a distinctive ring, replace it with another to hide the mark on your finger. If your coat or pocket bulges, it may reveal that you are carrying a weapon. And be careful your habits do not reveal that you are a law enforcement officer.

If you use a cover story, make sure it fits your dress, speech, and mannerisms. Be resourceful when your cover story must be used. If confronted by the subject, do not offer information. The subject may try to check the information and, perhaps, expose you.

Technical surveillance devices can be highly useful to you. These devices range from tape recorders and hidden microphones to small devices that can be hidden in a subject's clothing to transmit to a receiver. The devices let you know approximately where the subject is at all times. But be sure to get SJA advice before you use any type of electronic surveillance equipment.

PRECAUTIONS

Surveillants face two risks that can destroy weeks or months of preparation. One is the risk of being discovered. The other is the risk of losing the subject at a critical time. Even the most experienced investigator can be "burned" or lose a subject. However, certain precautions can help make your surveillance a success.

You should avoid direct eye contact with the subject. This will keep the subject from recalling your face should eye-to-eye contact be needed later. Sometimes looking away from the subject can make him suspicious. When that happens, focus on a point beyond the subject. This gives the impression of eye contact without actually having it.

Sudden or unnatural movements can call attention to you. Many times a subject will test to see if he is being observed. He may quickly change his course or enter a public vehicle or building. You must react quickly, but naturally, to these movements. It may be better to lose sight of a subject for a moment than to arouse his suspicion that he is being followed.

Hotels, theaters, restaurants, elevators, and public transportation can pose special problems for you. Carry enough money (and change) to pay for bus or cab fare, meals, or phone calls. You may have to move close to a subject when he or she enters a hotel or a theater. Enter restaurants behind a subject. Sit where you can see the subject easily. Order a meal which will be ready quickly, or the subject may leave before you are served. Be sure your meal can be eaten easily and hastily.

If a subject uses an elevator, do not press a floor button. Or choose the one for the top floor. That way you can exit behind the subject. If a subject enters a railroad station or bus depot ticket line, try to get close enough to learn his destination. Perhaps you can overhear his conversation with a clerk.

If a subject throws anything away, try to retrieve it. Obtain second sheets from pads the subject has used. But do not pick up an item if doing so could expose you.

If he enters a telephone booth, enter the next booth. Listen to his conversation. The subject may be pretending to call just to see if someone is following. If you enter a booth next to the subject, do not pretend to make a call. Deposit the required coins and dial a number. Then simulate your conversation.

You will have a tendency to believe you have been burned if the subject glances your way several times. You must overcome this. Normally, someone who thinks he is being observed will show his belief by taking actions to harass or lose you.

TECHNIQUES

There are many surveillance techniques. One technique of loose surveillance that has been shown to be quite useful, when you have time and the subject uses a set routine, is progressive surveillance. The subject is watched in one phase of his daily routine or for some length of time on one day. The cutoff point is recorded. The next day the surveillance is picked up at the previous day's cutoff. This process is repeated until the subject's actions have been thoroughly covered and noted. As you gain experience, you will use this and other techniques, and learn how to adapt, combine, and apply them.

The type of surveillance, the degree of risk, and the number of persons assigned to a job determine what technique to use. A one-man surveillance carries danger to the surveillant. The subject, his convoy, decoy, or associates may try to neutralize or physically eliminate the surveillant. It is always wise to have a second person ready to protect and to aid the main surveillant. Certain basic techniques can be used on foot and, with modification, in vehicles. These one-, two-, and three-man techniques allow surveillant to switch from foot surveillance to vehicle surveillance and vice versa. No one on foot walks everywhere. No one with a vehicle rides to every destination. The two types of surveillance must often be combined.

Foot Surveillance

If a one-man foot surveillance must be used, be cautious when you are on the same side of the street as the subject. Stay to the rear and vary your distance from the subject. Set your distance according to physical conditions like size of crowds and number of exits.

If the subject turns a corner, continue across the street, keeping the subject in view. Then, operating from across the street, you can fall in behind or move to the front or side of the subject. Decide which position will give you the best view. When the subject turns a corner, you may want to be abreast of him to see if he makes a contact or enters a building.

For a two-man foot surveillance, use the "AB" technique. The person right behind the subject has the A position. The other surveillant has the B position. When using the AB technique, A follows the subject and B follows A. B may be on the same side of the street as A. Or he may be on the opposite side of the street.

When both A and B are on the same side of the street, and the subject turns a corner to the right, A continues across the street. Then he signals B what action to take. The subject's actions may require B to take the A position, and A to take the B position. Signals between A and B should attract as little attention as possible.

When B is across the street and the subject turns the corner to the right--away from B--B crosses and takes the A position. This step should be prearranged so no signals will be needed. If the subject turns the corner to the left and crosses toward B, B drops back to avoid contact. B then waits for a signal from A before making the next move.

For a three-man foot surveillance, the "ABC" technique offers ease. And it is consistent with reasonable manpower resources. Use this technique for close foot surveillance unless you lack the manpower. The main advantage of the ABC technique is that it lets you cover the subject from two sides. As in the AB technique, A follows the subject and B follows A. C normally stays across the street and just to the rear of the subject.

The ABC technique allows several choices when the subject turns the corner. Assume A and B are behind the subject and C is across the street when the subject turns the corner away from C. A could keep going straight and B would take the A position. C would move across to the B position. A would stay across the street, moving as C had done before.

Another approach would be for C to move into the A position. A would go across and take up the C position, while B keeps his own. What if the subject turns left and crosses the street toward C? C drops back and A continues in the original direction and becomes C. Then B moves into the A position, and C becomes B.

Vehicle Surveillance

The techniques used for foot surveillance are also used for a vehicle surveillance. But applying these techniques to a vehicle surveillance must be done with care. Traffic congestion and traffic laws make actions more difficult. They also increase the risk of discovery. Two or more vehicle surveillants, like two or more foot surveillants, raise the likelihood of success. When possible, have two people in each vehicle. Teams within vehicles increase coverage and allow flexibility.

For all vehicle surveillances, you must familiarize yourself with the locale where you will operate. If you can, do a map study and make a ground recon. If time does not permit this, carry maps in the car. The person in the passenger's seat can navigate for the driver. Have coins for toll roads and bridges to make sure the surveillance is not hindered.

Choose a vehicle for surveillance duty that is mechanically sound. It should suit the locale where it will be used. It should have a radio, especially if two or more vehicles will be used. The radio allows contact between teams. You can also use it to call for help, if help is needed.

Your vehicle should not have official markings. Use a license plate of the county or state where the surveillance will take place. If possible, change your vehicle if the operation is of long duration. Consider using a rental car.

To decrease the risk of detection by the subject, disconnect the dome light of the car. This will keep the light from showing when the door is open. Operate the radio's microphone as covertly as you can. You can wire one of the headlights and the license plate light to be turned on or off separately from inside the vehicle. This changes the traffic pattern seen by the subject. But if traffic conditions are heavy, do not tamper with the headlights. Be sure to clear violations of traffic laws with local law enforcement agencies. Get the advice of the SJA if you need it.

At night it is often hard to be sure you are following the right vehicle. It helps if the subject's car is distinctive. If you get the chance, put a piece of reflectorized tape on the rear of the subject's car.

For a one-vehicle surveillance, you must remain close enough to the subject to see his actions. But you must be far enough away to escape detection. When the subject's car stops, one team member follows on foot. The subject will not expect to be followed by a person on foot if he suspects a vehicle is being used. Meanwhile the driver can look for a parking place where he can watch the suspect's vehicle. When the vehicle is parked, he can sit on the passenger side and appear to be waiting for the driver. This lessens the chance of attracting the subject's attention. He may change to the back seat. Or he may sometimes move the car to another parking place in the same zone of the subject.

If a subject turns a corner, you have two choices. You may keep going straight, cross the intersecting street, and make a U-shaped turn. The subject will not be alarmed by a car turning into the street behind him from a direction opposite to the way he was going before he made his turn. Or you may go straight, cross the intersecting street, and then go around the block. The subject will not be wary of a car coming from the front.

For a two-vehicle surveillance, the technique is similar to the AB foot surveillance. Two cars can tail the subject on the same street. Or one car can be on the same street and the other car travel abreast on a parallel street. The surveillant vehicles can also alternate the A position. This lessens the chance of raising the subject's suspicions.

To do any of these maneuvers, keep radio contact between the surveillant vehicles. The team in the car right behind the subject's vehicle is always the control, giving instructions to the other cars.

How to Conduct Surveillance

There are many different needs for the use of surveillance. Should a need arise for retail surveillance in which apprehension of a shoplifter or a person suspected of shoplifting some of the techniques to be discussed can be applied. In the event you have an occasion to conduct retail surveillance we suggest caution, planning and education as a necessary part of your planned surveillance procedure. There is a major difference you will encounter in this retail surveillance as opposed to the three types of surveillance we will be concentrating on in this section. The major difference is personal contact with the subject under surveillance. You must be prepared for possible physical confrontation in retail surveillance. Although this may happen occasionally, personal or physical confrontation is a rare occurrence in worker's comp, insurance defense or domestic surveillance if the surveillance is conducted properly.

Terms and definitions used in this article:

Target: The person, place or thing under surveillance.

Operative: The person conducting surveillance.

Contact: Any person the subject meets or confers with.

Convoy: A person employed by a subject to detect surveillance. Usually done by following the subject.

Decoy: A person who attempts to divert the operative's attention from the subject.

Burnt: Term indication that the subject has discovered the identity of an operative.

Stationary surveillance: The target is not expected to become mobile.

Mobile surveillance: The target is moving, either walking or in a vehicle.

Surveillance is the systematic observation of person, places, or things to obtain information. Surveillance is generally carried out without the knowledge of those under surveillance and is concerned primarily with people. Simply, surveillance is conducted in hopes that the activity, whatever the purpose of the surveillance, will occur.

Surveillance is conducted in one of two techniques either stationary or mobile. Mobile surveillance is conducted in one of two techniques either on foot or in a vehicle. One or all of these techniques of surveillance may be used on a surveillance to accurately document the target's movements either by personal observation, photographs or video.

Regardless of the technique of surveillance to be conducting the objective is the same, to gather and document information for personal knowledge or courtroom testimony.

The most common technique of surveillance employed by private investigators is a combination of stationary and mobile. Stationary because the subject has not moved or has not made an appearance before mobile surveillance is required. We will discuss the different techniques systematically.

SURVEILLANCE PREPARATION

The first order of business is securing the surveillance job. Selling the job as it were. All the surveillance techniques learned in this manual will do no good if one does not possess the expertise to sell one's self and secure the job. Remember when the potential client calls your office they may be shopping for confidence more than price.

Although a competitive price is important, your demeanor on the phone is what will sell the job. Get the potential client to discuss their problems their needs and goals of the surveillance on your initial phone contact so you can build rapport with the person before discussing hourly rates. Remember if it is a domestic call, is it probably one of the most difficult calls that person will have to make to a stranger.

Convince the person that you are not a stranger by your demeanor, understanding and knowledge of what it takes to get the job done. Once you have secured the job and your upfront money, then and only then should surveillance preparation will begin.

Once the job is secured and the upfront money is obtained then you should prepare a case history investigative form that contains all the vital information needed to identify the target.

First and foremost is to obtain an accurate address and description of the target including any distinguishing marks, tattoos etc. What vehicle will the target possibly be driving? What are the target's social habits? Information in the miscellaneous details section should include details of why the investigation is required. If domestic, the information should include why, what and who the spouse suspects.

If the investigation is a Worker's Compensation case the information should include details of the accident and the type of injury. The target's habits should also be listed. Pertinent telephone number should be included. This information is obtained from the client. Space should be provided for gathering additional information thru the investigators traditional channels such as the motor vehicle bureau, voter registration, directory assistance, etc.

EQUIPMENT

Now you have all the information needed to start the surveillance. Equipment needed for the job should be prepared with a checklist. The checklist should include, still camera, video camera, file, map, flashlight, pad and pencil, toilet facility (applies to males), window covers, binoculars and two way radios, at least one should be portable. Hats, sunglasses and a change of clothes are also recommended.

SURVEILLANCE VEHICLE

Advice on which vehicle is the perfect surveillance vehicle is plentiful. There are different opinions for each investigator you may talk with. Some recommendations that the author has received over the years are, a white truck, because white blends in and is unnoticeable or a van that is equipped with all the latest equipment. I have a friend that uses a red Cadillac and does well. The bottom line is that the vehicle no matter what color, style or type will not be of any use if the target notices any unusual vehicle in the area. The vehicle used is of little importance if the investigator uses the techniques and cautions outlined in this manual. If the vehicle is suspected then the investigator has to change vehicle in order to continue the surveillance in another location.

PREPARE TO FOLLOW

If the location is in close proximity to the investigative office, a drive-by a couple of days prior to starting the surveillance is recommended. This may not be possible in all surveillance cases. The investigator will have to make on the spot surveillance decisions as to what is the best location for parking and blending on most of the jobs.

The purpose of the drive-by is to log any vehicles for identification later and positive identification of the target's address and residence at the target's address. The investigators should log either by micro recorder or by physical notes any activity seen at the time of the drive-by. The investigator should make notes on any items that would indicate leisure activity or work activity along with a description of the house and its location within the residential block.

The investigator should make notes of the surrounding neighbors and any animals seen in the neighborhood. The investigator should note all possible surveillance locations including the rear and sides of the residence and if one vehicle will do the job.

The investigator should make note of all possible avenues that the target might take when leaving the location. The investigator should check all parallel routes in order to start the surveillance with knowledge of the immediate area.

BEGINNING THE SURVEILLANCE

The question always arises as to whether or not the investigator should notify the police when ever conducting surveillance. This is a question that has a different answer for different circumstances. My recommendation is that the investigator must do what they feel is necessary to protect their surveillance location.

There is no law that I know of in any state that requires notification of the police. After all this is America and we enjoy the same freedoms as any other businessperson does. We have encountered police departments that state that they have a policy that investigators check in with them before beginning investigations.

This so called policy is not law. The question the investigator should ask themselves on some surveillance jobs after assessing the surrounding area is "how much trouble do I want to bring upon myself and my surveillance?" The investigator should determine from the neighborhood if the threat of being exposed by police exist. The decision to call in and notify the police so they won't respond to a call from a neighbor may be a good one and then again it may not.

Golden rule number one is; "Never take your eyes off of the target."

My recommendation for the beginning location of any surveillance is to pick the farthest location from the target's location that will allow the investigator to see movement of any vehicles coming or going.

When the surveillance is to be conducted in a residential neighborhood it is a good idea to park with the rising sun or setting sun and in the shade so the vehicle won't be easy to see.

When it is possible, blend into a business parking lot and with other vehicles and place shades over in the windshield to make it appear that the vehicle is empty. Sometimes it becomes necessary to view at the target's location backwards in order to blend into the neighborhood. Watching in the rear view mirror while the investigators vehicle is pointed in the opposite direction is a bit more difficult because it narrows the field of vision but is just as effective.

Humans are creatures of habit.

Once the direction of travel of the target is established the investigator should conduct the surveillance in the opposite direction if possible. This will prevent the investigator from having to leave in a hurry to get out of the line of sight of the target and will prevent the investigator from taking their eye off of the target.

The investigator should record the license plates on any vehicle that arrives at the residence. Although it may not seem relevant at the time, the plate could be used to locate the target in the event the investigator loses sight of the target. If movement at the location is detected, the investigator should react by starting the video or moving closer to assess what the movement indicates.

Either the target is getting ready to leave the location or is getting ready to start activity that might be worthy of video or moving even closer to the target. The investigator must be prepared to drive aggressively while driving defensibly. Driving aggressive may require driving across a yellow light or even a red light, making U-turns where one would normally not make U-turns, cutting though parking lots etc. Mind you that this is not a recommendation but a reality. We never will recommend that an investigator break the law in any way in the pursuit of their duties.

Golden rule number Two; "if the target sees the investigator three times the investigator is burnt."

HANDLING CONFRONTATIONS

Animals and children are the biggest worry the investigator has when parked on surveillance. Dogs will bark, cows and horses will look and sometime walk towards the investigator. Children are as bold and will approach the investigator and sometime notify the neighborhood or the target that someone is parked in the neighborhood with a camera.

From time to time neighbors, kids and sometimes the target or a member of their family will confront the investigator. The investigator must have a story ready when the confrontation occurs.

Depending on the location of the investigator from the target, the statement to the confronter could very well be, when asked what the investigator is doing at the location, none of your business. However even if this is true it may not be the very best approach because it may cause the police to be summoned to the location.

Generally, the investigator could say he's working child custody, car repossession or even staking out a location for a bond jumper arrest or something simple such as "I'm on official business."

Should the police confront the investigator it is a good idea to tell the truth as to the reason for being at the location without giving out specifics. The investigator could withhold this information; but once again it depends on how much trouble and/or aggravation the investigator wants.

ONE VEHICLE TAILING THE TARGET

When using one investigator one vehicle, tailing a target's vehicle in the city and tailing the target's vehicle in the country require two different approaches. When tailing in the country, a distance must be maintained to keep from being burnt. On curves when the target is out of sight, the investigator must close the distance and then back off to a safe distance while maintaining eye contact with the vehicle.

This will prevent losing the vehicle should it turn off before the investigator has a chance to get a visual, whether the vehicle turns or continues straight. When tailing a target in the city the investigator must keep a closer vigilance on the moving target's vehicle because of the possibility of the investigator hitting a red light and losing the target. Keeping in mind the number one golden rule, "Never take your eyes off of the target" the investigator should keep as close to the target's vehicle as possible in city block stretches without traffic lights.

If traffic lights exist it is recommended that the investigator tailgate or at the very least do not leave room for any other vehicle to come between the investigator's and the target's vehicle eliminating the possibility of the investigator hitting the red light while the target moves across and out of sight. In the event both the investigator and the target are stopped at a traffic light and a vehicle is between the two.

The investigator should leave room between themselves and the odd vehicle in the event the odd vehicle stalls or does not move when the light changes. The investigator will have enough room to go around. The investigator should be aware as to whether or not the target is dragging the light in order to check to see if they are being followed.

When following a target in the city the investigator might want to keep the sun visor down blocking full view of the investigator in the target's rearview mirror. Since some targets will be more aware than others, this will keep the investigator from being identified in the event leaving the vehicle becomes necessary for a walking tail i.e. in a mall or shopping center.

Paying close attention to the vehicles that visit the target's residence or any vehicles that leave the target's residence when the tailing begins may save the investigator from being "burnt" during the tailing surveillance.

The two vehicles may meet in traffic and if the investigator has to quickly make a traffic light or quickly drive around a vehicle that is moving slow, the investigator may call attention to their movements if the second vehicle is traveling behind of along side of the target or the investigator.

The investigator has to be just as observant of what is happening around them as the investigator might expect the target to be observing. The investigator must be cautious as to what the target might be observing without being paranoid.

If the investigator becomes paranoid, then they are sure to lose the target. One reason investigators become paranoid is because people will look at them while they are on surveillance. This is a natural occurrence because it is human nature to look at someone when you drive by.

This natural occurrence should not necessarily be of concern unless the person stops at the target's residence or leaves the target's residence, drives-by and pays particular attention to the investigator's vehicle. If the target is suspicious for any reason they may make a series of turns to see if they are being followed or turn down a cul-de-sac.

The investigator if familiar with the area might want to wait for a time to allow the target to exit the cul-de-sac depending on the purpose of the surveillance. If the target does not exit in a reasonable amount of time the investigator will be forced to make a drive by into the cul-de-sac to observe where the vehicle is parked or any activity that the target may be engaged in.

The investigator should be sure to make notations of vehicles and a description of item in the yard for possible future use. What may not make any sense at the time may turn out to be significant when solving the question as to what the target is doing at the residence.

If a target pulls into a parking space the investigator should pull into a parking space a across the street or a couple of spaces either before or after the target. Park where it will be easy to reenter the flow of traffic whenever the target starts to move again.

If there are no parking spaces available, circle the block immediately, do not wait five or ten minutes and decide to find the perfect space. This is when the investigator will likely lose the target. This is the only time it will be recommended that the investigator take his eyes off of the subject.

Golden rule number three; "if you want to make something happen, take your eyes off of the target i.e., leave the area for a bathroom break, to grab a quick bite in the drive thru etc." more often than not the target will leave the location causing the investigator to report what they should try to avoid, I lost the target.

Of course, the investigator may not lose the target but I refer you back to Golden Rule # 1. Why take the chance?

FOOT SURVEILLANCE

Should the target enter a hotel, mall or possibly leaving the vehicle for the purpose of creating a diversion for any friends that may see the target and recognize their vehicle. The target may park the vehicle and meet someone in another location, take the bus or a taxi.

The investigator may choose to continue surveillance on foot depending on the purpose of the surveillance. Foot surveillance is sometimes referred to as shadowing. When shadowing the target on a long street with little foot traffic the investigator should give the target a bigger lead than in a crowded mall.

As when the target is in a vehicle approaching a traffic light, when the target approaches a corner the investigator should close the distance in the event the target turns and is out of sight of the investigator briefly.

The investigator is at a disadvantage if working alone because the target may exit their vehicle and walk into a mall only to exit on the other side and enter a vehicle of another person, a bus or have a taxi waiting for them.

If the surveillance is being conducted with two investigators, the investigator than takes the foot surveillance should have a portable radio to report back to the investigator who remained in the vehicle to take up the mobile surveillance.

There area generally less people to deal with in residential neighborhoods. However, the investigator can count on the outside neighbors to pay particular attention to the investigator if he or she is seen too many times, especially if the investigator is acting out of place and trying not to be noticed.

This is where a change of clothes comes in handy the investigator can change into a walking outfit and blend in without any suspicious being raised by the neighbor who is outside watering the lawn. It is recommended that when shadowing a target walking in a residential neighborhood the investigator should conduct the shadowing from across the street.

If the target enters an office building and enters an elevator, depending on the need to know, the investigator should enter the elevator with the target as required by Golden Rule # 1. Depending on how the surveillance has progressed thus far, the investigator should exit on the same floor as the target and walk in the opposite direction at some point the investigator can stop and turn as though they have walked in the wrong direction or have dropped something.

This will give the investigator the opportunity to see which office the target has entered without raising suspicion. If the office is a doctor's office the investigator can enter and pretend to sign the sign in log and take a seat to observe the target.

If the surveillance is to begin on the target when they leave the doctor's office it is a good idea to arrive at the doctor's office prior to the appointment time of the target. When the target arrives they must sign in and their name will be called when the nurse is ready for them.

This give the investigator a good look for identification purpose when the appointment is over and the surveillance is to begin. After identifying which office the target entered then the investigator can return to the lobby and wait for the target to exit the building.

If the target enters a hotel the investigator must blend in with the guest and attempt to follow the target until the room is established. Once the room number is established the investigator should register and check into a room at the hotel.

This will help the investigator justify being on the hotel property should a confrontation with hotel security occur. Once you establish that you are a hotel guest the hotel security will have no grounds to question or bother you.

The investigator should attempt to get the room across from the target and make observations through the peephole. Making contact with hotel personnel may not be a good idea unless the investigator has dealt with them on other occasions.

When two investigators are employ on foot surveillance, one should shadow on the same side of the street and the other one should shadow on the opposite side. The investigators should change positions on occasions to keep the target from becoming familiar with either of the investigators.

Surveillance

Surveillance is an advanced investigative technique that takes many hours of practice to master. I do not recommend that you conduct surveillance on a subject unless you are a licensed private investigator. You could get yourself into a lot of trouble by arousing the suspicion of someone who thinks you are in the act of committing a crime. Further, if you are not accomplished at conducting surveillance, there is a strong possibility that your subject will see you, which could cause major damage to your investigation.

My main reason for describing surveillance work is to give you a better idea how professional investigators work. If you should ever need to hire a private investigator to conduct surveillance, this chapter will give you a good idea of what to expect from them. Surveillance work is very demanding and great care is needed to achieve positive results.

Foot Surveillance

My opinion of a good, general definition of Surveillance is: "To surreptitiously determine the activities of a subject." This means following a subject without any suspicion, on their part, that you are following them.

Physical surveillance is one of the most common techniques used by investigators to obtain necessary information. Surveillance, or shadowing, involves following a person, both closely enough not to lose them (close tail), and far enough away to avoid detection (loose tail).

Effective surveillance requires much practice and a good measure of patience since you may find yourself tailing someone for hours, or even waiting for them just to appear.

A couple of terms in surveillance that you should be aware of are "getting warm" and "being burned." "Warm" means that the subject suspects that you are following them, while "burned" means that the subject knows you are following them and knows who it is. Experts agree that losing a subject is better than "burning" a case since you can usually locate a subject again. But once they know you are following them, your case is finished.

One thing to remember when conducting surveillance is to blend in with the crowd. Don't carry any objects, such as a briefcase, cigar or umbrella (unless it's raining) that could distinguish you from others around you.

In addition, it is rarely necessary to wear a disguise. Experts generally warn novices to avoid putting on a fake moustache or beard because, usually, they look fake. Make-up artists make good consultants if it should become necessary to disguise yourself.

If you want to change your appearance, you can do so by putting on or taking off a coat or hat. This is usually effective, but you also might want to carry a change of clothes in your car just in case. Having one or two pairs of glasses can also help.

Investigators often follow their subjects on foot and this surveillance method requires special techniques. The cardinal rule is "never lose sight of your subject." Sometimes, in heavy pedestrian traffic, this is easier said than done.

In heavy traffic, follow your subject by about eight to nine feet, much farther if there is little or no other foot traffic. Walking on the opposite side of the street may be a good way to follow someone without risking detection.

If your subject turns around, just act natural; don't panic and don't make any abrupt movements like darting into an alley or quickly hiding behind some object. If possible, simply stop and look in a shop window and use the reflection in the glass to observe your subject.

If that won't work, pass by your subject nonchalantly, stop a short distance ahead, look in a window and then take a casual look back toward your subject. But, it is a good idea not to meet their eyes since it will be easier for a subject to notice and remember you if your eyes briefly lock glances.

If your subject enters some public place like a restaurant, train, or bus, you will need to follow them inside. For these situations you will need to carry a sufficient amount of cash to cover your expenses. Credit cards can help in case your subject decides to take a train or plane to another city or state.

"Warm" subjects use a variety of tactics to discover if they are being followed. One way is to reverse their course of direction. Following on the opposite side of the street can help you avoid detection if your subject tries this.

Walking around a corner and stopping suddenly is another method subjects use to catch investigators on their trail. If this happens to you, just keep on walking around the corner, then turn back when it's safe.

A subject might intentionally drop a piece of paper on the ground to see if someone picks it up. Other ways subjects spot a tail include slipping into public places like restaurants, theatres, or hotels and exiting immediately through another door.

Getting on a subway, public transit, or bus and then jumping off just before the doors close is a common method. If this happens to you, just stay on until the next stop and hope you can find your subject again. Don't attempt to jump off with the subject.

Moving to a deserted area is an easy way for a subject to spot a tail since there is no concealment. In addition, a very suspicious subject may have another person around them acting as a lookout.

Some Surveillance Do's...

- Know as much about your subject as possible.

- Verify subject's address.

- Know the area where the surveillance will begin.

- Be properly equipped.

- Arrive early.

- When seated in a car, attract as little attention as possible.

- Watch subject's location carefully.

- Look ahead and anticipate anything.

- Watch the subject's rear closely. (the car, you fool)

- Keep intervening traffic under control when doing vehicle surveillance.

- Try to know beforehand the general direction that the subject will be heading.

Relax, take a deep, slow breath.

If, for example, your subject takes short trips to the same places at slow speeds everyday, your job will be much easier than if they are a fast and unpredictable driver who never visits the same place twice. If you know that the subject drives like a wild man, then you should consider a two-vehicle surveillance.

The type of vehicle you drive is important, as you do not wish to stand out. Your vehicle should be as similar as possible to other cars in the area. I have found that a later model two or four door sedan, or van, with a standard, non-flashy, neutral paint finish usually blends in nicely. Tan, dark, light blue, and white, are colors that don't call attention to themselves.

If you are working in an upper-class neighborhood, I would advise not using an older model car or rusty van as you would be drawing much attention to yourself. Whenever possible, use a newer model van as your surveillance unit.

Your vehicle should always be in excellent working condition and you should fill your gas tank before starting surveillance. It is very frustrating to have to stop because your gas gauge reads empty. You should have all your fluid levels and belts checked regularly. There is nothing worse than a vehicle that won't run right during a surveillance.

For vehicle surveillance that will last a few days, you might want to try switching units each day to avoid detection. Since you might not have more than one vehicle, you might borrow or rent a car or van from a low cost rental agency. Be aware that even if you are driving a rental car and your subject "makes" you, they could find out who you are through the rental agency. Therefore, you must use the same precautions as you would use driving your own vehicle.

Remember to keep essential equipment in your vehicle at all times. This includes flashlight, maps of the city and state, a camera, tape recorder, binoculars, and a packed overnight bag. Also, a pair of rubber-soled shoes will be of use if you have to leave the car and follow on foot.

Initiating the Surveillance

The way you begin your vehicle surveillance may decide the success or failure of your operation. Real-life surveillance is not like the movies where the surveillance vehicle parks across the street and starts up when the subject comes out. This is far too conspicuous and a deaf, dumb and blind subject probably would notice you.

It is much less risky to park down the block with a good telescope or set of binoculars. The surrounding geography may help you in this regard. Each new surveillance location usually has a perfect spot where the investigator can observe the subject come out to their car, and which also allows the investigator to follow the subject in any direction without concern.

If your subject is on a one way street, you may park just down the street or around the corner with a reasonable expectation that the subject will drive past you when they leave. This allows you to reduce your risk of detection when initiating surveillance.

Surveillance in progress...

While tailing a vehicle, keep at least one or two cars between you and the subject's car. Also, do not remain constantly behind the subject; change lanes often. Try not to appear fully in their rear-view mirror.

The distance between you and your subject will vary according to the traffic conditions and the type of area in which you find yourself. Dense city traffic requires you to stay very close to the subject. In rural areas you may have to keep a distance of hundreds of yards to avoid detection.

Always try to stay in the subject's blind spot whenever possible. This only works, of course, in city traffic and on roads that have more than one lane. The blind spot to the subject's right rear is usually the one allowing the least visibility.

Noticing whether the subject has a companion or is alone is important along with what the companion is doing. If the companion is turning their head around every few seconds, they may be watching for a "tail". Here you would have to be much more cautious.

Changing Appearances

While it is impossible to change a vehicle's appearance totally, there are some small things that can be done to reduce the sense of familiarity with it. The simple changing of positions by you and your partner(s) in the surveillance vehicle can modify your general appearance. Your partner can crouch down in the seat sometimes and you may even change your posture behind the wheel.

Also, you and your partner(s) could put on and remove caps and sunglasses. Depending on the weather you also can change coats or jackets. These things have a tendency to change the general appearance of the surveillance unit as a whole.

Strategies

With experience, you develop some preplanned moves that allow you to stay successfully with your subject, even under difficult situations. But sometimes, pure luck and inspiration play their part too.

If, for some reason, the subject stops, parks, or turns a corner before you can do so, don't panic. Drive past the subject, make the first turn you can and continue following from there, or park in the first available spot if you find the subject has parked.

Other strategies and terms you need to know include "leap frog", or "sandwich tailing" and "paralleling." The sandwich tail, or leap frog, is where two investigators participate in the tail; "A" is in front of the subject and "B" is far enough behind the subject that they remain undetected. "A" radios to "B" to tell them when the subject turns or parks.

After a while, or if "A" loses the subject, "B" closes the gap. When "A" is in position behind "B", then "B" passes the subject and takes over "A" 's original position. Of course, "A" then assumes the rear position. When properly carried out, this technique lowers suspicion and may be used for an extended period.

Much more difficult, paralleling is when the investigator tails a subject in a vehicle on a street parallel to the one the subject is driving on. Usually, the investigator will check at each intersection to see if the subject is still following the same course. If the subject isn't there, that means they either stopped on the last block, or turned the corner. The investigator must then discover the subject's exact location as quickly as possible.

When tailing an unsuspecting subject who is driving fast, it is best to follow in the same lane. Never allow too many vehicles to get between you and the subject. This is especially true if the subject is traveling in the fast or left turn lane. Suddenly, the subject may turn onto a side street and, unfortunately, lose you due to heavy oncoming traffic.

Serious problems can arise when approaching traffic signals. Remember, you are not driving a police or emergency vehicle and are liable for any traffic infractions that you may incur. Erratic driving also can arouse the suspicions of your subject. If your subject does not suspect a "tail", it is not uncommon to follow the vehicle almost directly behind. This is especially advantageous in heavy, city traffic.

When approaching traffic lights at an intersection it is helpful to watch the pedestrian cross-walk signals. These let you know how fresh or stale your green light is. If the pedestrian signal shows a white or green light, you know that you have a fresh green light.

You don't have to hurry as much to get through the intersection. But, if the pedestrian signal shows solid or blinking red, you have a stale green traffic light that could turn yellow at any moment. Here, you have to get through the intersection, behind or next to your subject, as soon as possible.

In residential areas, it is somewhat easy to maintain a "loose tail" and observe parked cars from a considerable distance with the use of binoculars. But, you must use extreme caution and never let anyone see you using binoculars. This will arouse enough suspicion for the neighbors to call the police.

When observing the subject and their associates, make complete detailed notes at the time or as soon as possible, noting complete descriptions of clothing and physical appearances. If appropriate, photograph what you see whenever possible, as photographic evidence is difficult to repute in a Court of Law. We will be discussing note taking and photography later in the book.

Perhaps you have prior information that your subject will be traveling to a specific location, such as another home, hotel or motel. If this is the case, you may not need to attempt to follow the vehicle. You might proceed ahead of them and locate an appropriate place of hiding before their arrival.

Night Surveillance

Night surveillance poses some problems, and also some relief from other problems. The lower visibility works both ways. It is harder for the subject to see who is following, but the investigator has more trouble keeping track of the subject's car.

One problem with night vehicle surveillance is that your headlights will be very visible from a long distance. This isn't a problem if there is other traffic because headlights look even more alike than tail lights, but in a rural area they stand out.
One solution is to have your headlights wired so that they can be operated independently from one another. (This may be illegal in some areas.) It is done usually with two toggle switches. When your subject goes around a corner, you simply turn off one of your headlights. If your subject should be paying attention, your vehicle will appear as a completely different one at night.

If the investigation is of considerable importance, then sophisticated equipment may be rented or purchased for the occasion. Such sophisticated equipment might include an electronic tracking device, night vision starlight scope or an expensive high-speed telephoto lens for the camera.

Extended periods of surveillance should be conducted by several different investigators because fatigue can play tricks on one's imagination. Remember to be well equipped and have fresh replacement batteries for the appropriate equipment. The greatest teacher in this type of investigation is experience. The more you attempt something, the more efficient you become.

Stakeout Surveillance

The Hollywood or television version of a stakeout is two men in a car parked some 30 feet away from the subject's premises, watching through the windshield. In real life, two men in a car might as well hang out a sign saying "Stake Out In Progress" because they would be that obvious. Usually a nervous neighbor will call the police.

Using a car as a fixed observation post is very amateurish, and is a method of last resort. Standing in a doorway is also conspicuous, although it may become useful when following a subject who goes into a building and will soon be coming back out.

Temporary Stakeouts

There must be a better way, and there is! A temporary stakeout works much better if you can blend in with other people in the area. One way of doing so is to go into a nearby cafe, store or restaurant. When you do this, the subject would have to pick you out of a crowd to "make" you. This is much more difficult than spotting a lone figure in a doorway.

Behavior is as important as physical surroundings. Your behavior must be appropriate for a given situation. That is why standing in a doorway or sitting in a parked car is so conspicuous.

People don't normally stand in doorways unless it's raining or snowing or they're waiting for a bus. People normally park their car, lock it and leave. Anyone who sits in a car for more than a couple of minutes will stand out because it is not a normal thing.

One exception is a male-female team. They don't stand out if they sit in a car together. Anyone who sees them will interpret their behavior as that of friends or lovers, especially if they are talking.

At night on a dark street they can avoid seeming out of place by hugging and kissing. Obviously, in the same situation and in most neighborhoods, a team of two men hugging and kissing would attract attention.

Setting up a temporary observation post is a matter of quick improvisation. Often, there are props available nearby. A shoeshine stand or a stand-up lunch counter is often nearby in a city. A telephone booth might be another prop. A gas station is yet another opportunity.

Using a phone booth for a few minutes' cover is more than just picking up the hand set and pretending to talk. It helps to have a notebook open and pretend to be writing. A briefcase is a useful prop for this situation. If the phone booth is occupied, even better. Simply stand next to it as if you are waiting to use the phone. This will enable you to look around and remain normal and less conspicuous.

If no props seem available, you might lift the hood of your car and appear to be working on your engine. A stalled motorist won't usually arouse suspicion, but this improvised maneuver shouldn't last for too long.

Semi-Fixed Stakeouts

Sometimes it's possible to establish a somewhat more permanent position for a stakeout. I mentioned cars being the worst possible choice for a stakeout, but other vehicles can be much better. Any vehicle that does not permit easy observation of the inside will do, when it blends in with the surroundings.

Vans and campers are very common surveillance vehicles and are ideal. If you can borrow or use a van, you will have a tremendous advantage. You might rent a van, but if you do so often, you might be better off buying one.

The ideal set up is a van with lightly tinted windows at the sides and back. Combine this with heavy, dark curtains over each window and an opaque curtain or partition between the front seats and rear compartment. The tinted windows prevent people from easily seeing that curtains are opening and closing. The curtains prevent you from being silhouetted. When there are two windows on opposite sides of the van, people can see you moving between them.

It is critical to remain back from the windows when observing, just as you would in a room. The interior of the van should be darker than the light level outside to make seeing in more difficult. Curtains also serve the purpose of keeping the van darker inside. If the stakeout takes place overnight, it's important to make sure no lights come on when any van door opens, as the slightest light might give you away.

The van windows should be clean, not only for observation, but to enable you to take clear photographs when the opportunity arises. When using camera or binoculars, be sure to remain far enough inside to avoid direct sunlight reflection from the lenses. A ray of sunlight can reflect very brightly if the angle is right, thus giving your presence away.

If you expect your stakeout to last a long time, it is good to prepare in advance. You should plan for food, drink and toilet facilities. If your van isn't camperized, you'll have to improvise. In a pinch, some granola bars and a canteen of water will do for a short while.

A milk carton or jar might serve for urination unless you are staked out for more than twenty-four hours. Here, you should have a camper's porta-potti. It is important not to risk blowing the stakeout by leaving your post due to a call of nature.

If you have a camperized van, you can set your stakeout up in style. Presumably, you'll have a refrigerator or icebox, a stove, and even a toilet. This enables you to maintain the observation post for days at a time in comfort.

In such a case, your main problems will be that of staying awake and avoiding signs of occupancy. You'll have to be careful about noise and be aware that any moving around inside the vehicle may make it rock. If anyone passes by and notices movement or talking, it could give you away.

Parking could be a problem. First, the vehicle must "fit in" and appear normal in the area. A lavish motor home seems out of place in a poor section of the city. A rusted "hippy van" doesn't fit very well into a middle or upper-class neighborhood. There may be local parking regulations that will impede your operation. Watch out for parking meters and time restricted parking zones.

Parking distance is important. People are less likely to pay attention to vehicles parked a block or two away than within a few yards of them. If the parking place is a logical one, such as a shopping center parking lot, your surveillance vehicle will remain psychologically invisible.

The Fixed Stakeout

The basic prerequisite for a fixed observation post is to know the territory. Knowing the layout of the area is important because it allows you to choose the best possible observation post. Knowing your subject's building and all its exits enables you to cover it best. It may be necessary to set up more than one observation point if you need to cover several sides of a building.

In certain instances you will need to rent a room or an apartment to carry out your surveillance. You'll want to keep your true purpose a secret from the landlord. They may talk to, or even be a friend of your subject.

Another danger is having the landlord think that you are doing something suspicious. Unless you behave fairly naturally, someone might suspect that you are dealing drugs or doing something illegal and bring in police surveillance or even direct questioning.

Most likely you will need to move in some equipment and supplies, even for the smaller stakeouts. Some of these items might be:

· food

· drink

· Digital or Video Camera

· Binoculars or Telescope

· Misc. Electronic Equipment

While the sight of a person carrying a cooler or cardboard box doesn't ordinarily arouse suspicion, a pair of binoculars might. Remember to transport any optical or other specialized equipment in a box or bag to avoid revealing your true purpose.

Avoiding detection while at the observation post is essential. The first thing you should do upon entering the surveillance area is to draw all the blinds, curtains and drapes almost shut, and turn off any lights that are on.

Set up your post so that you can see the target area while back from the window some distance. Never put your face close to the window or draw back the drapes to get a better view. Select your field of view and leave it that way.

You may use a small, weak flashlight at night if you are careful not to shine it out the window. Turning on the room lights in a residential neighborhood may seem normal during the night, but in a commercial area it would be a giveaway.

Rural Observation Posts

Wide open spaces give you more freedom but also expose you to easier observation by your subject or others. When selecting an observation post, you may choose a gully, rock formation or shrubbery. An important point is that you should choose a spot that gives you cover from all angles. Someone might come along, see you before you can hide, and blow your cover.

People living in rural areas usually know their neighbors and immediately spot anyone who doesn't belong. Thick woods usually give good cover. It may be necessary to approach the post at night to reduce the chances of detection by anyone. This may mean that warm clothing is necessary with food and drink.

Finding a place to leave your vehicle can be a serious problem. If there are no campgrounds nearby, it might be necessary to have a friend drive you to a point near your cover and drop you off.

It is most likely going too far to wear camouflage clothing and camouflage colors on your face. If anyone sees you it would immediately arouse suspicion. Much better is dark clothing and the removal of anything shiny, reflective or bright, such as a belt buckle.

Noise carries far on a quiet night, therefore, it is best to leave behind things that rattle or make noise such as coins and other objects. Choice of clothing material is important too, because some fabrics, such as nylon, are noisy when rubbed against brush. Dacron or cotton, and even wool, is much better.

In an extreme situation it may become necessary to dig a foxhole and camouflage it with branches. If this does become necessary, it is best to dig at night and have all loose soil and other evidence of digging covered up or scattered by first light.

A Lesson in Surveillance:

First you will need a target. Someone you hate, someone that you wish to expose, someone you want to blackmail. This could be a boss, a co-worker, a friend, or an ex-lover.

Second you will need a manual still camera with a zoom lens. If you can't get your hands on a zoom lens a 50mm lens will work and will work much better than a zoom in low-light conditions.

Third you will need a car and someone to drive it, the more nondescript the better. If you have 1975 Nova, complete with a body painted in rust and a trunk held down by a bungee cord, leave it and find something else.

Always try and choose a car that fits both your subject and the areas in which you'll be following him. If you plan on tailing your target more than a few days a week you'd be best advised to switch cars frequently.

Harassment is easily prosecuted and most states have stalking laws in effect.

And lastly you'll need a plan. Are you tailing someone for profit? Or are you seeking retribution? Or are you doing this all out of sheer boredom? Whatever you find to be your reason, make sure you find a way to bring that plan it into reality.

Now, I suggest to you to make your first subject a completely random target. Continue watching only random people until you feel comfortable enough to hide yourself from someone that may know you. The best way to choose a random target is by picking one straight out of a phone book.

Therefore if you were caught on your first project, you'd have absolutely no connection to the person you have been watching. I don't recommend choosing a 'random' person that you have seen. I.E. if you see the perfect target, that just happens to be a woman, in the parking lot of a grocery store you may find yourself losing your professionalism to your own voyeuristic tendencies.

Simply put, if you are interested in Pointless Espionage you are a Voyeur. And if you build up an attraction for your target, you are now a stalker. Pick a random person to start, case closed.

As you follow your subject you should have either a small notebook and pen that you can conceal on yourself, or a small mini cassette recorder that you can use to log your notes on your subject.

Using a digital recorder is ideal because it gives you hands free note taking and allows you to keep your eyes on your subject at all times. Your notes and your pictures are your evidence, so remember to be as detailed as possible. Including dates, times, locations, license plate numbers, etc.

If you happen to lose your target for an extended period of time, your notes may give you a clue as to their usual whereabouts and habits... allowing you to pick up the tail.

After you have graduated from your first practice missions you may find it difficult finding the address of your 'Prime Target' by going through the proper channels.

If you don't have a point in which you can start tracking your target (i.e. a frequented public place) you may need to use other means. If your target isn't in the yellow pages, or on an online version, try a detective website

If you don't have any trusted friends in the Police Department or at the Phone Company, and if you've got the resources, you may want to try a lost person's search agency. These agencies usually advertise on TV and are on average discreet, fast, and classified.

A Note on Tailing:

If you intend to follow someone for an extended period of time inside of your car, remember to top off you gas tank. You can't afford to run out of gas during a mission. I also shouldn't have to tell you by now how to be discreet. If you're tailing someone in a car, put some space in between your two cars. If you can, stay behind another car or in another lane.

Try to anticipate their turns, this shouldn't be hard. People, when switching lanes, often hesitate before putting on their turn signals. Don't look for the signal, look at the tires and the driver. Forgive me for using a sports metaphor, but keep your eyes on the ball.

If you want a real challenge follow the person by driving ahead of them. In this way your target will avoid most suspicions that they are being followed. Drive like a normal person; speed up, slow down, tailgate, and pass them.

If you don't they'll probably think you're a cop and slow down. At this point you may be noticed if you don't go around them as everyone else would do.

You should always bring a few different sets of clothes with you when you attempt to shadow someone. At some point you may be following a subject to a beach where without a bathing suit, you'll stand out.

The same can be said for a fancy restaurant or club where you won't fit in without a formal style of dress. You must learn to prepare for many different situations.

The most difficult thing to do is sit in a car in the middle of the night and be discreet as you watch someone. If you are parked in a street overnight, relax, you're probably going to be there for a few hours. Try to minimize your food and liquid intake. You may lose sight of your subject if you are forced to take a bathroom break.

At four in the morning it's hard to pass the time if you're alone without falling asleep. And anytime you spend in a car in the middle of night, especially in a suburban neighborhood, will attract attention to you and your activities. If you are a woman it may be a lot easier for you.

In a suburban area a man sitting behind the steering wheel of a car will definitely attract more attention than a woman sitting in the passenger side. By sitting in the passenger side of a car you are implying that you are waiting for someone to return, and if you're a woman, people will think that you're waiting for your husband to return to the car and pay you far less attention.

If you have the means try getting your hands on a van and stay away from tinted windows, they wind up drawing more attention to your car. Ideally you may try getting a room in a neighboring building or hotel that you can surveil from.

Don't go climbing trees and telephone poles to get a better position, there is always an easier way.

You should always have a cover story in the event that you are stopped and questioned by Police or Neighbors.

You may want to print up business cards in the event that you are stopped during the day as well as working on a small run down or your product or service that you can repeat on command.

You may also want to print up false identification cards that you can present in place of your real one. (I.E. a fake Private Investigator or Press Pass ID.)

If you're caught snooping around someone's property, my personal favorite cover is to bring a broken dog leash with you and claim that your dog has run away from you. Memorize the name, color, and breed of your imaginary dog to recite on command.

So if you've got you target, your camera, and your car- get started!

And remember this is practice for a larger goal. So if you've read this guide and become interested in Pointless Espionage, I ask you to go out, find a target, and build a file.

Are You Being Followed?

When the police follow you on foot, they operate in teams of three or more, all in radio contact and coordinated from a station or a car. They can be very hard to spot, because if one of them thinks that you have seen him/her they will drop behind and let another take over. Always when being followed, the way to flush a tail is to do something illogical, such as jump on a bus and then jump off again immediately and see who follows you.

Go up an escalator and then come down again. Take a lift up and down. Cross a road twice. Take a route that is more complicated than necessary. There is no reason for anyone else to do any of these things unless they are following you.

You could have a friend follow you at a distance over a prearranged route to see if they can see anyone else following. Geddit? To lose a tail, head for very crowded areas such as shopping centers, high streets, department stores, etc. and try and slip in and out of crowds and exits.

In a car the same thing applies. Car tails are often done in a "box", whereby three or four cars will follow ahead, behind and parallel to you. You may not see them but they will always be where you want to go. Going round a roundabout more than once or taking four consecutive left or right turns are classic methods of telling if you are being tailed.

Whether on foot or in a car the ideal situation is to get to somewhere isolated, such as long, empty roads or areas of parkland, so that anyone tailing you will stick out like a sore thumb.

Chapter 6 Survival

Introduction

The following paragraphs expand on the meaning of each letter of the word survival. Study and remember what each letter signifies because you may some day have to make it work for you.

S -Size Up the Situation

If you are in a combat situation, find a place where you can conceal yourself from the enemy. Remember, security takes priority. Use your senses of hearing, smell, and sight to get a feel for the battlefield. What is the enemy doing? Advancing? Holding in place? Retreating? You will have to consider what is developing on the battlefield when you make your survival plan.

Size Up Your Surroundings

Determine the pattern of the area. Get a feel for what is going on around you. Every environment, whether forest, jungle, or desert, has a rhythm or pattern. This rhythm or pattern includes animal and bird noises and movements and insect sounds. It may also include enemy traffic and civilian movements.

Size Up Your Physical Condition

The pressure of the battle you were in or the trauma of being in a survival situation may have caused you to overlook wounds you received. Check your wounds and give yourself first aid. Take care to prevent further bodily harm. For instance, in any climate, drink plenty of water to prevent dehydration. If you are in a cold or wet climate, put on additional clothing to prevent hypothermia.

Size Up Your Equipment

Perhaps in the heat of battle, you lost or damaged some of your equipment. Check to see what equipment you have and what condition it is in.

Now that you have sized up your situation, surroundings, physical condition, and equipment, you are ready to make your survival plan. In doing so, keep in mind your basic physical needs--water, food, and shelter.

U -Use All Your Senses, Undue Haste Makes Waste

You may make a wrong move when you react quickly without thinking or planning. That move may result in your capture or death. Don't move just for the sake of taking action. Consider all aspects of your situation (size up your situation) before you make a decision and a move. If you act in haste, you may forget or lose some of your equipment. In your haste you may also become disoriented so that you don't know which way to go. Plan your moves. Be ready to move out quickly without endangering yourself if the enemy is near you. Use all your senses to evaluate the situation. Note sounds and smells. Be sensitive to temperature changes. Be observant.

R -Remember Where You Are

Spot your location on your map and relate it to the surrounding terrain. This is a basic principle that you must always follow. If there are other persons with you, make sure they also know their location. Always know who in your group, vehicle, or aircraft has a map and compass. If that person is killed, you will have to get the map and compass from him. Pay close attention to where you are and to where you are going. Do not rely on others in the group to keep track of the route. Constantly orient yourself. Always try to determine, as a minimum, how your location relates to--

The location of enemy units and controlled areas.

The location of friendly units and controlled areas.

The location of local water sources (especially important in the desert).

Areas that will provide good cover and concealment.

This information will allow you to make intelligent decisions when you are in a survival and evasion situation.

V -Vanquish Fear and Panic

The greatest enemies in a combat survival and evasion situation are fear and panic. If uncontrolled, they can destroy your ability to make an intelligent decision. They may cause you to react to your feelings and imagination rather than to your situation. They can drain your energy and thereby cause other negative emotions. Previous survival and evasion training and self-confidence will enable you to vanquish fear and panic.

I –Improvise

In the United States, we have items available for all our needs. Many of these items are cheap to replace when damaged. Our easy come, easy go, easy-to-replace culture makes it unnecessary for us to improvise. This inexperience in improvisation can be an enemy in a survival situation. Learn to improvise. Take a tool designed for a specific purpose and see how many other uses you can make of it.

Learn to use natural objects around you for different needs. An example is using a rock for a hammer. No matter how complete a survival kit you have with you, it will run out or wear out after a while.

Your imagination must take over when your kit wears out.

V -Value Living

All of us were born kicking and fighting to live, but we have become used to the soft life. We have become creatures of comfort. We dislike inconveniences and discomforts. What happens when we are faced with a survival situation with its stresses, inconveniences, and discomforts? This is when the will to live- placing a high value on living-is vital. The experience and knowledge you have gained through life and your Army training will have a bearing on your will to live. Stubbornness, a refusal to give in to problems and obstacles that face you, will give you the mental and physical strength to endure.

A -Act Like the Natives

The natives and animals of a region have adapted to their environment. To get a feel of the area, watch how the people go about their daily routine. When and what do they eat? When, where, and how do they get their food? When and where do they go for water? What time do they usually go to bed and get up? These actions are important to you when you are trying to avoid capture.

Animal life in the area can also give you clues on how to survive. Animals also require food, water, and shelter. By watching them, you can find sources of water and food.

WARNING

Animals cannot serve as an absolute guide to what you can eat and drink. Many animals eat plants that are toxic to humans.

Keep in mind that the reaction of animals can reveal your presence to the enemy.

If in a friendly area, one way you can gain rapport with the natives is to show interest in their tools and how they get food and water. By studying the people, you learn to respect them, you often make valuable friends, and, most important, you learn how to adapt to their environment and increase your chances of survival.

L -Live by Your Wits, But for Now, Learn Basic Skills

Without training in basic skills for surviving and evading on the battlefield, your chances of living through a combat survival and evasion situation are slight.

Learn these basic skills now--not when you are headed for or are in the battle. How you decide to equip yourself before deployment will impact on whether or not you survive. You need to know about the environment to which you are going, and you must practice basic skills geared to that environment. For instance, if you are going to a desert, you need to know how to get water in the desert.

Practice basic survival skills during all training programs and exercises. Survival training reduces fear of the unknown and gives you self-confidence. It teaches you to live by your wits.

Develop a survival pattern that lets you beat the enemies of survival. This survival pattern must include food, water, shelter, fire, first aid, and signals placed in order of importance. For example, in a cold environment, you would need a fire to get warm; a shelter to protect you from the cold, wind, and rain or snow; traps or snares to get food; a means to signal friendly aircraft; and first aid to maintain health. If injured, first aid has top priority no matter what climate you are in.

Change your survival pattern to meet your immediate physical needs as the environment changes.

As you read the rest of these chapters, keep in mind the keyword SURVIVAL and the need for a survival pattern.

Chapter 7 Psychology of Survival

It takes much more than the knowledge and skills to build shelters, get food, make fires, and travel without the aid of standard navigational devices to live successfully through a survival situation. Some people with little or no survival training have managed to survive life-threatening circumstances.

Some people with survival training have not used their skills and died. A key ingredient in any survival situation is the mental attitude of the individual(s) involved. Having survival skills is important; having the will to survive is essential. Without a desire to survive, acquired skills serve little purpose and invaluable knowledge goes to waste.

There is a psychology to survival. The soldier in a survival environment faces many stresses that ultimately impact on his mind. These stresses can produce thoughts and emotions that, if poorly understood, can transform a confident, well-trained soldier into an indecisive, ineffective individual with questionable ability to survive.

Thus, every soldier must be aware of and be able to recognize those stresses commonly associated with survival. Additionally, it is imperative that soldiers be aware of their reactions to the wide variety of stresses associated with survival. This chapter will identify and explain the nature of stress, the stresses of survival, and those internal reactions soldiers will naturally experience when faced with the stresses of a real-world survival situation.

The knowledge you, the soldier, gain from this chapter and other chapters in this manual, will prepare you to come through the toughest times alive.

A LOOK AT STRESS

Before we can understand our psychological reactions in a survival setting, it is helpful to first know a little bit about stress.

Stress is not a disease that you cure and eliminate. Instead, it is a condition we all experience. Stress can be described as our reaction to pressure. It is the name given to the experience we have as we physically, mentally, emotionally, and spiritually respond to life's tensions.

Need for Stress

We need stress because it has many positive benefits. Stress provides us with challenges; it gives us chances to learn about our values and strengths. Stress can show our ability to handle pressure without breaking; it tests our adaptability and flexibility; it can stimulate us to do our best. Because we usually do not consider unimportant events stressful, stress can also be an excellent indicator of the significance we attach to an event-- in other words, it highlights what is important to us.

We need to have some stress in our lives, but too much of anything can be bad. The goal is to have stress, but not an excess of it. Too much stress can take its toll on people and organizations. Too much stress leads to distress. Distress causes an uncomfortable tension that we try to escape and, preferably, avoid. Listed below are a few of the common signs of distress you may find in your fellow soldiers or yourself when faced with too much stress:

Difficulty making decisions.

Angry outbursts.

Forgetfulness.

Low energy level.

Constant worrying.

Propensity for mistakes.

Thoughts about death or suicide.

Trouble getting along with others.

Withdrawing from others.

Hiding from responsibilities.

Carelessness.

As you can see, stress can be constructive or destructive. It can encourage or discourage, move us along or stop us dead in our tracks, and make life meaningful or seemingly meaningless. Stress can inspire you to operate successfully and perform at your maximum efficiency in a survival situation. It can also cause you to panic and forget all your training. Key to your survival is your ability to manage the inevitable stresses you will encounter. The survivor is the soldier who works with his stresses instead of letting his stresses work on him.

Survival Stressors

Any event can lead to stress and, as everyone has experienced, events don't always come one at a time. Often, stressful events occur simultaneously. These events are not stress, but they produce it and are called "stressors." Stressors are the obvious cause while stress is the response. Once the body recognizes the presence of a stressor, it then begins to act to protect itself.

In response to a stressor, the body prepares either to "fight or flee." This preparation involves an internal SOS sent throughout the body. As the body responds to this SOS, several actions take place. The body releases stored fuels (sugar and fats) to provide quick energy; breathing rate increases to supply more oxygen to the blood; muscle tension increases to prepare for action; blood clotting mechanisms are activated to reduce bleeding from cuts; senses become more acute (hearing becomes more sensitive, eyes become big, smell becomes sharper) so that you are more aware of your surrounding and heart rate and blood pressure rise to provide more blood to the muscles. This protective posture lets a person cope with potential dangers; however, a person cannot maintain such a level of alertness indefinitely.

Stressors are not courteous; one stressor does not leave because another one arrives. Stressors add up. The cumulative effect of minor stressors can be a major distress if they all happen too close together. As the body's resistance to stress wears down and the sources of stress continue (or increase), eventually a state of exhaustion arrives. At this point, the ability to resist stress or use it in a positive way gives out and signs of distress appear. Anticipating stressors and developing strategies to cope with them are two ingredients in the effective management of stress. It is therefore essential that the soldier in a survival setting be aware of the types of stressors he will encounter. Let's take a look at a few of these.

Injury, Illness, or Death

Injury, illness, and death are real possibilities a survivor has to face. Perhaps nothing is more stressful than being alone in an unfamiliar environment where you could die from hostile action, an accident, or from eating something lethal. Illness and injury can also add to stress by limiting your ability to maneuver, get food and drink, find shelter, and defend yourself. Even if illness and injury don't lead to death, they add to stress through the pain and discomfort they generate. It is only by con-trolling the stress associated with the vulnerability to injury, illness, and death that a soldier can have the courage to take the risks associated with survival tasks.

Uncertainly and Lack of Control

Some people have trouble operating in settings where everything is not clear-cut. The only guarantee in a survival situation is that nothing is guaranteed. It can be extremely stressful operating on limited information in a setting where you have limited control of your surroundings. This uncertainty and lack of control also add to the stress of being ill, injured, or killed.

Environment

Even under the most ideal circumstances, nature is quite formidable. In survival, a soldier will have to contend with the stressors of weather, terrain, and the variety of creatures inhabiting an area. Heat, cold, rain, winds, mountains, swamps, deserts, insects, dangerous reptiles, and other animals are just a few of the challenges awaiting the soldier working to survive. Depending on how a soldier handles the stress of his environment, his surroundings can be either a source of food and protection or can be a cause of extreme discomfort leading to injury, illness, or death.

Hunger and Thirst

Without food and water a person will weaken and eventually die. Thus, getting and preserving food and water takes on increasing importance as the length of time in a survival setting increases. For a soldier used to having his provisions issued, foraging can be a big source of stress.

Fatigue

Forcing yourself to continue surviving is not easy as you grow more tired. It is possible to become so fatigued that the act of just staying awake is stressful in itself.

Isolation

There are some advantages to facing adversity with others. As soldiers we learn individual skills, but we train to function as part of a team. Although we, as soldiers, complain about higher headquarters, we become used to the information and guidance it provides, especially during times of confusion. Being in contact with others also provides a greater sense of security and a feeling someone is available to help if problems occur. A significant stressor in survival situations is that often a person or team has to rely solely on its own resources.

The survival stressors mentioned in this section are by no means the only ones you may face. Remember, what is stressful to one person may not be stressful to another. Your experiences, training, personal outlook on life, physical and mental conditioning, and level of self-confidence contribute to what you will find stressful in a survival environment. The object is not to avoid stress, but rather to manage the stressors of survival and make them work for you.

We now have a general knowledge of stress and the stressors common to survival; the next step is to examine our reactions to the stressors we may face.

NATURAL REACTIONS

Man has been able to survive many shifts in his environment throughout the centuries. His ability to adapt physically and mentally to a changing world kept him alive while other species around him gradually died off. The same survival mechanisms that kept our forefathers alive can help keep us alive as well! However, these survival mechanisms that can help us can also work against us if we don't understand and anticipate their presence.

It is not surprising that the average person will have some psychological reactions in a survival situation. We will now examine some of the major internal reactions you and anyone with you might experience with the survival stressors addressed in the earlier paragraphs. Let's begin.

Fear

Fear is our emotional response to dangerous circumstances that we believe have the potential to cause death, injury, or illness. This harm is not just limited to physical damage; the threat to one's emotional and mental well-being can generate fear as well. For the soldier trying to survive, fear can have a positive function if it encourages him to be cautious in situations where recklessness could result in injury. Unfortunately, fear can also immobilize a person. It can cause him to become so frightened that he fails to perform activities essential for survival. Most soldiers will have some degree of fear when placed in unfamiliar surroundings under adverse conditions. There is no shame in this! Each soldier must train himself not to be overcome by his fears. Ideally, through realistic training, we can acquire the knowledge and skills needed to increase our confidence and thereby manage our fears.

Anxiety

Associated with fear is anxiety. Because it is natural for us to be afraid, it is also natural for us to experience anxiety. Anxiety can be an uneasy, apprehensive feeling we get when faced with dangerous situations (physical, mental, and emotional). When used in a healthy way, anxiety urges us to act to end, or at least master, the dangers that threaten our existence. If we were never anxious, there would be little motivation to make changes in our lives. The soldier in a survival setting reduces his anxiety by performing those tasks that will ensure his coming through the ordeal alive. As he reduces his anxiety, the soldier is also bringing under control the source of that anxiety-- his fears. In this form, anxiety is good; however, anxiety can also have a devastating impact. Anxiety can overwhelm a soldier to the point where he becomes easily confused and has difficulty thinking. Once this happens, it becomes more and more difficult for him to make good judgments and sound decisions. To survive, the soldier must learn techniques to calm his anxieties and keep them in the range where they help, not hurt.

Anger and Frustration

Frustration arises when a person is continually thwarted in his attempts to reach a goal. The goal of survival is to stay alive until you can reach help or until help can reach you. To achieve this goal, the soldier must complete some tasks with minimal resources.

It is inevitable, in trying to do these tasks, that something will go wrong; that something will happen beyond the soldier's control; and that with one's life at stake, every mistake is magnified in terms of its importance. Thus, sooner or later, soldiers will have to cope with frustration when a few of their plans run into trouble. One outgrowth of this frustration is anger.

There are many events in a survival situation that can frustrate or anger a soldier. Getting lost, damaged or forgotten equipment, the weather, inhospitable terrain, enemy patrols, and physical limitations are just a few sources of frustration and anger.

Frustration and anger encourage impulsive reactions, irrational behavior, poorly thought-out decisions, and, in some instances, an "I quit" attitude (people sometimes avoid doing something they can't master). If the soldier can harness and properly channel the emotional intensity associated with anger and frustration, he can productively act as he answers the challenges of survival.

If the soldier does not properly focus his angry feelings, he can waste much energy in activities that do little to further either his chances of survival or the chances of those around him.

Depression

It would be a rare person indeed who would not get sad, at least momentarily, when faced with the privations of survival. As this sadness deepens, we label the feeling "depression." Depression is closely linked with frustration and anger. The frustrated person becomes more and more angry as he fails to reach his goals. If the anger does not help the person to succeed, then the frustration level goes even higher. A destructive cycle between anger and frustration continues until the person becomes worn down-physically, emotionally, and mentally. When a person reaches this point, he starts to give up, and his focus shifts from "What can I do" to "There is nothing I can do."

Depression is an expression of this hopeless, helpless feeling. There is nothing wrong with being sad as you temporarily think about your loved ones and remember what life is like back in "civilization" or "the world." Such thoughts, in fact, can give you the desire to try harder and live one more day.

On the other hand, if you allow yourself to sink into a depressed state, then it can sap all your energy and, more important, your will to survive. It is imperative that each soldier resist succumbing to depression.

Loneliness and Boredom

Man is a social animal. This means we, as human beings, enjoy the company of others. Very few people want to be alone all the time! As you are aware, there is a distinct chance of isolation in a survival setting. This is not bad. Loneliness and boredom can bring to the surface qualities you thought only others had. The extent of your imagination and creativity may surprise you.

When required to do so, you may discover some hidden talents and abilities. Most of all, you may tap into a reservoir of inner strength and fortitude you never knew you had. Conversely, loneliness and boredom can be another source of depression. As a soldier surviving alone, or with others, you must find ways to keep your mind productively occupied.

Additionally, you must develop a degree of self-sufficiency. You must have faith in your capability to "go it alone."

Guilt

The circumstances leading to your being in a survival setting are sometimes dramatic and tragic. It may be the result of an accident or military mission where there was a loss of life. Perhaps you were the only, or one of a few, survivors. While naturally relieved to be alive, you simultaneously may be mourning the deaths of others who were less fortunate.

It is not uncommon for survivors to feel guilty about being spared from death while others were not. This feeling, when used in a positive way, has encouraged people to try harder to survive with the belief they were allowed to live for some greater purpose in life.

Sometimes, survivors tried to stay alive so that they could carry on the work of those killed. Whatever reason you give yourself, do not let guilt feelings prevent you from living. The living who abandon their chance to survive accomplish nothing. Such an act would be the greatest tragedy.

PREPARING YOURSELF

Your mission as a soldier or partisan in a survival situation is to stay alive. As you can see, you are going to experience an assortment of thoughts and emotions. These can work for you, or they can work to your downfall. Fear, anxiety, anger, frustration, guilt, depression, and loneliness are all possible reactions to the many stresses common to survival.

These reactions, when controlled in a healthy way, help to increase a soldier's likelihood of surviving. They prompt the soldier to pay more attention in training, to fight back when scared, to take actions that ensure sustenance and security, to keep faith with his fellow soldiers, and to strive against large odds.

When the survivor cannot control these reactions in a healthy way, they can bring him to a standstill. Instead of rallying his internal resources, the soldier listens to his internal fears. This soldier experiences psychological defeat long before he physically succumbs. Remember, survival is natural to everyone; being unexpectedly thrust into the life and death struggle of survival is not.

Don't be afraid of your "natural reactions to this unnatural situation." Prepare yourself to rule over these reactions so they serve your ultimate interest-- staying alive with the honor and dignity associated with being an American soldier.

It involves preparation to ensure that your reactions in a survival setting are productive, not destructive. The challenge of survival has produced countless examples of heroism, courage, and self-sacrifice. These are the qualities it can bring out in you if you have prepared yourself. Below are a few tips to help prepare yourself psychologically for survival. Through studying this manual and attending survival training you can develop the survival attitude.

Know Yourself

Through training, family, and friends take the time to discover who you are on the inside. Strengthen your stronger qualities and develop the areas that you know are necessary to survive.

Anticipate Fears

Don't pretend that you will have no fears. Begin thinking about what would frighten you the most if forced to survive alone. Train in those areas of concern to you. The goal is not to eliminate the fear, but to build confidence in your ability to function despite your fears.

Be Realistic

Don't be afraid to make an honest appraisal of situations. See circumstances as they are, not as you want them to be. Keep your hopes and expectations within the estimate of the situation. When you go into a survival setting with unrealistic expectations, you may be laying the groundwork for bitter disappointment.

Follow the adage, "Hope for the best, prepare for the worst." It is much easier to adjust to pleasant surprises about one's unexpected good fortunes than to be upset by one's unexpected harsh circumstances.

Adopt a Positive Attitude

Learn to see the potential good in everything. Looking for the good not only boosts morale, it also is excellent for exercising your imagination and creativity.

Remind Yourself What Is at Stake

Remember, failure to prepare yourself psychologically to cope with survival leads to reactions such as depression, carelessness, inattention, loss of confidence, poor decision-making, and giving up before the body gives in. At stake is your life and the lives of others who are depending on you to do your share.

Train

Through military training and life experiences, begin today to prepare yourself to cope with the rigors of survival. Demonstrating your skills in training will give you the confidence to call upon them should the need arise. Remember, the more realistic the training, the less overwhelming an actual survival setting will be.

Learn Stress Management Techniques

People under stress have a potential to panic if they are not well-trained and not prepared psychologically to face whatever the circumstances may be. While we often cannot control the survival circumstances in which we find ourselves, it is within our ability to control our response to those circumstances.

Learning stress management techniques can enhance significantly your capability to remain calm and focused as you work to keep yourself and others alive. A few good techniques to develop include relaxation skills, time management skills, assertiveness skills, and cognitive restructuring skills (the ability to control how you view a situation).

Remember, "the will to survive" can also be considered to be "the refusal to give up."

Chapter 8 Survival Planning

SURVIVAL PLANNING AND SURVIVAL KITS

Survival planning is nothing more than realizing something could happen that would put you in a survival situation and, with that in mind, taking steps to increase your chances of survival. Thus, survival planning means preparation.

Preparation means having survival items and knowing how to use them People who live in snow regions prepare their vehicles for poor road conditions. They put snow tires on their vehicles, add extra weight in the back for traction, and they carry a shovel, salt, and a blanket.

Another example of preparation is finding the emergency exits on an aircraft when you board it for a flight. Preparation could also mean knowing your intended route of travel and familiarizing yourself with the area. Finally, emergency planning is essential.

IMPORTANCE OF PLANNING

Detailed prior planning is essential in potential survival situations. Including survival considerations in mission planning will enhance your chances of survival if an emergency occurs.

For example, if your job re-quires that you work in a small, enclosed area that limits what you can carry on your person, plan where you can put your rucksack or your load-bearing equipment. Put it where it will not prevent you from getting out of the area quickly, yet where it is readily accessible.

One important aspect of prior planning is preventive medicine. Ensuring that you have no dental problems and that your immunizations are current will help you avoid potential dental or health problems.

A dental problem in a survival situation will reduce your ability to cope with other problems that you face. Failure to keep your shots current may mean your body is not immune to diseases that are prevalent in the area.

Preparing and carrying a survival kit is as important as the considerations mentioned above. All Army aircraft normally have survival kits on board for the type area(s) over which they will fly.

There are kits for over-water survival, for hot climate survival, and an aviator survival vest. If you are not an aviator, you will probably not have access to the survival vests or survival kits.

However, if you know what these kits contain, it will help you to plan and to prepare your own survival kit.

Even the smallest survival kit, if properly prepared, is invaluable when faced with a survival problem.

Before making your survival kit, however, consider your unit's mission, the operational environment, and the equipment and vehicles assigned to your unit.

SURVIVAL KITS

The environment is the key to the types of items you will need in your survival kit. How much equipment you put in your kit depends on how you will carry the kit. A kit carried on your body will have to be smaller than one carried in a vehicle.

Always layer your survival kit, keeping the most important items on your body. For example, your map and compass should always be on your body. Carry less important items on your load-bearing equipment. Place bulky items in the rucksack.

In preparing your survival kit, select items you can use for more than one purpose. If you have two items that will serve the same function, pick the one you can use for another function. Do not duplicate items, as this increases your kit's size and weight.

Your survival kit need not be elaborate. You need only functional items that will meet your needs and a case to hold the items. For the case, you might want to use a Band-Aid box, a first aid case, an ammunition pouch, or another suitable case. This case should be--

Water repellent or waterproof.

Easy to carry or attach to your body.

Suitable to accept various sized components.

Durable.

In your survival kit, you should have--

First aid items.

Water purification tablets or drops.

Fire starting equipment.

Signaling items.

Food procurement items.

Shelter items.

Some examples of these items are--

Lighter, metal match, waterproof matches.

Snare wire.

Signaling mirror.

Wrist compass.

Fish and snare line.

Fishhooks.

Candle.

Small hand lens.

Oxytetracycline tablets (diarrhea or infection).

Water purification tablets.

Solar blanket.

Surgical blades.

Butterfly sutures.

Condoms for water storage.

Chap Stick.

Needle and thread.

Knife.

Always include a weapon. Consider your mission and the environment in which your unit will operate. Then prepare your survival kit.

Chapter 9 Shelters

A shelter can protect you from the sun, insects, wind, rain, snow, hot or cold temperatures, and enemy observation. It can give you a feeling of well-being. It can help you maintain your will to survive.

In some areas, your need for shelter may take precedence over your need for food and possibly even your need for water. For example, prolonged exposure to cold can cause excessive fatigue and weakness (exhaustion). An exhausted person may develop a "passive" outlook, thereby losing the will to survive.

The most common error in making a shelter is to make it too large. A shelter must be large enough to protect you. It must also be small enough to contain your body heat, especially in cold climates.

SHELTER SITE SELECTION

When you are in a survival situation and realize that shelter is a high priority, start looking for shelter as soon as possible. As you do so, remember what you will need at the site. Two requisites are--

It must contain material to make the type of shelter you need.

It must be large enough and level enough for you to lie down comfortably.

When you consider these requisites, however, you cannot ignore your tactical situation or your safety. You must also consider whether the site—

Provides concealment from enemy observation.

Has camouflaged escape routes.

Is suitable for signaling, if necessary.

Provides protection against wild animals and rocks and dead trees that might fall.

Is free from insects, reptiles, and poisonous plants.

You must also remember the problems that could arise in your environment. For instance--

Avoid flash flood areas in foothills.

Avoid avalanche or rockslide areas in mountainous terrain.

Avoid sites near bodies of water that are below the high water mark.

In some areas, the season of the year has a strong bearing on the site you select. Ideal sites for a shelter differ in winter and summer. During cold winter months you will want a site that will protect you from the cold and wind, but will have a source of fuel and water. During summer months in the same area you will want a source of water, but you will want the site to be almost insect free.

When considering shelter site selection, use the word BLISS as a guide.

B - Blend in with the surroundings.

L - Low silhouette.
I - Irregular shape.

S - Small.

S - Secluded location.

TYPES OF SHELTERS

When looking for a shelter site, keep in mind the type of shelter (protection) you need. However, you must also consider--

How much time and effort you need to build the shelter.

If the shelter will adequately protect you from the elements (sun, wind, rain, snow).

If you have the tools to build it. If not, can you make improvised tools?

If you have the type and amount of materials needed to build it.

To answer these questions, you need to know how to make various types of shelters and what materials you need to make them.

Poncho Lean-To

It takes only a short time and minimal equipment to build this lean-to (Figure 5-1). You need a poncho, 2 to 3 meters of rope or parachute suspension line, three stakes about 30 centimeters long, and two trees or two poles 2 to 3 meters apart. Before selecting the trees you will use or the location of your poles, check the wind direction. Ensure that the back of your lean-to will be into the wind.

To make the lean-to--

Tie off the hood of the poncho. Pull the drawstring tight, roll the hood longways, fold it into thirds, and tie it off with the drawstring.

Cut the rope in half. On one long side of the poncho, tie half of the rope to the corner grommet. Tie the other half to the other corner grommet.

Attach a drip stick (about a 10-centimeter stick) to each rope about 2.5 centimeters from the grommet. These drip sticks will keep rainwater from running down the ropes into the lean-to. Tying strings (about 10 centimeters long) to each grommet along the poncho's top edge will allow the water to run to and down the line without dripping into the shelter.

Tie the ropes about waist high on the trees (uprights). Use a round turn and two half hitches with a quick-release knot.

Spread the poncho and anchor it to the ground, putting sharpened sticks through the grommets and into the ground.

If you plan to use the lean-to for more than one night, or you expect rain, make a center support for the lean-to. Make this support with a line. Attach one end of the line to the poncho hood and the other end to an overhanging branch. Make sure there is no slack in the line.

Another method is to place a stick upright under the center of the lean-to. This method, however, will restrict your space and movements in the shelter.

For additional protection from wind and rain, place some brush, your rucksack, or other equipment at the sides of the lean-to.

To reduce heat loss to the ground, place some type of insulating material, such as leaves or pine needles, inside your lean-to.

Note: When at rest, you lose as much as 80 percent of your body heat to the ground.

To increase your security from enemy observation, lower the lean-to's silhouette by making two changes. First, secure the support lines to the trees at knee height (not at waist height) using two knee-high sticks in the two center grommets (sides of lean-to). Second, angle the poncho to the ground, securing it with sharpened sticks, as above.

Poncho Tent

This tent provides a low silhouette. It also protects you from the elements on two sides. It has, however, less usable space and observation area than a lean-to, decreasing your reaction time to enemy detection. To make this tent, you need a poncho, two 1.5- to 2.5-meter ropes, six sharpened sticks about 30 centimeters long, and two trees 2 to 3 meters apart.

To make the tent--

Tie off the poncho hood in the same way as the poncho lean-to.

Tie a 1.5- to 2.5-meter rope to the center grommet on each side of the poncho.

Tie the other ends of these ropes at about knee height to two trees 2 to 3 meters apart and stretch the poncho tight.

Draw one side of the poncho tight and secure it to the ground pushing sharpened sticks through the grommets.

Follow the same procedure on the other side.

If you need a center support, use the same methods as for the poncho lean-to. Another center support is an A-frame set outside but over the center of the tent. Use two 90- to 120-centimeter-long sticks, one with a forked end, to form the A-frame. Tie the hood's drawstring to the A-frame to support the center of the tent.

Three-Pole Parachute Tepee

If you have a parachute and three poles and the tactical situation allows, make a parachute tepee. It is easy and takes very little time to make this tepee. It provides protection from the elements and can act as a signaling device by enhancing a small amount of light from a fire or candle. It is large enough to hold several people and their equipment and to allow sleeping, cooking, and storing firewood.

You can make this tepee using parts of or a whole personnel main or reserve parachute canopy. If using a standard personnel parachute, you need three poles 3.5 to 4.5 meters long and about 5 centimeters in diameter.

Lay the poles on the ground and lash them together at one end.

Stand the framework up and spread the poles to form a tripod.

For more support, place additional poles against the tripod. Five or six additional poles work best, but do not lash them to the tripod.

Determine the wind direction and locate the entrance 90 degrees or more from the mean wind direction.

Lay out the parachute on the "backside" of the tripod and locate the bridle loop (nylon web loop) at the top (apex) of the canopy.

Place the bridle loop over the top of a free-standing pole. Then place the pole back up against the tripod so that the canopy's apex is at the same height as the lashing on the three poles.

Wrap the canopy around one side of the tripod. The canopy should be of double thickness, as you are wrapping an entire parachute. You need only wrap half of the tripod, as the remainder of the canopy will encircle the tripod in the opposite direction.

Construct the entrance by wrapping the folded edges of the canopy around two free-standing poles. You can then place the poles side by side to close the tepee's entrance.

Place all extra canopy underneath the tepee poles and inside to create a floor for the shelter.

Leave a 30- to 50-centimeter opening at the top for ventilation if you intend to have a fire inside the tepee.

One-Pole Parachute Tepee

You need a 14-gore section (normally) of canopy, stakes, a stout center pole, and inner core and needle to construct this tepee. You cut the suspension lines except for 40- to 45-centimeter lengths at the canopy's lower lateral band.

Select a shelter site and scribe a circle about 4 meters in diameter on the ground.

Stake the parachute material to the ground using the lines remaining at the lower lateral band.

After deciding where to place the shelter door, emplace a stake and tie the first line (from the lower lateral band) securely to it.

Stretch the parachute material taut to the next line, emplace a stake on the scribed line, and tie the line to it.

Continue the staking process until you have tied all the lines.

Loosely attach the top of the parachute material to the center pole with a suspension line you previously cut and, through trial and error, determine the point at which the parachute material will be pulled tight once the center pole is upright.

Then securely attach the material to the pole.

Using a suspension line (or inner core), sew the end gores together leaving 1 or 1.2 meters for a door.

No-Pole Parachute Tepee
You use the same materials, except for the center pole, as for the one-pole parachute tepee.

Tie a line to the top of parachute material with a previously cut suspension line.

Throw the line over a tree limb, and tie it to the tree trunk.

Starting at the opposite side from the door, emplace a stake on the scribed 3.5- to 4.3-meter circle.

Tie the first line on the lower lateral band.

Continue emplacing the stakes and tying the lines to them.

After staking down the material, unfasten the line tied to the tree trunk, tighten the tepee material by pulling on this line, and tie it securely to the tree trunk.

One-Man Shelter

A one-man shelter you can easily make using a parachute requires a tree and three poles. One pole should be about 4.5 meters long and the other two about 3 meters long.

Secure the 4.5-meter pole to the tree at about waist height.

Lay the two 3-meter poles on the ground on either side of and in the same direction as the 4.5-meter pole.

Lay the folded canopy over the 4.5 meter pole so that about the same amount of material hangs on both sides.

Tuck the excess material under the 3-meter poles, and spread it on the ground inside to serve as a floor.

Stake down or put a spreader between the two 3-meter poles at the shelter's entrance so they will not slide inward.

Use any excess material to cover the entrance.

The parachute cloth makes this shelter wind resistant, and the shelter is small enough that it is easily warmed. A candle, used carefully, can keep the inside temperature comfortable. This shelter is unsatisfactory, however, when snow is falling as even a light snowfall will cave it in.

Parachute Hammock

You can make a hammock using 6 to 8 gores of parachute canopy and two trees about 4.5 meters apart

Field-Expedient Lean-To

If you are in a wooded area and have enough natural materials, you can make a field-expedient lean-to without the aid of tools or with only a knife. It takes longer to make this type of shelter than it does to make other types, but it will protect you from the elements.

You will need two trees (or upright poles) about 2 meters apart; one pole about 2 meters long and 2.5 centimeters in diameter; five to eight poles about 3 meters long and 2.5 centimeters in diameter for beams; cord or vines for securing the horizontal support to the trees; and other poles, saplings, or vines to crisscross the beams.

Tie the 2-meter pole to the two trees at waist to chest height. This is the horizontal support. If a standing tree is not available, construct a biped using Y-shaped sticks or two tripods.

Place one end of the beams (3-meter poles) on one side of the horizontal support. As with all lean-to type shelters, be sure to place the lean-to's backside into the wind.

Crisscross saplings or vines on the beams.

Cover the framework with brush, leaves, pine needles, or grass, starting at the bottom and working your way up like shingling.

Place straw, leaves, pine needles, or grass inside the shelter for bedding.
In cold weather, add to your lean-to's comfort by building a fire reflector wall. Drive four 1.5-meter-long stakes into the ground to support the wall. Stack green logs on top of one another between the support stakes.

Form two rows of stacked logs to create an inner space within the wall that you can fill with dirt. This action not only strengthens the wall but makes it more heat reflective. Bind the top of the support stakes so that the green logs and dirt will stay in place.

With just a little more effort you can have a drying rack. Cut a few 2-centimeter-diameter poles (length depends on the distance between the lean-to's horizontal support and the top of the fire reflector wall).

Lay one end of the poles on the lean-to support and the other end on top of the reflector wall. Place and tie into place smaller sticks across these poles. You now have a place to dry clothes, meat, or fish.

Swamp Bed

In a marsh or swamp, or any area with standing water or continually wet ground, the swamp bed keeps you out of the water. When selecting such a site, consider the weather, wind, tides, and available materials.

Look for four trees clustered in a rectangle, or cut four poles (bamboo is ideal) and drive them firmly into the ground so they form a rectangle. They should be far enough apart and strong enough to support your height and weight, to include equipment.

Cut two poles that span the width of the rectangle. They, too, must be strong enough to support your weight.

Secure these two poles to the trees (or poles). Be sure they are high enough above the ground or water to allow for tides and high water.

Cut additional poles that span the rectangle's length. Lay them across the two side poles, and secure them.

Cover the top of the bed frame with broad leaves or grass to form a soft sleeping surface.

Build a fire pad by laying clay, silt, or mud on one corner of the swamp bed and allow it to dry.

Another shelter designed to get you above and out of the water or wet ground uses the same rectangular configuration as the swamp bed. You very simply lay sticks and branches lengthwise on the inside of the trees (or poles) until there is enough material to raise the sleeping surface above the water level.

Natural Shelters

Do not overlook natural formations that provide shelter. Examples are caves, rocky crevices, clumps of bushes, small depressions, large rocks on leeward sides of hills, large trees with low-hanging limbs, and fallen trees with thick branches. However, when selecting a natural formation--

Stay away from low ground such as ravines, narrow valleys, or creek beds. Low areas collect the heavy cold air at night and are therefore colder than the surrounding high ground. Thick, brushy, low ground also harbors more insects.

Check for poisonous snakes, ticks, mites, scorpions, and stinging ants.

Look for loose rocks, dead limbs, coconuts, or other natural growth than could fall on your shelter.

Debris Hut

For warmth and ease of construction, this shelter is one of the best. When shelter is essential to survival, build this shelter.

To make a debris hut

Build it by making a tripod with two short stakes and a long ridgepole or by placing one end of a long ridgepole on top of a sturdy base.

Secure the ridgepole (pole running the length of the shelter) using the tripod method or by anchoring it to a tree at about waist height.

Prop large sticks along both sides of the ridgepole to create a wedge-shaped ribbing effect. Ensure the ribbing is wide enough to accommodate your body and steep enough to shed moisture.

Place finer sticks and brush crosswise on the ribbing. These form a latticework that will keep the insulating material (grass, pine needles, leaves) from falling through the ribbing into the sleeping area.

Add light, dry, if possible, soft debris over the ribbing until the insulating material is at least 1 meter thick--the thicker the better.

Place a 30-centimeter layer of insulating material inside the shelter.

At the entrance, pile insulating material that you can drag to you once inside the shelter to close the entrance or build a door.

As a final step in constructing this shelter, add shingling material or branches on top of the debris layer to prevent the insulating material from blowing away in a storm.

Tree-Pit Snow Shelter

If you are in a cold, snow-covered area where evergreen trees grow and you have a digging tool, you can make a tree-pit shelter

To make this shelter--

Find a tree with bushy branches that provides overhead cover.

Dig out the snow around the tree trunk until you reach the depth and diameter you desire, or until you reach the ground.

Pack the snow around the top and the inside of the hole to provide support.

Find and cut other evergreen boughs. Place them over the top of the pit to give you additional overhead cover. Place evergreen boughs in the bottom of the pit for insulation.

Beach Shade Shelter

This shelter protects you from the sun, wind, rain, and heat. It is easy to make using natural materials.

Find and collect driftwood or other natural material to use as support beams and as a digging tool.

Select a site that is above the high water mark.

Scrape or dig out a trench running north to south so that it receives the least amount of sunlight. Make the trench long and wide enough for you to lie down comfortably.

Mound soil on three sides of the trench. The higher the mound, the more space inside the shelter.

Lay support beams (driftwood or other natural material) that span the trench on top of the mound to form the framework for a roof.

Enlarge the shelter's entrance by digging out more sand in front of it.

Use natural materials such as grass or leaves to form a bed inside the shelter.

Desert Shelters

In an arid environment, consider the time, effort, and material needed to make a shelter. If you have material such as a poncho, canvas, or a parachute, use it along with such terrain features as rock outcropping, mounds of sand, or a depression between dunes or rocks to make your shelter.

Using rock outcroppings--

Anchor one end of your poncho (canvas, parachute, or other material) on the edge of the outcrop using rocks or other weights.

Extend and anchor the other end of the poncho so it provides the best possible shade.

In a sandy area--

Build a mound of sand or use the side of a sand dune for one side of the shelter.

Anchor one end of the material on top of the mound using sand or other weights.

Extend and anchor the other end of the material so it provides the best possible shade.

Note: If you have enough material, fold it in half and form a 30-centimeter to 45-centimeter airspace between the two halves. This airspace will reduce the temperature under the shelter.

A belowground shelter can reduce the midday heat as much as 16 to 22 degrees C (30 to 40 degrees F). Building it, however, requires more time and effort than for other shelters. Since your physical effort will make you sweat more and increase dehydration, construct it before the heat of the day.

Find a low spot or depression between dunes or rocks. If necessary, dig a trench 45 to 60 centimeters deep and long and wide enough for you to lie in comfortably.

Pile the sand you take from the trench to form a mound around three sides.

On the open end of the trench, dig out more sand so you can get in and out of your shelter easily.

Cover the trench with your material.

Secure the material in place using sand, rocks, or other weights.

If you have extra material, you can further decrease the midday temperature in the trench by securing the material 30 to 45 centimeters above the other cover. This layering of the material will reduce the inside temperature 11 to 22 degrees C (20 to 40 degrees F).

Another type of below ground shade shelter is of similar construction, except all sides are open to air currents and circulation. For maximum protection, you need a minimum of two layers of parachute material.

White is the best color to reflect heat; the innermost layer should be of darker material.

Chapter 10 Water Procurement

Water is one of your most urgent needs in a survival situation. You can't live long without it, especially in hot areas where you lose water rapidly through perspiration. Even in cold areas, you need a minimum of 2 liters of water each day to maintain efficiency.

More than three-fourths of your body is composed of fluids. Your body loses fluid as a result of heat, cold, stress, and exertion. To function effectively, you must replace the fluid your body loses. So, one of your first goals is to obtain an adequate supply of water.

WATER SOURCES

Almost any environment has water present to some degree. Figure 6-1 lists possible sources of water in various environments. It also provides information on how to make the water potable.

Environment	Source of Water	Means of Obtaining and/or Making Potable	Remarks
Frigid areas	Snow and ice	Melt and purify.	**Do not eat** without melting! Eating snow and ice can reduce body temperature and will lead to more dehydration.
			Snow and ice are no purer than the water from which they come.
			Sea ice that is gray in color or opaque is salty. Do not use it without desalting it. Sea ice that is crystalline with a bluish cast has little salt in it.
At sea	Sea	Use desalter kit.	**Do not** drink seawater without desalting.
	Rain	Catch rain in tarps or in other water-holding material or containers.	If tarp or water-holding material has become encrusted with salt, wash it in the sea before using (very little salt will remain on it).
	Sea ice		See remarks above for frigid areas.

Figure 6-1. Water sources in different environments.

Environment	Source of Water	Means of Obtaining and/or Making Potable	Remarks
Beach	Ground	Dig hole deep enough to allow water to seep in; obtain rocks, build fire, and heat rocks; drop hot rocks in water; hold cloth over hole to absorb steam; wring water from cloth.	Alternate method if a container or bark pot is available: Fill container or pot with seawater; build fire and boil water to produce steam; hold cloth over container to absorb steam; wring water from cloth.
Desert	Ground • in valleys and low areas • at foot of concave banks of dry river beads • at foot of cliffs or rock outcrops • at first depression behind first sand dune of dry desert lakes • wherever you find damp surface sand • wherever you find green vegetation	Dig holes deep enough to allow water to seep in.	In a sand dune belt, any available water will be found beneath the original valley floor at the edge of dunes.
	Cacti	Cut off the top of a barrel cactus and mash or squeeze the pulp. **CAUTION: Do not eat pulp. Place pulp in mouth, suck out juice, and discard pulp.**	Without a machete, cutting into a cactus is difficult and takes time since you must get past the long, strong spines and cut through the tough rind.

Figure 6-1. Water sources in different environments (continued).

167

Environment	Source of Water	Means of Obtaining and/or Making Potable	Remarks
Desert (continued)	Depressions or holes in rocks		Periodic rainfall may collect in pools, seep into fissures, or collect in holes in rocks.
	Fissures in rock	Insert flexible tubing and siphon water. If fissure is large enough, you can lower a container into it.	
	Porous rock	Insert flexible tubing and siphon water.	
	Condensation on metal	Use cloth to absorb water, then wring water from cloth.	Extreme temperature variations between night and day may cause condensation on metal surfaces.
			Following are signs to watch for in the desert to help you find water:
			• All trails lead to water. You should follow in the direction in which the trails converge. Signs of camps, campfire ashes, animal droppings, and trampled terrain may mark trails.
			• Flocks of birds will circle over water holes. Some birds fly to water holes at dawn and sunset. Their flight at these times is generally fast and close to the ground. Bird tracks or chirping sounds in the evening or early morning sometimes indicate that water is nearby.

Figure 6-1. Water sources in different environments (continued).

Note: If you do not have a canteen, a cup, a can, or other type of container, improvise one from plastic or water-resistant cloth. Shape the plastic or cloth

168

into a bowl by pleating it. Use pins or other suitable items--even your hands--to hold the pleats.

If you do not have a reliable source to replenish your water supply, stay alert for ways in which your environment can help you.

CAUTION

Do not substitute the fluids listed in Figure 6-2 for water.

Fluid	Remarks
Alcoholic beverages	Dehydrate the body and cloud judgment.
Urine	Contains harmful body wastes. Is about 2 percent salt.
Blood	Is salty and considered a food; therefore, requires additional body fluids to digest. May transmit disease.
Seawater	Is about 4 percent salt. It takes about 2 liters of body fluids to rid the body of waste from 1 liter of seawater. Therefore, by drinking seawater you deplete your body's water supply, which can cause death.

Figure 6-2. The effects of substitute fluids.

Heavy dew can provide water. Tie rags or tufts of fine grass around your ankles and walk through dew-covered grass before sunrise. As the rags or grass tufts absorb the dew, wring the water into a container. Repeat the process until you have a supply of water or until the dew is gone. Australian natives sometimes mop up as much as a liter an hour this way.

Bees or ants going into a hole in a tree may point to a water-filled hole. Siphon the water with plastic tubing or scoop it up with an improvised dipper. You can also stuff cloth in the hole to absorb the water and then wring it from the cloth.

Water sometimes gathers in tree crotches or rock crevices. Use the above procedures to get the water. In arid areas, bird droppings around a crack in the rocks may indicate water in or near the crack.

Green bamboo thickets are an excellent source of fresh water. Water from green bamboo is clear and odorless. To get the water, bend a green bamboo stalk, tie it down, and cut off the top (Figure 6-3). The water will drip freely during the night. Old, cracked bamboo may contain water.

Figure 6-3. Water from green bamboo.

CAUTION

Purify the water before drinking it.

Wherever you find banana or plantain trees, you can get water. Cut down the tree, leaving about a 30-

centimeter stump, and scoop out the center of the stump so that the hollow is bowl-shaped. Water from the roots will immediately start to fill the hollow. The first three fillings of water will be bitter, but succeeding fillings will be palatable. The stump (Figure 6-4) will supply water for up to four days. Be sure to cover it to keep out insects.

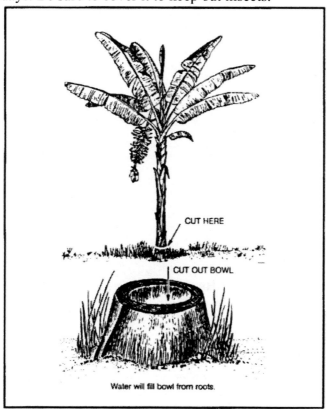

CUT HERE

CUT OUT BOWL

Water will fill bowl from roots.

Figure 6-4. Water from plantain or banana tree stump.

Some tropical vines can give you water. Cut a notch in the vine as high as you can reach, then cut the vine off close to the ground. Catch the dropping liquid in a container or in your mouth (Figure 6-5).

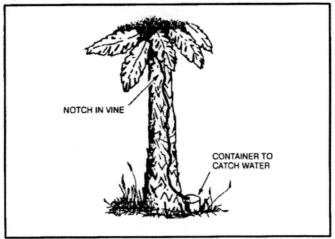

NOTCH IN VINE

CONTAINER TO CATCH WATER

Figure 6-5. Water from a vine.

CAUTION

Do not drink the liquid if it is sticky, milky, or bitter tasting.

The milk from green (unripe) coconuts is a good thirst quencher. However, the milk from mature coconuts contains an oil that acts as a laxative. Drink in moderation only.

In the American tropics you may find large trees whose branches support air plants. These air plants may hold a considerable amount of rainwater in their overlapping, thickly growing leaves. Strain the water through a cloth to remove insects and debris.

You can get water from plants with moist pulpy centers. Cut off a section of the plant and squeeze or smash the pulp so that the moisture runs out. Catch the liquid in a container.

Plant roots may provide water. Dig or pry the roots out of the ground, cut them into short pieces, and smash the pulp so that the moisture runs out. Catch the liquid in a container.

Fleshy leaves, stems, or stalks, such as bamboo, contain water. Cut or notch the stalks at the base of a joint to drain out the liquid.

The following trees can also provide water:

Palms. Palms, such as the buri, coconut, sugar, rattan, and nips, contain liquid. Bruise a lower frond and pull it down so the tree will "bleed" at the injury.

Traveler's tree. Found in Madagascar, this tree has a cuplike sheath at the base of its leaves in which water collects.

Umbrella tree. The leaf bases and roots of this tree of western tropical Africa can provide water.

Baobab tree. This tree of the sandy plains of northern Australia and Africa collects water in its bottlelike trunk during the wet season. Frequently, you can find clear, fresh water in these trees after weeks of dry weather.

CAUTION

Do not keep the sap from plants longer than 24 hours. It begins fermenting, becoming dangerous as a water source.

STILL CONSTRUCTION

You can use stills in various areas of the world. They draw moisture from the ground and from plant material. You need certain materials to build a still, and you need time to let it collect the water. It takes about 24 hours to get 0.5 to 1 liter of water.

Aboveground Still

To make the aboveground still, you need a sunny slope on which to place the still, a clear plastic bag, green leafy vegetation, and a small rock

Fill the bag with air by turning the opening into the breeze or by "scooping" air into the bag.

Fill the plastic bag half to three-fourths full of green leafy vegetation. Be sure to remove all hard sticks or sharp spines that might puncture the bag.

CAUTION

Do not use poisonous vegetation. It will provide poisonous liquid.

Place a small rock or similar item in the bag.

Close the bag and tie the mouth securely as close to the end of the bag as possible to keep the maximum amount of air space. If you have a piece of tubing, a small straw, or a hollow reed, insert one end in the mouth of the bag before you tie it securely. Then tie off or plug the tubing so that air will not escape. This tubing will allow you to drain out condensed water without untying the bag.

Place the bag, mouth downhill, on a slope in full sunlight. Position the mouth of the bag slightly higher than the low point in the bag.

Settle the bag in place so that the rock works itself into the low point in the bag.

To get the condensed water from the still, loosen the tie around the bag's mouth and tip the bag so that the water collected around the rock will drain out. Then retie the mouth securely and reposition the still to allow further condensation.

Change the vegetation in the bag after extracting most of the water from it. This will ensure maximum output of water.

Belowground Still

To make a belowground still, you need a digging tool, a container, a clear plastic sheet, a drinking tube, and a rock.

Select a site where you believe the soil will contain moisture (such as a dry stream bed or a low spot where rainwater has collected). The soil at this site should be easy to dig, and sunlight must hit the site most of the day.

Dig a bowl-shaped hole about 1 meter across and 60 centimeters deep.

Dig a sump in the center of the hole. The sump's depth and perimeter will depend on the size of the container that you have to place in it. The bottom of the sump should allow the container to stand upright.
Anchor the tubing to the container's bottom by forming a loose overhand knot in the tubing.

Place the container upright in the sump.

Extend the unanchored end of the tubing up, over, and beyond the lip of the hole.

Place the plastic sheet over the hole, covering its edges with soil to hold it in place.

Place a rock in the center of the plastic sheet.

Lower the plastic sheet into the hole until it is about 40 centimeters below ground level. It now forms an inverted cone with the rock at its apex. Make sure that the cone's apex is directly over your container. Also make sure the plastic cone does not touch the sides of the hole because the earth will absorb the condensed water.

Put more soil on the edges of the plastic to hold it securely in place and to prevent the loss of moisture.

Plug the tube when not in use so that the moisture will not evaporate.

You can drink water without disturbing the still by using the tube as a straw.

You may want to use plants in the hole as a moisture source. If so, dig out additional soil from the sides of the hole to form a slope on which to place the plants. Then proceed as above.

If polluted water is your only moisture source, dig a small trough outside the hole about 25 centimeters from the still's lip. Dig the trough about 25 centimeters deep and 8 centimeters wide. Pour the polluted water in the trough. Be sure you do not spill any polluted water around the rim of the hole where the plastic sheet touches the soil. The trough holds the polluted water and the soil filters it as the still draws it. The water then condenses on the plastic and drains into the container. This process works extremely well when your only water source is salt water.

You will need at least three stills to meet your individual daily water intake needs.

WATER PURIFICATION

Rainwater collected in clean containers or in plants is usually safe for drinking. However, purify water from lakes, ponds, swamps, springs, or streams, especially the water near human settlements or in the tropics.

When possible, purify all water you got from vegetation or from the ground by using iodine or chlorine, or by boiling.

Using water purification tablets. (Follow the directions provided.)

Placing 5 drops of 2 percent tincture of iodine in a canteen full of clear water. If the canteen is full of cloudy or cold water, use 10 drops. (Let the canteen of water stand for 30 minutes before drinking.)

Boiling water for 1 minute at sea level, adding 1 minute for each additional 300 meters above sea level, or boil for 10 minutes no matter where you are.

By drinking nonpotable water you may contract diseases or swallow organisms that can harm you. Examples of such diseases or organisms are--

Dysentery. Severe, prolonged diarrhea with bloody stools, fever, and weakness.

Cholera and typhoid. You may be susceptible to these diseases regardless of inoculations.

Flukes. Stagnant, polluted water--especially in tropical areas--often contains blood flukes. If you swallow flukes, they will bore into the bloodstream, live as parasites, and cause disease.

Leeches. If you swallow a leech, it can hook onto the throat passage or inside the nose. It will suck blood, create a wound, and move to another area. Each bleeding wound may become infected.

WATER FILTRATION DEVICES

If the water you find is also muddy, stagnant, and foul smelling, you can clear the water--

By placing it in a container and letting it stand for 12 hours.

By pouring it through a filtering system.

Note: These procedures only clear the water and make it more palatable. You will have to purify it.

To make a filtering system, place several centimeters or layers of filtering material such as sand, crushed rock, charcoal, or cloth in bamboo, a hollow log, or an article of clothing.

Remove the odor from water by adding charcoal from your fire. Let the water stand for 45 minutes before drinking it.

Chapter 11 Firecraft

In many survival situations, the ability to start a fire can make the difference between living and dying. Fire can fulfill many needs. It can provide warmth and comfort. It not only cooks and preserves food, it also provides warmth in the form of heated food that saves calories our body normally uses to produce body heat.

You can use fire to purify water, sterilize bandages, signal for rescue, and provide protection from animals. It can be a psychological boost by providing peace of mind and companionship. You can also use fire to produce tools and weapons.

Fire can cause problems, as well. The enemy can detect the smoke and light it produces. It can cause forest fires or destroy essential equipment. Fire can also cause burns or carbon monoxide poisoning when used in shelters.

BASIC FIRE PRINCIPLES

To build a fire, it helps to understand the basic principles of a fire. Fuel (in a nongaseous state) does not burn directly. When you apply heat to a fuel, it produces a gas. This gas, combined with oxygen in the air, burns.

Understanding the concept of the fire triangle is very important in correctly constructing and maintaining a fire. The three sides of the triangle represent air, heat, and fuel. If you remove any of these, the fire will go out. The correct ratio of these components is very important for a fire to burn at its greatest capability. The only way to learn this ratio is to practice.

SITE SELECTION AND PREPARATION

You will have to decide what site and arrangement to use. Before building a fire consider--

The area (terrain and climate) in which you are operating.

The materials and tools available.

Time: how much time you have?

Need: why you need a fire?

Security: how close is the enemy?

Look for a dry spot that--

Is protected from the wind.

Is suitably placed in relation to your shelter (if any).

Will concentrate the heat in the direction you desire.

Has a supply of wood or other fuel available.

If you are in a wooded or brush-covered area, clear the brush and scrape the surface soil from the spot you have selected. Clear a circle at least 1 meter in diameter so there is little chance of the fire spreading.

If time allows, construct a fire wall using logs or rocks. This wall will help to reflector direct the heat where you want it.

It will also reduce flying sparks and cut down on the amount of wind blowing into the fire. However, you will need enough wind to keep the fire burning.

CAUTION

Do not use wet or porous rocks as they may explode when heated.

In some situations, you may find that an underground fireplace will best meet your needs. It conceals the fire and serves well for cooking food.

To make an underground fireplace or Dakota fire hole.

Dig a hole in the ground.

On the upwind side of this hole, poke or dig a large connecting hole for ventilation.

Build your fire in the hole.

If you are in a snow-covered area, use green logs to make a dry base for your fire. Trees with wrist-sized trunks are easily broken in extreme cold. Cut or break several green logs and lay them side by side on top of the snow. Add one or two more layers. Lay the top layer of logs opposite those below it.

FIRE MATERIAL SELECTION

You need three types of materials to build a fire-- tinder, kindling, and fuel.

Tinder is dry material that ignites with little heat--a spark starts a fire. The tinder must be absolutely dry to be sure just a spark will ignite it. If you only have a device that generates sparks, charred cloth will be almost essential. It holds a spark for long periods, allowing you to put tinder on the hot area to generate a small flame.

You can make charred cloth by heating cotton cloth until it turns black, but does not burn. Once it is black, you must keep it in an airtight container to keep it dry. Prepare this cloth well in advance of any survival situation. Add it to your individual survival kit.

Kindling is readily combustible material that you add to the burning tinder. Again, this material should be absolutely dry to ensure rapid burning. Kindling increases the fire's temperature so that it will ignite less combustible material.

Fuel is less combustible material that burns slowly and steadily once ignited.

HOW TO BUILD A FIRE

There are several methods for laying a fire, each of which has advantages. The situation you find yourself in will determine which fire to use.

Tepee

To make this fire, arrange the tinder and a few sticks of kindling in the shape of a tepee or cone. Light the center. As the tepee burns, the outside logs will fall inward, feeding the fire. This type of fire burns well even with wet wood.

Lean-To

To lay this fire, push a green stick into the ground at a 30-degree angle. Point the end of the stick in the direction of the wind. Place some tinder deep under this lean-to stick. Lean pieces of kindling against the lean-to stick. Light the tinder. As the kindling catches fire from the tinder, add more kindling.

Cross-Ditch

To use this method, scratch a cross about 30 centimeters in size in the ground. Dig the cross 7.5 centimeters deep. Put a large wad of tinder in the middle of the cross. Build a kindling pyramid above the tinder. The shallow ditch allows air to sweep under the tinder to provide a draft.

Pyramid

To lay this fire, place two small logs or branches parallel on the ground. Place a solid layer of small logs across the parallel logs. Add three or four more layers of logs or branches, each layer smaller than and at a right angle to the layer below it. Make a starter fire on top of the pyramid. As the starter fire burns, it will ignite the logs below it. This gives you a fire that burns downward, requiring no attention during the night.

There are several other ways to lay a fire that are quite effective. Your situation and the material available in the area may make another method more suitable.

HOW TO LIGHT A FIRE

Always light your fire from the upwind side. Make sure to lay your tinder, kindling, and fuel so that your fire will burn as long as you need it. Igniters provide the initial heat required to start the tinder burning. They fall into two categories: modern methods and primitive methods.

Modern Methods

Modem igniters use modem devices--items we normally think of to start a fire.

Matches

Make sure these matches are waterproof. Also, store them in a waterproof container along with a dependable striker pad.

Convex Lens

Use this method only on bright, sunny days. The lens can come from binoculars, camera, telescopic sights, or magnifying glasses. Angle the lens to concentrate the sun's rays on the tinder. Hold the lens over the same spot until the tinder begins to smolder. Gently blow or fan the tinder into flame, and apply it to the fire lay.

Metal Match

Place a flat, dry leaf under your tinder with a portion exposed. Place the tip of the metal match on the dry leaf, holding the metal match in one hand and a knife in the other. Scrape your knife against the metal match to produce sparks. The sparks will hit the tinder. When the tinder starts to smolder, proceed as above.

Battery

Use a battery to generate a spark. Use of this method depends on the type of battery available. Attach a wire to each terminal. Touch the ends of the bare wires together next to the tinder so the sparks will ignite it.

Gunpowder

Often, you will have ammunition with your equipment. If so, carefully extract the bullet from the shell casing, and use the gunpowder as tinder. A spark will ignite the powder. Be extremely careful when extracting the bullet from the case.

Primitive Methods

Primitive igniters are those attributed to our early ancestors.

Flint and Steel

The direct spark method is the easiest of the primitive methods to use. The flint and steel method is the most reliable of the direct spark methods. Strike a flint or other hard, sharp-edged rock edge with a piece of carbon steel (stainless steel will not produce a good spark). This method requires a loose-jointed wrist and practice. When a spark has caught in the tinder, blow on it. The spark will spread and burst into flames.

Fire-Plow

The fire-plow is a friction method of ignition. You rub a hardwood shaft against a softer wood base. To use this method, cut a straight groove in the base and plow the blunt tip of the shaft up and down the groove. The plowing action of the shaft pushes out small particles of wood fibers. Then, as you apply more pressure on each stroke, the friction ignites the wood particles.

Bow and Drill

The technique of starting a fire with a bow and drill is simple, but you must exert much effort and be persistent to produce a fire. You need the following items to use this method:

Socket. The socket is an easily grasped stone or piece of hardwood or bone with a slight depression in one side. Use it to hold the drill in place and to apply downward pressure.

Drill. The drill should be a straight, seasoned hardwood stick about 2 centimeters in diameter and 25 centimeters long. The top end is round and the low end blunt (to produce more friction).

Fire board. Its size is up to you. A seasoned softwood board about 2.5 centimeters thick and 10 centimeters wide is preferable. Cut a depression about 2 centimeters from the edge on one side of the board. On the underside, make a V-shaped cut from the edge of the board to the depression.

Bow. The bow is a resilient, green stick about 2.5 centimeters in diameter and a string. The type of wood is not important. The bowstring can be any type of cordage. You tie the bowstring from one end of the bow to the other, without any slack.

To use the bow and drill, first prepare the fire lay. Then place a bundle of tinder under the V-shaped cut in the fire board. Place one foot on the fire board. Loop the bowstring over the drill and place the drill in the precut depression on the fire board.

Place the socket, held in one hand, on the top of the drill to hold it in position. Press down on the drill and saw the bow back and forth to twirl the drill. Once you have established a smooth motion, apply more downward pressure and work the bow faster. This action will grind hot black powder into the tinder, causing a spark to catch. Blow on the tinder until it ignites.

Note: Primitive fire-building methods are exhaustive and require practice to ensure success.

HELPFUL HINTS

Use nonaromatic seasoned hardwood for fuel, if possible.

Collect kindling and tinder along the trail.

Add insect repellent to the tinder.

Keep the firewood dry.

Dry damp firewood near the fire.

Bank the fire to keep the coals alive overnight.

Carry lighted punk, when possible.

Be sure the fire is out before leaving camp.

Do not select wood lying on the ground. It may appear to be dry but generally doesn't provide enough friction.

Chapter 12 Food Procurement

After water, man's most urgent requirement is food. In contemplating virtually any hypothetical survival situation, the mind immediately turns to thoughts of food. Unless the situation occurs in an arid environment, even water, which is more important to maintaining body functions, will almost always follow food in our initial thoughts.

The survivor must remember that the three essentials of survival--water, food, and shelter--are prioritized according to the estimate of the actual situation. This estimate must not only be timely but accurate as well. Some situations may well dictate that shelter precede both food and water.

ANIMALS FOR FOOD

Unless you have the chance to take large game, concentrate your efforts on the smaller animals, due to their abundance. The smaller animal species are also easier to prepare. You must not know all the animal species that are suitable as food. Relatively few are poisonous, and they make a smaller list to remember.

What is important is to learn the habits and behavioral patterns of classes of animals. For example, animals that are excellent choices for trapping, those that inhabit a particular range and occupy a den or nest, those that have somewhat fixed feeding areas, and those that have trails leading from one area to another.

Larger, herding animals, such as elk or caribou, roam vast areas and are somewhat more difficult to trap. Also, you must understand the food choices of a particular species.

You can, with relatively few exceptions, eat anything that crawls, swims, walks, or flies. The first obstacle is overcoming your natural aversion to a particular food source. Historically, people in starvation situations have resorted to eating everything imaginable for nourishment.

A person who ignores an otherwise healthy food source due to a personal bias, or because he feels it is unappetizing, is risking his own survival. Although it may prove difficult at first, a survivor must eat what is available to maintain his health.

Insects

The most abundant life-form on earth, insects are easily caught. Insects provide 65 to 80 percent protein compared to 20 percent for beef. This fact makes insects an important, if not overly appetizing, food source. Insects to avoid include all adults that sting or bite, hairy or brightly colored insects, and caterpillars and insects that have a pungent odor. Also avoid spiders and common disease carriers such as ticks, flies, and mosquitoes.

Rotting logs lying on the ground are excellent places to look for a variety of insects including ants, termites, beetles, and grubs, which are beetle larvae. Do not overlook insect nests on or in the ground. Grassy areas, such as fields, are good areas to search because the insects are easily seen. Stones, boards, or other materials lying on the ground provide the insects with good nesting sites. Check these sites. Insect larvae are also edible. Insects such as beetles and grasshoppers that have a hard outer shell will have parasites. Cook them before eating. Remove any wings and barbed legs also. You can eat most insects raw.

The taste varies from one species to another. Wood grubs are bland, while some species of ants store honey in their bodies, giving them a sweet taste. You can grind a collection of insects into a paste. You can mix them with edible vegetation. You can cook them to improve their taste.

Worms

Worms (Annelidea) are an excellent protein source. Dig for them in damp humus soil or watch for them on the ground after a rain. After capturing them, drop them into clean, potable water for a few minutes. The worms will naturally purge or wash themselves out, after which you can eat them raw.

Crustaceans

Freshwater shrimp range in size from 0.25 centimeter up to 2.5 centimeters. They can form rather large colonies in mats of floating algae or in mud bottoms of ponds and lakes.

Crayfish are akin to marine lobsters and crabs. You can distinguish them by their hard exoskeleton and five pairs of legs, the front pair having oversized pincers. Crayfish are active at night, but you can locate them in the daytime by looking under and around stones in streams.

You can also find them by looking in the soft mud near the chimney like breathing holes of their nests. You can catch crayfish by tying bits of offal or internal organs to a string. When the crayfish grabs the bait, pull it to shore before it has a chance to release the bait.

You find saltwater lobsters, crabs, and shrimp from the surf's edge out to water 10 meters deep. Shrimp may come to a light at night where you can scoop them up with a net.

You can catch lobsters and crabs with a baited trap or a baited hook. Crabs will come to bait placed at the edge of the surf, where you can trap or net them. Lobsters and crabs are nocturnal and caught best at night.

Mollusks

This class includes octopuses and freshwater and saltwater shellfish such as snails, clams, mussels, bivalves, barnacles, periwinkles, chitons, and sea urchins. You find bivalves similar to our freshwater mussel and terrestrial and aquatic snails worldwide under all water conditions.

River snails or freshwater periwinkles are plentiful in rivers, streams, and lakes of northern coniferous forests. These snails may be pencil point or globular in shape.

In fresh water, look for mollusks in the shallows, especially in water with a sandy or muddy bottom. Look for the narrow trails they leave in the mud or for the dark elliptical slit of their open valves.

Near the sea, look in the tidal pools and the wet sand. Rocks along beaches or extending as reefs into deeper water often bear clinging shellfish. Snails and limpets cling to rocks and seaweed from the low water mark upward. Large snails, called chitons, adhere tightly to rocks above the surf line.

Mussels usually form dense colonies in rock pools, on logs, or at the base of boulders.

CAUTION

Mussels may be poisonous in tropical zones during the summer!

Steam, boil, or bake mollusks in the shell. They make excellent stews in combination with greens and tubers.

CAUTION

Do not eat shellfish that are not covered by water at high tide!

Fish

Fish represent a good source of protein and fat. They offer some distinct advantages to the survivor or evader. They are usually more abundant than mammal wildlife, and the ways to get them are silent. To be successful at catching fish, you must know their habits.

For instance, fish tend to feed heavily before a storm. Fish are not likely to feed after a storm when the water is muddy and swollen. Light often attracts fish at night. When there is a heavy current, fish will rest in places where there is an eddy, such as near rocks.

Fish will also gather where there are deep pools, under overhanging brush, and in and around submerged foliage, logs, or other objects that offer them shelter.

There are no poisonous freshwater fish. However, the catfish species has sharp, needlelike protrusions on its dorsal fins and barbels. These can inflict painful puncture wounds that quickly become infected.

Cook all freshwater fish to kill parasites. Also cook saltwater fish caught within a reef or within the influence of a freshwater source as a precaution. Any marine life obtained farther out in the sea will not contain parasites because of the saltwater environment. You can eat these raw.

Certain saltwater species of fish have poisonous flesh. In some species the poison occurs seasonally in others, it is permanent. Examples of poisonous saltwater fish are the porcupine fish, triggerfish, cowfish, thorn fish, oilfish, red snapper, jack, and puffer. The barracuda, while not actually poisonous itself, may transmit ciguatera (fish poisoning) if eaten raw.

Amphibians

Frogs and salamanders are easily found around bodies of fresh water. Frogs seldom move from the safety of the water's edge. At the first sign of danger, they plunge into the water and bury themselves in the mud and debris. There are few poisonous species of frogs.

Avoid any brightly colored frog or one that has a distinct "X" mark on it's back. Do not confuse toads with frogs. You normally find toads in drier environments. Several species of toads secrete a poisonous substance through their skin as a defense against attack. Therefore, to avoid poisoning, do not handle or eat toads.

Salamanders are nocturnal. The best time to catch them is at night using a light. They can range in size from a few centimeters to well over 60 centimeters in length. Look in water around rocks and mud banks for salamanders.

Reptiles

Reptiles are a good protein source and relatively easy to catch. You should cook them, but in an emergency, you can eat them raw. Their raw flesh may transmit parasites, but because reptiles are cold-blooded, they do not carry the blood diseases of the warm-blooded animals.

The box turtle is a commonly encountered turtle that you should not eat. It feeds on poisonous mushrooms and may build up a highly toxic poison in its flesh. Cooking does not destroy this toxin.

Avoid the hawksbill turtle, found in the Atlantic Ocean, because of its poisonous thorax gland. Poisonous snakes, alligators, crocodiles, and large sea turtles present obvious hazards to the survivor.

Birds

All species of birds are edible, although the flavor will vary considerably. You may skin fish-eating birds to improve their taste. As with any wild animal, you must understand birds' common habits to have a realistic chance of capturing them. You can take pigeons, as well as some other species, from their roost at night by hand.

During the nesting season, some species will not leave the nest even when approached. Knowing where and when the birds nest makes catching them easier. Birds tend to have regular flyways going from the roost to a feeding area, to water, and so forth.

Careful observation should reveal where these flyways are and indicate good areas for catching birds in nets stretched across the flyways. Roosting sites and waterholes are some of the most promising areas for trapping or snaring.

Nesting birds present another food source--eggs. Remove all but two or three eggs from the clutch, marking the ones that you leave. The bird will continue to lay more eggs to fill the clutch. Continue removing the fresh eggs, leaving the ones you marked.

Mammals

Mammals are excellent protein sources and, for Americans, the most tasty food source. There are some drawbacks to obtaining mammals. In a hostile environment, the enemy may detect any traps or snares placed on land.

The amount of injury an animal can inflict is in direct proportion to its size. All mammals have teeth and nearly all will bite in self-defense. Even a squirrel can inflict a serious wound and any bite presents a serious risk of infection. Also, a mother can be extremely aggressive in defense of her young. Any animal with no route of escape will fight when cornered.

All mammals are edible; however, the polar bear and bearded seal have toxic levels of vitamin A in their livers. The platypus, native to Australia and Tasmania, is an egg-laying, semi-aquatic mammal that has poisonous glands. Scavenging mammals, such as the opossum, may carry diseases.

TRAPS AND SNARES

For an unarmed survivor or evader, or when the sound of a rifle shot could be a problem, trapping or snaring wild game is a good alternative. Several well-placed traps have the potential to catch much more game than a man with a rifle is likely to shoot.

To be effective with any type of trap or snare, you must--

Be familiar with the species of animal you intend to catch.

Be capable of constructing a proper trap.

Not alarm the prey by leaving signs of your presence.

There are no catchall traps you can set for all animals. You must determine what species are in a given area and set your traps specifically with those animals in mind. Look for the following:

Runs and trails.

Tracks.

Droppings.

Chewed or rubbed vegetation.

Nesting or roosting sites.

Feeding and watering areas.

Position your traps and snares where there is proof that animals pass through. You must determine if it is a "run" or a "trail." A trail will show signs of use by several species and will be rather distinct.

A run is usually smaller and less distinct and will only contain signs of one species. You may construct a perfect snare, but it will not catch anything if haphazardly placed in the woods. Animals have bedding areas, waterholes, and feeding areas with trails leading from one to another. You must place snares and traps around these areas to be effective.

For an evader in a hostile environment, trap and snare concealment is important. It is equally important, however, not to create a disturbance that will alarm the animal and cause it to avoid the trap.

Therefore, if you must dig, remove all fresh dirt from the area. Most animals will instinctively avoid a pitfall-type trap. Prepare the various parts of a trap or snare away from the site, carry them in, and set them up. Such actions make it easier to avoid disturbing the local vegetation, thereby alerting the prey.

Do not use freshly cut, live vegetation to construct a trap or snare. Freshly cut vegetation will "bleed" sap that has an odor the prey will be able to smell. It is an alarm signal to the animal.

You must remove or mask the human scent on and around the trap you set. Although birds do not have a developed sense of smell, nearly all mammals depend on smell even more than on sight. Even the slightest human scent on a trap will alarm the prey and cause it to avoid the area. Actually removing the scent from a trap is difficult but masking it is relatively easy.

Use the fluid from the gall and urine bladders of previous kills. Do not use human urine. Mud, particularly from an area with plenty of rotting vegetation, is also good. Use it to coat your hands when handling the trap and to coat the trap when setting it.

In nearly all parts of the world, animals know the smell of burned vegetation and smoke. It is only when a fire is actually burning that they become alarmed. Therefore, smoking the trap parts is an effective means to mask your scent. If one of the above techniques is not practical, and if time permits, allow a trap to weather for a few days and then set it.

Do not handle a trap while it is weathering. When you position the trap, camouflage it as naturally as possible to prevent detection by the enemy and to avoid alarming the prey.

Traps or snares placed on a trail or run should use channelization. To build a channel, construct a funnel-shaped barrier extending from the sides of the trail toward the trap, with the narrowest part nearest the trap.

Channelization should be inconspicuous to avoid alerting the prey. As the animal gets to the trap, it cannot turn left or right and continues into the trap. Few wild animals will back up, preferring to face the direction of travel. Channelization does not have to be an impassable barrier.

You only have to make it inconvenient for the animal to go over or through the barrier. For best effect, the channelization should reduce the trail's width to just slightly wider than the targeted animal's body. Maintain this constriction at least as far back from the trap as the animal's body length, then begin the widening toward the mouth of the funnel.

Use of Bait

Baiting a trap or snare increases your chances of catching an animal. When catching fish, you must bait nearly all the devices. Success with an un-baited trap depends on its placement in a good location. A baited trap can actually draw animals to it. The bait should be something the animal knows.

This bait, however, should not be so readily available in the immediate area that the animal can get it close by. For example, baiting a trap with corn in the middle of a corn field would not be likely to work. Likewise, if corn is not grown in the region, a corn-baited trap may arouse an animal's curiosity and keep it alerted while it ponders the strange food.

Under such circumstances it may not go for the bait. One bait that works well on small mammals is the peanut butter from a meal, ready-to-eat (MRE) ration. Salt is also a good bait. When using such baits, scatter bits of it around the trap to give the prey a chance to sample it and develop a craving for it.

The animal will then overcome some of its caution before it gets to the trap.

If you set and bait a trap for one species but another species takes the bait without being caught, try to determine what the animal was. Then set a proper trap for that animal, using the same bait.

Note: Once you have successfully trapped an animal, you will not only gain confidence in your ability, you also will have resupplied yourself with bait for several more traps.

Trap and Snare Construction

Traps and snares crush, choke, hang, or entangle the prey. A single trap or snare will commonly incorporate two or more of these principles. The mechanisms that provide power to the trap are almost always very simple. The struggling victim, the force of gravity, or a bent sapling's tension provides the power.

The heart of any trap or snare is the trigger. When planning a trap or snare, ask yourself how it should affect the prey, what is the source of power, and what will be the most efficient trigger.

Your answers will help you devise a specific trap for a specific species. Traps are designed to catch and hold or to catch and kill. Snares are traps that incorporate a noose to accomplish either function.

Simple Snare

A simple snare consists of a noose placed over a trail or den hole and attached to a firmly planted stake. If the noose is some type of cordage placed upright on a game trail, use small twigs or blades of grass to hold it up.

Filaments from spider webs are excellent for holding nooses open. Make sure the noose is large enough to pass freely over the animal's head. As the animal continues to move, the noose tightens around its neck. The more the animal struggles, the tighter the noose gets.

This type of snare usually does not kill the animal. If you use cordage, it may loosen enough to slip off the animal's neck. Wire is therefore the best choice for a simple snare.

Drag Noose

Use a drag noose on an animal run. Place forked sticks on either side of the run and lay a sturdy cross member across them. Tie the noose to the cross member and hang it at a height above the animal's head.

(Nooses designed to catch by the head should never be low enough for the prey to step into with a foot.) As the noose tightens around the animal's neck, the animal pulls the cross member from the forked sticks and drags it along. The surrounding vegetation quickly catches the cross member and the animal becomes entangled.

Twitch-Up

A twitch-up is a supple sapling, which, when bent over and secured with a triggering device, will provide power to a variety of snares. Select a hardwood sapling along the trail. A twitch-up will work much faster and with more force if you remove all the branches and foliage.

Twitch-Up Snare

A simple twitch-up snare uses two forked sticks, each with a long and short leg. Bend the twitch-up and mark the trail below it. Drive the long leg of one forked stick firmly into the ground at that point.

Ensure the cut on the short leg of this stick is parallel to the ground. Tie the long leg of the remaining forked stick to a piece of cordage secured to the twitch-up. Cut the short leg so that it catches on the short leg of the other forked stick. Extend a noose over the trail.

Set the trap by bending the twitch-up and engaging the short legs of the forked sticks. When an animal catches its head in the noose, it pulls the forked sticks apart, allowing the twitch-up to spring up and hang the prey.

Note: Do not use green sticks for the trigger. The sap that oozes out could glue them together.

Squirrel Pole

A squirrel pole is a long pole placed against a tree in an area showing a lot of squirrel activity. Place several wire nooses along the top and sides of the pole so that a squirrel trying to go up or down the pole will have to pass through one or more of them.

Position the nooses (5 to 6 centimeters in diameter) about 2.5 centimeters off the pole. Place the top and bottom wire nooses 45 centimeters from the top and bottom of the pole to prevent the squirrel from getting its feet on a solid surface. If this happens, the squirrel will chew through the wire. Squirrels are naturally curious.

After an initial period of caution, they will try to go up or down the pole and will get caught in a noose. The struggling animal will soon fall from the pole and strangle. Other squirrels will soon follow and, in this way, you can catch several squirrels. You can emplace multiple poles to increase the catch.

Ojibwa Bird Pole

An Ojibwa bird pole is a snare used by native Americans for centuries. To be effective, place it in a relatively open area away from tall trees. For best results, pick a spot near feeding areas, dusting areas, or watering holes.

Cut a pole 1.8 to 2.1 meters long and trim away all limbs and foliage. Do not use resinous wood such as pine. Sharpen the upper end to a point, then drill a small diameter hole 5 to 7.5 centimeters down from the top.

Cut a small stick 10 to 15 centimeters long and shape one end so that it will almost fit into the hole. This is the perch. Plant the long pole in the ground with the pointed end up.

Tie a small weight, about equal to the weight of the targeted species, to a length of cordage. Pass the free end of the cordage through the hole, and tie a slip noose that covers the perch.

Tie a single overhand knot in the cordage and place the perch against the hole. Allow the cordage to slip through the hole until the overhand knot rests against the pole and the top of the perch.

The tension of the overhand knot against the pole and perch will hold the perch in position. Spread the noose over the perch, ensuring it covers the perch and drapes over on both sides.

Most birds prefer to rest on something above ground and will land on the perch. As soon as the bird lands, the perch will fall, releasing the over-hand knot and allowing the weight to drop.

The noose will tighten around the bird's feet, capturing it. If the weight is too heavy, it will cut the bird's feet off, allowing it to escape.

Noosing Wand

A noose stick or "noosing wand" is useful for capturing roosting birds or small mammals. It requires a patient operator. This wand is more a weapon than a trap. It consists of a pole (as long as you can effectively handle) with a slip noose of wire or stiff cordage at the small end. To catch an animal, you slip the noose over the neck of a roosting bird and pull it tight. You can also place it over a den hole and hide in a nearby blind.

When the animal emerges from the den, you jerk the pole to tighten the noose and thus capture the animal. Carry a stout club to kill the prey.

Treadle Spring Snare

Use a treadle snare against small game on a trail. Dig a shallow hole in the trail. Then drive a forked stick (fork down) into the ground on each side of the hole on the same side of the trail. Select two fairly straight sticks that span the two forks. Position these two sticks so that their ends engage the forks.

Place several sticks over the hole in the trail by positioning one end over the lower horizontal stick and the other on the ground on the other side of the hole. Cover the hole with enough sticks so that the prey must step on at least one of them to set off the snare.

Tie one end of a piece of cordage to a twitch-up or to a weight suspended over a tree limb. Bend the twitch-up or raise the suspended weight to determine where you will tie a 5 centimeter or so long trigger.

Form a noose with the other end of the cordage. Route and spread the noose over the top of the sticks over the hole. Place the trigger stick against the horizontal sticks and route the cordage behind the sticks so that the tension of the power source will hold it in place.

Adjust the bottom horizontal stick so that it will barely hold against the trigger. A the animal places its foot on a stick across the hole, the bottom horizontal stick moves down, releasing the trigger and allowing the noose to catch the animal by the foot.

Because of the disturbance on the trail, an animal will be wary. You must therefore use channelization.

Figure 4 Deadfall

The figure 4 is a trigger used to drop a weight onto a prey and crush it. The type of weight used may vary, but it should be heavy enough to kill or incapacitate the prey immediately. Construct the figure 4 using three notched sticks. These notches hold the sticks together in a figure 4 pattern when under tension. Practice making this trigger beforehand; it requires close tolerances and precise angles in its construction.

Paiute Deadfall

The Paiute deadfall is similar to the figure 4 but uses a piece of cordage and a catch stick. It has the advantage of being easier to set than the figure 4. Tie one end of a piece of cordage to the lower end of the diagonal stick. Tie the other end of the cordage to another stick about 5 centimeters long.

This 5-centimeter stick is the catch stick. Bring the cord halfway around the vertical stick with the catch stick at a 90-degree angle. Place the bait stick with one end against the drop weight, or a peg driven into the ground, and the other against the catch stick. When a prey disturbs the bait stick, it falls free, releasing the catch stick. As the diagonal stick flies up, the weight falls, crushing the prey.

Bow Trap

A bow trap is one of the deadliest traps. It is dangerous to man as well as animals. To construct this trap, build a bow and anchor it to the ground with pegs. Adjust the aiming point as you anchor the bow.

Lash a toggle stick to the trigger stick. Two upright sticks driven into the ground hold the trigger stick in place at a point where the toggle stick will engage the pulled bow string. Place a catch stick between the toggle stick and a stake driven into the ground.

Tie a trip wire or cordage to the catch stick and route it around stakes and across the game trail where you tie it off. When the prey trips the trip wire, the bow looses an arrow into it. A notch in the bow serves to help aim the arrow.

WARNING

This is a lethal trap. Approach it with caution and from the rear only!

Pig Spear Shaft

To construct the pig spear shaft, select a stout pole about 2.5 meters long . At the smaller end, firmly lash several small stakes. Lash the large end tightly to a tree along the game trail. Tie a length of cordage to another tree across the trail.

Tie a sturdy, smooth stick to the other end of the cord. From the first tree, tie a trip wire or cord low to the ground, stretch it across the trail, and tie it to a catch stick. Make a slip ring from vines or other suitable material.

Encircle the trip wire and the smooth stick with the slip ring. Emplace one end of another smooth stick within the slip ring and its other end against the second tree. Pull the smaller end of the spear shaft across the trail and position it between the short cord and the smooth stick.

As the animal trips the trip wire, the catch stick pulls the slip ring off the smooth sticks, releasing the spear shaft that springs across the trail and impales the prey against the tree.

WARNING

This is a lethal trap. Approach it with caution!

Bottle Trap

A bottle trap is a simple trap for mice and voles. Dig a hole 30 to 45 centimeters deep that is wider at the bottom than at the top. Make the top of the hole as small as possible. Place a piece of bark or wood over the hole with small stones under it to hold it up 2.5 to 5 centimeters off the ground. Mice or voles will hide under the cover to escape danger and fall into the hole. They cannot climb out because of the wall's backward slope. Use caution when checking this trap; it is an excellent hiding place for snakes.

KILLING DEVICES

There are several killing devices that you can construct to help you obtain small game to help you survive. The rabbit stick, the spear, the bow and arrow, and the sling are such devices.

Rabbit Stick

One of the simplest and most effective killing devices is a stout stick as long as your arm, from fingertip to shoulder, called a "rabbit stick." You can throw it either overhand or sidearm and with considerable force. It is very effective against small game that stops and freezes as a defense.

Spear

You can make a spear to kill small game and to fish. Jab with the spear, do not throw it.

Bow and Arrow

A good bow is the result of many hours of work. You can construct a suitable short-term bow fairly easily. When it loses its spring or breaks, you can replace it. Select a hardwood stick about one meter long that is free of knots or limbs.

Carefully scrape the large end down until it has the same pull as the small end. Careful examination will show the natural curve of the stick. Always scrape from the side that faces you, or the bow will break the first time you pull it.

Dead, dry wood is preferable to green wood. To increase the pull, lash a second bow to the first, front to front, forming an "X" when viewed from the side. Attach the tips of the bows with cordage and only use a bowstring on one bow.

Select arrows from the straightest dry sticks available. The arrows should be about half as long as the bow. Scrape each shaft smooth all around. You will probably have to straighten the shaft.

You can bend an arrow straight by heating the shaft over hot coals. Do not allow the shaft to scorch or bum. Hold the shaft straight until it cools.

You can make arrowheads from bone, glass, metal, or pieces of rock. You can also sharpen and fire harden the end of the shaft. To fire harden wood, hold it over hot coals, being careful not to bum or scorch the wood.

You must notch the ends of the arrows for the bowstring. Cut or file the notch; do not split it. Fletching (adding feathers to the notched end of an arrow) improves the arrow's flight characteristics, but is not necessary on a field-expedient arrow.

Sling

You can make a sling by tying two pieces of cordage, about sixty centimeters long, at opposite ends of a palm-sized piece of leather or cloth. Place a rock in the cloth and wrap one cord around the middle finger and hold in your palm.

Hold the other cord between the forefinger and thumb. To throw the rock, spin the sling several times in a circle and release the cord between the thumb and forefinger. Practice to gain proficiency. The sling is very effective against small game.

FISHING DEVICES

You can make your own fishhooks, nets and traps and use several methods to obtain fish in a survival situation.

Improvised Fishhooks

You can make field-expedient fishhooks from pins, needles, wire, small nails, or any piece of metal. You can also use wood, bone, coconut shell, thorns, flint, seashell, or tortoise shell. You can also make fishhooks from any combination of these items.
To make a wooden hook, cut a piece of hardwood about 2.5 centimeters long and about 6 millimeters in diameter to form the shank. Cut a notch in one end in which to place the point. Place the point (piece of bone, wire, nail) in the notch. Hold the point in the notch and tie securely so that it does not move out of position. This is a fairly large hook. To make smaller hooks, use smaller material.

A gorge is a small shaft of wood, bone, metal, or other material. It is sharp on both ends and notched in the middle where you tie cordage. Bait the gorge by placing a piece of bait on it lengthwise. When the fish swallows the bait, it also swallows the gorge.

Stakeout

A stakeout is a fishing device you can use in a hostile environment . To construct a stakeout, drive two supple saplings into the bottom of the lake, pond, or stream with their tops just below the water surface. Tie a cord between them and slightly below the surface. Tie two short cords with hooks or gorges to this cord, ensuring that they cannot wrap around the poles or each other. They should also not slip along the long cord. Bait the hooks or gorges.

Gill Net

If a gill net is not available, you can make one using parachute suspension line or similar material. Remove the core lines from the suspension line and tie the easing between two trees. Attach several core lines to the easing by doubling them over and tying them with prusik knots or girth hitches.

The length of the desired net and the size of the mesh determine the number of core lines used and the space between them. Starting at one end of the easing, tie the second and the third core lines together using an overhand knot.

Then tie the fourth and fifth, sixth and seventh, and so on, until you reach the last core line. You should now have all core lines tied in pairs with a single core line hanging at each end. Start the second row with the first core line, tie it to the second, the third to the fourth, and so on

To keep the rows even and to regulate the size of the mesh, tie a guideline to the trees. Position the guideline on the opposite side of the net you are working on. Move the guideline down after completing each row.

The lines will always hang in pairs and you always tie a cord from one pair to a cord from an adjoining pair. Continue tying rows until the net is the desired width. Thread a suspension line easing along the bottom of the net to strengthen it.

Fish Traps

You may trap fish using several methods. Fish baskets are one method. You construct them by lashing several sticks together with vines into a funnel shape. You close the top, leaving a hole large enough for the fish to swim through.

You can also use traps to catch saltwater fish, as schools regularly approach the shore with the incoming tide and often move parallel to the shore. Pick a location at high tide and build the trap at low tide.

On rocky shores, use natural rock pools. On coral islands, use natural pools on the surface of reefs by blocking the openings as the tide recedes. On sandy shores, use sandbars and the ditches they enclose. Build the trap as a low stone wall extending outward into the water and forming an angle with the shore.

Spearfishing

If you are near shallow water (about waist deep) where the fish are large and plentiful, you can spear them. To make a spear, cut a long, straight sapling. Sharpen the end to a point or attach a knife, jagged piece of bone, or sharpened metal. You can also make a spear by splitting the shaft a few inches down from the end and inserting a piece of wood to act as a spreader.

You then sharpen the two separated halves to points. To spear fish, find an area where fish either gather or where there is a fish run. Place the spear point into the water and slowly move it toward the fish. Then, with a sudden push, impale the fish on the stream bottom.

Do not try to lift the fish with the spear, as it with probably slip off and you will lose it; hold the spear with one hand and grab and hold the fish with the other.

Do not throw the spear, especially if the point is a knife. You cannot afford to lose a knife in a survival situation. Be alert to the problems caused by light refraction when looking at objects in the water.

Chop Fishing

At night, in an area with a good fish density, you can use a light to attract fish. Then, armed with a machete or similar weapon, you can gather fish using the back side of the blade to strike them. Do not use the sharp side as you will cut them in two pieces and end up losing some of the fish.

Fish Poison

Another way to catch fish is by using poison. Poison works quickly. It allows you to remain concealed while it takes effect. It also enables you to catch several fish at one time. When using fish poison, be sure to gather all of the affected fish, because many dead fish floating downstream could arouse suspicion.

Some plants that grow in warm regions of the world contain rotenone, a substance that stuns or kills cold-blooded animals but does not harm persons who eat the animals. The best place to use rotenone, or rotenone-producing plants, is in ponds or the headwaiters of small streams containing fish.

Rotenone works quickly on fish in water 21 degrees C (70 degrees F) or above. The fish rise helplessly to the surface. It works slowly in water 10 to 21 degrees C (50 to 70 degrees F) and is ineffective in water below 10 degrees C (50 degrees F). The following plants, used as indicated, will stun or kill fish:

Anamirta cocculus. This woody vine grows in southern Asia and on islands of the South Pacific. Crush the bean-shaped seeds and throw them in the water.

Croton tiglium. This shrub or small tree grows in waste areas on islands of the South Pacific. It bears seeds in three angled capsules. Crush the seeds and throw them into the water.

Barringtonia. These large trees grow near the sea in Malaya and parts of Polynesia. They bear a fleshy one-seeded fruit. Crush the seeds and bark and throw into the water.

Derris eliptica. This large genus of tropical shrubs and woody vines is the main source of commercially produced rotenone. Grind the roots into a powder and mix with water. Throw a large quantity of the mixture into the water.

Duboisia. This shrub grows in Australia and bears white clusters of flowers and berrylike fruit. Crush the plants and throw them into the water.

Tephrosia. This species of small shrubs, which bears beanlike pods, grows throughout the tropics. Crush or bruise bundles of leaves and stems and throw them into the water.

Lime. You can get lime from commercial sources and in agricultural areas that use large quantities of it. You may produce your own by burning coral or seashells. Throw the lime into the water.

Nut husks. Crush green husks from butternuts or black walnuts. Throw the husks into the water.

PREPARATION OF FISH AND GAME FOR COOKING AND STORAGE

You must know how to prepare fish and game for cooking and storage in a survival situation. Improper cleaning or storage can result in inedible fish or game.

Fish

Do not eat fish that appears spoiled. Cooking does not ensure that spoiled fish will be edible. Signs of spoilage are--

Sunken eyes.

Peculiar odor.

Suspicious color. (Gills should be red to pink. Scales should be a pronounced shade of gray, not faded.)

Dents stay in the fish's flesh after pressing it with your thumb.

Slimy, rather than moist or wet body.

Sharp or peppery taste.

Eating spoiled or rotten fish may cause diarrhea, nausea, cramps, vomiting, itching, paralysis, or a metallic taste in the mouth. These symptoms appear suddenly, one to six hours after eating. Induce vomiting if symptoms appear.

Fish spoils quickly after death, especially on a hot day. Prepare fish for eating as soon as possible after catching it. Cut out the gills and large blood vessels that lie near the spine. Gut fish that is more than 10 centimeters long. Scale or skin the fish.

You can impale a whole fish on a stick and cook it over an open fire. However, boiling the fish with the skin on is the best way to get the most food value. The fats and oil are under the skin and, by boiling, you can save the juices for broth.

You can use any of the methods used to cook plant food to cook fish. Pack fish into a ball of clay and bury it in the coals of a fire until the clay hardens. Break open the clay ball to get to the cooked fish. Fish is done when the meat flakes off. If you plan to keep the fish for later, smoke or fry it. To prepare fish for smoking, cut off the head and remove the backbone.

Snakes

To skin a snake, first cut off its head and bury it. Then cut the skin down the body 15 to 20 centimeters. Peel the skin back, then grasp the skin in one hand and the body in the other and pull apart. On large, bulky snakes it may be necessary to slit the belly skin. Cook snakes in the same manner as small game. Remove the entrails and discard. Cut the snake into small sections and boil or roast it.

Birds

After killing the bird, remove its feathers by either plucking or skinning. Remember, skinning removes some of the food value. Open up the body cavity and remove its entrails, saving the craw (in seed-eating birds), heart, and liver. Cut off the feet. Cook by boiling or roasting over a spit. Before cooking scavenger birds, boil them at least 20 minutes to kill parasites.

Skinning and Butchering Game

Bleed the animal by cutting its throat. If possible, clean the carcass near a stream. Place the carcass belly up and split the hide from throat to tail, cutting around all sexual organs. Remove the musk glands to avoid tainting the meat.

For smaller mammals, cut the hide around the body and insert two fingers under the hide on both sides of the cut and pull both pieces off.

Note: When cutting the hide, insert the knife blade under the skin and turn the blade up so that only the hide gets cut. This will also prevent cutting hair and getting it on the meat.

Remove the entrails from smaller game by splitting the body open and pulling them out with the fingers.

Do not forget the chest cavity. For larger game, cut the gullet away from the diaphragm. Roll the entrails out of the body. Cut around the anus, then reach into the lower abdominal cavity, grasp the lower intestine, and pull to remove.

Remove the urine bladder by pinching it off and cutting it below the fingers. If you spill urine on the meat, wash it to avoid tainting the meat. Save the heart and liver. Cut these open and inspect for signs of worms or other parasites.

Also inspect the liver's color; it could indicate a diseased animal. The liver's surface should be smooth and wet and its color deep red or purple. If the liver appears diseased, discard it. However, a diseased liver does not indicate you cannot eat the muscle tissue.

Cut along each leg from above the foot to the previously made body cut. Remove the hide by pulling it away from the carcass, cutting the connective tissue where necessary. Cut off the head and feet.

Cut larger game into manageable pieces. First, slice the muscle tissue connecting the front legs to the body. There are no bones or joints connecting the front legs to the body on four-legged animals. Cut the hindquarters off where they join the body. You must cut around a large bone at the top of the leg and cut to the ball and socket hip joint.

Cut the ligaments around the joint and bend it back to separate it. Remove the large muscles (the tenderloin) that lie on either side of the spine. Separate the ribs from the backbone. There is less work and less wear on your knife if you break the ribs first, then cut through the breaks.

Cook large meat pieces over a spit or boil them. You can stew or boil smaller pieces, particularly those that remain attached to bone after the initial butchering, as soup or broth.

You can cook body organs such as the heart, liver, pancreas, spleen, and kidneys using the same methods as for muscle meat. You can also cook and eat the brain. Cut the tongue out, skin it, boil it until tender, and eat it.

Smoking Meat

To smoke meat, prepare an enclosure around a fire. Two ponchos snapped together will work. The fire does not need to be big or hot.

The intent is to produce smoke, not heat. Do not use resinous wood in the fire because its smoke will ruin the meat. Use hardwoods to produce good smoke. The wood should be somewhat green.

If it is too dry, soak it. Cut the meat into thin slices, no more than 6 centimeters thick, and drape them over a framework. Make sure none of the meat touches another piece. Keep the poncho enclosure around the meat to hold the smoke and keep a close watch on the fire.

Do not let the fire get too hot. Meat smoked overnight in this manner will last about 1 week. Two days of continuous smoking will preserve the meat for 2 to 4 weeks. Properly smoked meat will look like a dark, curled, brittle stick and you can eat it without further cooking. You can also use a pit to smoke meat.

Drying Meat

To preserve meat by drying, cut it into 6-millimeter strips with the grain. Hang the meat strips on a rack in a sunny location with good air flow. Keep the strips out of the reach of animals and cover them to keep blowflies off. Allow the meat to dry thoroughly before eating. Properly dried meat will have a dry, crisp texture and will not feel cool to the touch.

Other Preservation Methods

You can also preserve meats using the freezing or brine and salt methods.

Freezing

In cold climates, you can freeze and keep meat indefinitely. Freezing is not a means of preparing meat. You must still cook it before eating.

Brine and Salt

You can preserve meat by soaking it thoroughly in a saltwater solution. The solution must cover the meat. You can also use salt by itself. Wash off the salt before cooking.

Chapter 13 Field-Expedient Weapons, Tools, And Equipment

As a partisan you know the importance of proper care and use of your weapons, tools, and equipment. This is especially true of your knife. You must always keep it sharp and ready to use.

A knife is your most valuable tool in a survival situation. Imagine being in a survival situation without any weapons, tools, or equipment except your knife. It could happen! You might even be without a knife. You would probably feel helpless, but with the proper knowledge and skills, you can easily improvise needed items.

In survival situations, you may have to fashion any number and type of field-expedient tools and equipment to survive. Examples of tools and equipment that could make your life much easier are ropes, rucksacks, clothes, nets, and so on.

Weapons serve a dual purpose. You use them to obtain and prepare food and to provide self-defense. A weapon can also give you a feeling of security and provide you with the ability to hunt on the move.

CLUBS

You hold clubs, you do not throw them. As a field-expedient weapon, the club does not protect you from enemy soldiers. It can, however, extend your area of defense beyond your fingertips. It also serves to increase the force of a blow without injuring yourself. There are three basic types of clubs. They are the simple, weighted, and sling club.

Simple Club

A simple club is a staff or branch. It must be short enough for you to swing easily, but long enough and strong enough for you to damage whatever you hit. Its diameter should fit comfortably in your palm, but it should not be so thin as to allow the club to break easily upon impact. A straight-grained hardwood is best if you can find it.

Weighted Club

A weighted club is any simple club with a weight on one end. The weight may be a natural weight, such as a knot on the wood, or something added, such as a stone lashed to the club.

To make a weighted club, first find a stone that has a shape that will allow you to lash it securely to the club. A stone with a slight hourglass shape works well. If you cannot find a suitably shaped stone, you must fashion a groove or channel into the stone by a technique known as pecking. By repeatedly rapping the club stone with a smaller hard stone, you can get the desired shape.

Next, find a piece of wood that is the right length for you. A straight-grained hardwood is best. The length of the wood should feel comfortable in relation to the weight of the stone. Finally, lash the stone to the handle.

There are three techniques for lashing the stone to the handle: split handle, forked branch, and wrapped handle. The technique you use will depend on the type of handle you choose.

Sling Club

A sling club is another type of weighted club. A weight hangs 8 to 10 centimeters from the handle by a strong, flexible lashing. This type of club both extends the user's reach and multiplies the force of the blow.

OTHER EXPEDIENT WEAPONS

You can make other field-expedient weapons such as the throwing stick, archery equipment, and the bola.

Throwing Stick

The throwing stick, commonly known as the rabbit stick, is very effective against small game (squirrels, chipmunks, and rabbits). The rabbit stick itself is a blunt stick, naturally curved at about a 45-degree angle. Select a stick with the desired angle from heavy hardwood such as oak.

Shave off two opposite sides so that the stick is flat like a boomerang. You must practice the throwing technique for accuracy and speed. First, align the target by extending the nonthrowing arm in line with the mid to lower section of the target.

Slowly and repeatedly raise the throwing arm up and back until the throwing stick crosses the back at about a 45-degree angle or is in line with the nonthrowing hip. Bring the throwing arm forward until it is just slightly above and parallel to the nonthrowing arm. This will be the throwing stick's release point. Practice slowly and repeatedly to attain accuracy.

Archery Equipment

You can make a bow and arrow from materials available in your survival area.

While it may be relatively simple to make a bow and arrow, it is not easy to use one. You must practice using it a long time to be reasonably sure that you will hit your target. Also, a field-expedient bow will not last very long before you have to make a new one. For the time and effort involved, you may well decide to use another type of field-expedient weapon.

Bola

The bola is another field-expedient weapon that is easy to make. It is especially effective for capturing running game or low-flying fowl in a flock. To use the bola, hold it by the center knot and twirl it above your head. Release the knot so that the bola flies toward your target.

When you release the bola, the weighted cords will separate. These cords will wrap around and immobilize the fowl or animal that you hit.

LASHING AND CORDAGE

Many materials are strong enough for use as lashing and cordage. A number of natural and man-made materials are available in a survival situation. For example, you can make a cotton web belt much more useful by unraveling it. You can then use the string for other purposes (fishing line, thread for sewing, and lashing).

Natural Cordage Selection

Before making cordage, there are a few simple tests you can do to determine you material's suitability. First, pull on a length of the material to test for strength. Next, twist it between your fingers and roll the fibers together. If it withstands this handling and does not snap apart, tie an overhand knot with the fibers and gently tighten. If the knot does not break, the material is usable.

Lashing Material

The best natural material for lashing small objects is sinew. You can make sinew from the tendons of large game, such as deer. Remove the tendons from the game and dry them completely.

Smash the dried tendons so that they separate into fibers. Moisten the fibers and twist them into a continuous strand. If you need stronger lashing material, you can braid the strands. When you use sinew for small lashings, you do not need knots as the moistened sinew is sticky and it hardens when dry.

You can shred and braid plant fibers from the inner bark of some trees to make cord. You can use the linden, elm, hickory, white oak, mulberry, chestnut, and red and white cedar trees. After you make the cord, test it to be sure it is strong enough for your purpose. You can make these materials stronger by braiding several strands together.

You can use rawhide for larger lashing jobs. Make rawhide from the skins of medium or large game. After skinning the animal, remove any excess fat and any pieces of meat from the skin. Dry the skin completely.

You do not need to stretch it as long as there are no folds to trap moisture. You do not have to remove the hair from the skin. Cut the skin while it is dry. Make cuts about 6 millimeters wide. Start from the center of the hide and make one continuous circular cut, working clockwise to the hide's outer edge.

Soak the rawhide for 2 to 4 hours or until it is soft. Use it wet, stretching it as much as possible while applying it. It will be strong and durable when it dries.

RUCKSACK CONSTRUCTION

The materials for constructing a rucksack or pack are almost limitless. You can use wood, bamboo, rope, plant fiber, clothing, animal skins, canvas, and many other materials to make a pack.

There are several construction techniques for rucksacks. Many are very elaborate, but those that are simple and easy are often the most readily made in a survival situation.

Horseshoe Pack

This pack is simple to make and use and relatively comfortable to carry over one shoulder. Lay available square-shaped material, such as poncho, blanket, or canvas, flat on the ground. Lay items on one edge of the material. Pad the hard items. Roll the material (with the items) toward the opposite edge and tie both ends securely. Add extra ties along the length of the bundle. You can drape the pack over one shoulder with a line connecting the two ends.

Square Pack

This pack is easy to construct if rope or cordage is available. Otherwise, you must first make cordage. To make this pack, construct a square frame from bamboo, limbs, or sticks. Size will vary for each person and the amount of equipment carried.

Chapter 14 Clothing and Cooking

You can use many materials for clothing and insulation. Both man-made materials, such as parachutes, and natural materials, such as skins and plant materials, are available and offer significant protection.

Animal Skins

The selection of animal skins in a survival situation will most often be limited to what you manage to trap or hunt. However, if there is an abundance of wildlife, select the hides of larger animals with heavier coats and large fat content. Do not use the skins of infected or diseased animals if at all possible. Since they live in the wild, animals are carriers of pests such as ticks, lice, and fleas.

Because of these pests, use water to thoroughly clean any skin obtained from any animal. If water is not available, at least shake out the skin thoroughly. As with rawhide, lay out the skin, and remove all fat and meat. Dry the skin completely. Use the hind quarter joint areas to make shoes and mittens or socks. Wear the hide with the fur to the inside for its insulating factor.

Plant Fibers

Several plants are sources of insulation from cold. Cattail is a marshland plant found along lakes, ponds, and the backwaters of rivers. The fuzz on the tops of the stalks forms dead air spaces and makes a good down-like insulation when placed between two pieces of material. Milkweed has pollenlike seeds that act as good insulation. The husk fibers from coconuts are very good for weaving ropes and, when dried, make excellent tinder and insulation.

COOKING AND EATING UTENSILS

Many materials may be used to make equipment for the cooking, eating, and storing of food.

Bowls

Use wood, bone, horn, bark, or other similar material to make bowls. To make wooden bowls, use a hollowed out piece of wood that will hold your food and enough water to cook it in. Hang the wooden container over the fire and add hot rocks to the water and food. Remove the rocks as they cool and add more hot rocks until your food is cooked.

CAUTION

Do not use rocks with air pockets, such as limestone and sandstone. They may explode while heating in the fire.

You can also use this method with containers made of bark or leaves. However, these containers will burn above the waterline unless you keep them moist or keep the fire low.

A section of bamboo works very well, if you cut out a section between two sealed joints.

CAUTION

A sealed section of bamboo will explode if heated because of trapped air and water in the section.

Forks, Knives, and Spoons

Carve forks, knives, and spoons from nonresinous woods so that you do not get a wood resin aftertaste or do not taint the food. Nonresinous woods include oak, birch, and other hardwood trees.

Note: Do not use those trees that secrete a syrup or resinlike liquid on the bark or when cut.

Pots

You can make pots from turtle shells or wood. As described with bowls, using hot rocks in a hollowed out piece of wood is very effective. Bamboo is the best wood for making cooking containers.

To use turtle shells, first thoroughly boil the upper portion of the shell. Then use it to heat food and water over a flame.

Water Bottles

Make water bottles from the stomachs of larger animals. Thoroughly flush the stomach out with water, then tie off the bottom. Leave the top open, with some means of fastening it closed.

One of the most difficult survival situations is a cold weather scenario. Remember, cold weather is an adversary that can be as dangerous as an enemy soldier.

Every time you venture into the cold, you are pitting yourself against the elements. With a little knowledge of the environment, proper plans, and appropriate equipment, you can overcome the elements. As you remove one or more of these factors, survival becomes increasingly difficult.

Remember, winter weather is highly variable. Prepare yourself to adapt to blizzard conditions even during sunny and clear weather.

Cold is a far greater threat to survival than it appears. It decreases your ability to think and weakens your will to do anything except to get warm.

Cold is an insidious enemy; as it numbs the mind and body, it subdues the will to survive. Cold makes it very easy to forget your ultimate goal--to survive.

Chapter 15 Cold Weather Survival

Cold regions include arctic and sub-arctic areas and areas immediately adjoining them. You can classify about 48 percent of the northern hemisphere's total landmass as a cold region due to the influence and extent of air temperatures.

Ocean currents affect cold weather and cause large areas normally included in the temperate zone to fall within the cold regions during winter periods. Elevation also has a marked effect on defining cold regions.

Within the cold weather regions, you may face two types of cold weather environments--wet or dry. Knowing in which environment your area of operations falls will affect planning and execution of a cold weather operation.

Wet Cold Weather Environments

Wet cold weather conditions exist when the average temperature in a 24-hour period is -10 degrees C or above. Characteristics of this condition are freezing during the colder night hours and thawing during the day.

Even though the temperatures are warmer during this condition, the terrain is usually very sloppy due to slush and mud. You must concentrate on protecting yourself from the wet ground and from freezing rain or wet snow.

Dry Cold Weather Environments

Dry cold weather conditions exist when the average temperature in a 24-hour period remains below -10 degrees C. Even though the temperatures in this condition are much lower than normal, you do not have to contend with the freezing and thawing. In these conditions, you need more layers of inner clothing to protect you from temperatures as low as -60 degrees C. Extremely hazardous conditions exist when wind and low temperature combine.

WINDCHILL

Windchill increases the hazards in cold regions. Windchill is the effect of moving air on exposed flesh. For instance, with a 27.8-kph (15-knot) wind and a temperature of -10 degrees C, the equivalent windchill temperature is -23 degrees C.

Remember, even when there is no wind, you will create the equivalent wind by skiing, running, being towed on skis behind a vehicle, working around aircraft that produce wind blasts.

BASIC PRINCIPLES OF COLD WEATHER SURVIVAL

It is more difficult for you to satisfy your basic water, food, and shelter needs in a cold environment than in a warm environment. Even if you have the basic requirements, you must also have adequate protective clothing and the will to survive.

The will to survive is as important as the basic needs. There have been incidents when trained and well-equipped individuals have not survived cold weather situations because they lacked the will to live. Conversely, this will has sustained individuals less well-trained and equipped.

There are many different items of cold weather equipment and clothing issued by the U.S. Army today. Specialized units may have access to newer, lightweight gear such as polypropylene underwear, GORE-TEX outerwear and boots, and other special equipment.

Remember, however, the older gear will keep you warm as long as you apply a few cold weather principles. If the newer types of clothing are available, use them. If not, then your clothing should be entirely wool, with the possible exception of a windbreaker.

You must not only have enough clothing to protect you from the cold, you must also know how to maximize the warmth you get from it. For example, always keep your head covered. You can lose 40 to 45 percent of body heat from an unprotected head and even more from the unprotected neck, wrist, and ankles.

These areas of the body are good radiators of heat and have very little insulating fat. The brain is very susceptible to cold and can stand the least amount of cooling. Because there is much blood circulation in the head, most of which is on the surface, you can lose heat quickly if you do not cover your head.

There are four basic principles to follow to keep warm. An easy way to remember these basic principles is to use the word COLD--

C - Keep clothing clean.

O - Avoid overheating.

L - Wear clothes loose and in layers.

D - Keep clothing dry.

C -
Keep clothing clean. This principle is always important for sanitation and comfort. In winter, it is also important from the standpoint of warmth. Clothes matted with dirt and grease lose much of their insulation value. Heat can escape more easily from the body through the clothing's crushed or filled up air pockets.

O -
Avoid overheating. When you get too hot, you sweat and your clothing absorbs the moisture. This affects your warmth in two ways: dampness decreases the insulation quality of clothing, and as sweat evaporates, your body cools. Adjust your clothing so that you do not sweat. Do this by partially opening your parka or jacket, by removing an inner layer of clothing, by removing heavy outer

mittens, or by throwing back your parka hood or changing to lighter headgear. The head and hands act as efficient heat dissipaters when overheated.

L -

Wear your clothing loose and in layers. Wearing tight clothing and footgear restricts blood circulation and invites cold injury. It also decreases the volume of air trapped between the layers, reducing its insulating value. Several layers of lightweight clothing are better than one equally thick layer of clothing, because the layers have dead-air space between them. The dead-air space provides extra insulation. Also, layers of clothing allow you to take off or add clothing layers to prevent excessive sweating or to increase warmth.

D -

Keep clothing dry. In cold temperatures, your inner layers of clothing can become wet from sweat and your outer layer, if not water repellent, can become wet from snow and frost melted by body heat. Wear water repellent outer clothing, if available. It will shed most of the water collected from melting snow and frost.

Before entering a heated shelter, brush off the snow and frost. Despite the precautions you take, there will be times when you cannot keep from getting wet. At such times, drying your clothing may become a major problem. On the march, hang your damp mittens and socks on your rucksack.

Sometimes in freezing temperatures, the wind and sun will dry this clothing.

You can also place damp socks or mittens, unfolded, near your body so that your body heat can dry them. In a campsite, hang damp clothing inside the shelter near the top, using drying lines or improvised racks. You may even be able to dry each item by holding it before an open fire.

Dry leather items slowly. If no other means are available for drying your boots, put them between your sleeping bag shell and liner. Your body heat will help to dry the leather.

A heavy, down-lined sleeping bag is a valuable piece of survival gear in cold weather. Ensure the down remains dry. If wet, it loses a lot of its insulation value. If you do not have a sleeping bag, you can make one out of parachute cloth or similar material and natural dry material, such as leaves, pine needles, or moss. Place the dry material between two layers of the material.

Other important survival items are a knife; waterproof matches in a waterproof container, preferably one with a flint attached; a durable compass; map; watch; waterproof ground cloth and cover; flashlight; binoculars; dark glasses; fatty emergency foods; food gathering gear; and signaling items.

Remember, a cold weather environment can be very harsh. Give a good deal of thought to selecting the right equipment for survival in the cold. If unsure of an item you have never used, test it in an "overnight backyard" environment before venturing further. Once you have selected items that are essential for your survival, do not lose them after you enter a cold weather environment.

HYGIENE

Although washing yourself may be impractical and uncomfortable in a cold environment, you must do so. Washing helps prevent skin rashes that can develop into more serious problems.

In some situations, you may be able to take a snow bath. Take a handful of snow and wash your body where sweat and moisture accumulate, such as under the arms and between the legs, and then wipe yourself dry.

If possible, wash your feet daily and put on clean, dry socks. Change your underwear at least twice a week. If you are unable to wash your underwear, take it off, shake it, and let it air out for an hour or two.

If you are using a previously used shelter, check your body and clothing for lice each night. If your clothing has become infested, use insecticide powder if you have any. Otherwise, hang your clothes in the cold, then beat and brush them. This will help get rid of the lice, but not the eggs.

If you shave, try to do so before going to bed. This will give your skin a chance to recover before exposing it to the elements.

MEDICAL ASPECTS

When you are healthy, your inner core temperature (torso temperature) remains almost constant at 37 degrees C (98.6 degrees F). Since your limbs and head have less protective body tissue than your torso, their temperatures vary and may not reach core temperature.

Your body has a control system that lets it react to temperature extremes to maintain a temperature balance. There are three main factors that affect this temperature balance--heat production, heat loss, and evaporation.

The difference between the body's core temperature and the environment's temperature governs the heat production rate. Your body can get rid of heat better than it can produce it. Sweating helps to control the heat balance. Maximum sweating will get rid of heat about as fast as maximum exertion produces it.

Shivering causes the body to produce heat. It also causes fatigue that, in turn, leads to a drop in body temperature. Air movement around your body affects heat loss. It has been calculated that a naked man exposed to still air at or about 0 degrees C can maintain a heat balance if he shivers as hard as he can. However, he can't shiver forever.

It has also been calculated that a man at rest wearing the maximum arctic clothing in a cold environment can keep his internal heat balance during temperatures well below freezing. To withstand really cold conditions for any length of time, however, he will have to become active or shiver.

COLD INJURIES

The best way to deal with injuries and sicknesses is to take measures to prevent them from happening in the first place. Treat any injury or sickness that occurs as soon as possible to prevent it from worsening.

The knowledge of signs and symptoms and the use of the buddy system are critical in maintaining health. Following are cold injuries that can occur.

Hypothermia

Hypothermia is the lowering of the body temperature at a rate faster than the body can produce heat. Causes of hypothermia may be general exposure or the sudden wetting of the body by falling into a lake or spraying with fuel or other liquids.

The initial symptom is shivering. This shivering may progress to the point that it is uncontrollable and interferes with an individual's ability to care for himself. This begins when the body's core (rectal) temperature falls to about 35.5 degrees C (96 degrees F).

When the core temperature reaches 35 to 32 degrees C (95 to 90 degrees F), sluggish thinking, irrational reasoning, and a false feeling of warmth may occur. Core temperatures of 32 to 30 degrees C (90 to 86 degrees F) and below result in muscle rigidity, unconsciousness, and barely detectable signs of life. If the victim's core temperature falls below 25 degrees C (77 degrees F), death is almost certain.

To treat hypothermia, re-warm the entire body. If there are means available, re-warm the person by first immersing the trunk area only in warm water of 37.7 to 43.3 degrees C (100 to 110 degrees F).

CAUTION

Re-warming the total body in a warm water bath should be done only in a hospital environment because of the increased risk of cardiac arrest and re-warming shock.

One of the quickest ways to get heat to the inner core is to give warm water enemas. Such an action, however, may not be possible in a survival situation. Another method is to wrap the victim in a warmed sleeping bag with another person who is already warm; both should be naked.

CAUTION

The individual placed in the sleeping bag with victim could also become a hypothermia victim if left in the bag too long.

If the person is conscious, give him hot, sweetened fluids. One of the best sources of calories is honey or dextrose; if unavailable, use sugar, cocoa, or a similar soluble sweetener.

CAUTION

Do not force an unconscious person to drink.

There are two dangers in treating hypothermia—re-warming too rapidly and "after drop." Re-warming too rapidly can cause the victim to have circulatory problems, resulting in heart failure.

After drop is the sharp body core temperature drop that occurs when taking the victim from the warm water. Its probable cause is the return of previously stagnant limb blood to the core (inner torso) area as recirculation occurs.

Concentrating on warming the core area and stimulating peripheral circulation will lessen the effects of after drop. Immersing the torso in a warm bath, if possible, is the best treatment.

Frostbite

This injury is the result of frozen tissues. Light frostbite involves only the skin that takes on a dull whitish pallor. Deep frostbite extends to a depth below the skin. The tissues become solid and immovable. Your feet, hands, and exposed facial areas are particularly vulnerable to frostbite.

The best frostbite prevention, when you are with others, is to use the buddy system. Check your buddy's face often and make sure that he checks yours. If you are alone, periodically cover your nose and lower part of your face with your mittened hand.

The following pointers will aid you in keeping warm and preventing frostbite when it is extremely cold or when you have less than adequate clothing:

Face. Maintain circulation by twitching and wrinkling the skin on your face making faces. Warm with your hands.

Ears. Wiggle and move your ears. Warm with your hands.

Hands. Move your hands inside your gloves. Warm by placing your hands close to your body.

Feet. Move your feet and wiggle your toes inside your boots.

A loss of feeling in your hands and feet is a sign of frostbite. If you have lost feeling for only a short time, the frostbite is probably light.

Otherwise, assume the frostbite is deep. To re-warm a light frostbite, use your hands or mittens to warm your face and ears. Place your hands under your armpits. Place your feet next to your buddy's stomach. A deep frostbite injury, if thawed and refrozen, will cause more damage than a non-medically trained person can handle.

Trench Foot and Immersion Foot

These conditions result from many hours or days of exposure to wet or damp conditions at a temperature just above freezing. The symptoms are a sensation of pins and needles, tingling, numbness, and then pain. The skin will initially appear wet, soggy, white, and shriveled.

As it progresses and damage appears, the skin will take on a red and then a bluish or black discoloration. The feet become cold, swollen, and have a waxy appearance. Walking becomes difficult and the feet feel heavy and numb. The nerves and muscles sustain the main damage, but gangrene can occur. In extreme cases, the flesh dies and it may become necessary to have the foot or leg amputated.

The best prevention is to keep your feet dry. Carry extra socks with you in a waterproof packet. You can dry wet socks against your torso (back or chest). Wash your feet and put on dry socks daily.

Dehydration

When bundled up in many layers of clothing during cold weather, you may be unaware that you are losing body moisture. Your heavy clothing absorbs the moisture that evaporates in the air. You must drink water to replace this loss of fluid.

Your need for water is as great in a cold environment as it is in a warm environment. One way to tell if you are becoming dehydrated is to check the color of your urine on snow. If your urine makes the snow dark yellow, you are becoming dehydrated and need to replace body fluids. If it makes the snow light yellow to no color, your body fluids have a more normal balance.

Cold Diuresis

Exposure to cold increases urine output. It also decreases body fluids that you must replace.

Sunburn

Exposed skin can become sunburned even when the air temperature is below freezing. The sun's rays reflect at all angles from snow, ice, and water, hitting sensitive areas of skin--lips, nostrils, and eyelids. Exposure to the sun results in sunburn more quickly at high altitudes than at low altitudes. Apply sunburn cream or lip salve to your face when in the sun.

Snow Blindness

The reflection of the sun's ultraviolet rays off a snow-covered area causes this condition. The symptoms of snow blindness are a sensation of grit in the eyes, pain in and over the eyes that increases with eyeball movement, red and teary eyes, and a headache that intensifies with continued exposure to light. Prolonged exposure to these rays can result in permanent eye damage. To treat snow blindness, bandage your eyes until the symptoms disappear.

You can prevent snow blindness by wearing sunglasses. If you don't have sunglasses, improvise. Cut slits in a piece of cardboard, thin wood, tree bark, or other available material. Putting soot under your eyes will help reduce shine and glare.

Constipation

It is very important to relieve yourself when needed. Do not delay because of the cold condition. Delaying relieving yourself because of the cold, eating dehydrated foods, drinking too little liquid, and irregular eating habits can cause you to become constipated. Although not disabling, constipation can cause some discomfort. Increase your fluid intake to at least 2 liters above your normal 2 to 3 liters daily intake and, if available, eat fruit and other foods that will loosen the stool.

Insect Bites

Insect bites can become infected through constant scratching. Flies can carry various disease-producing germs. To prevent insect bites, use insect repellent, netting, and wear proper clothing.

SHELTERS

Your environment and the equipment you carry with you will determine the type of shelter you can build. You can build shelters in wooded areas, open country, and barren areas. Wooded areas usually provide the best location, while barren areas have only snow as building material. Wooded areas provide timber for shelter construction, wood for fire, concealment from observation, and protection from the wind.

Note: In extreme cold, do not use metal, such as an aircraft fuselage, for shelter. The metal will conduct away from the shelter what little heat you can generate.

Shelters made from ice or snow usually require tools such as ice axes or saws. You must also expend much time and energy to build such a shelter. Be sure to ventilate an enclosed shelter, especially if you intend to build a fire in it. Always block a shelter's entrance, if possible, to keep the heat in and the wind out.

Use a rucksack or snow block. Construct a shelter no larger than needed. This will reduce the amount of space to heat. A fatal error in cold weather shelter construction is making the shelter so large that it steals body heat rather than saving it. Keep shelter space small.

Never sleep directly on the ground. Lay down some pine boughs, grass, or other insulating material to keep the ground from absorbing your body heat.

Never fall asleep without turning out your stove or lamp. Carbon monoxide poisoning can result from a fire burning in an unventilated shelter. Carbon monoxide is a great danger. It is colorless and odorless. Any time you have an open flame, it may generate carbon monoxide.

Always check your ventilation. Even in a ventilated shelter, incomplete combustion can cause carbon monoxide poisoning. Usually, there are no symptoms. Unconsciousness and death can occur without warning. Sometimes, however, pressure at the temples, burning of the eyes, headache, pounding pulse, drowsiness, or nausea may occur.

The one characteristic, visible sign of carbon monoxide poisoning is a cherry red coloring in the tissues of the lips, mouth, and inside of the eyelids. Get into fresh air at once if you have any of these symptoms.

There are several types of field-expedient shelters you can quickly build or employ. Many use snow for insulation.

Snow Cave Shelter

The snow cave shelter is a most effective shelter because of the insulating qualities of snow. Remember that it takes time and energy to build and that you will get wet while building it. First, you need to find a drift about 3 meters deep into which you can dig.

While building this shelter, keep the roof arched for strength and to allow melted snow to drain down the sides. Build the sleeping platform higher than the entrance. Separate the sleeping platform from the snow cave's walls or dig a small trench between the platform and the wall.

This platform will prevent the melting snow from wetting you and your equipment. This construction is especially important if you have a good source of heat in the snow cave. Ensure the roof is high enough so that you can sit up on the sleeping platform. Block the entrance with a snow block or other material and use the lower entrance area for cooking.

The walls and ceiling should be at least 30 centimeters thick. Install a ventilation shaft. If you do not have a drift large enough to build a snow cave, you can make a variation of it by piling snow into a mound large enough to dig out.

Snow Trench Shelter

The idea behind this shelter is to get you below the snow and wind level and use the snow's insulating qualities. If you are in an area of compacted snow, cut snow blocks and use them as overhead cover. If not, you can use a poncho or other material. Build only one entrance and use a snow block or rucksack as a door.

Snow Block and Parachute Shelter

Use snow blocks for the sides and parachute material for overhead cover. If snowfall is heavy, you will have to clear snow from the top at regular intervals to prevent the collapse of the parachute material.

Snow House or Igloo

In certain areas, the natives frequently use this type of shelter as hunting and fishing shelters. They are efficient shelters but require some practice to make them properly. Also, you must be in an area that is suitable for cutting snow blocks and have the equipment to cut them (snow saw or knife).

Lean-To Shelter

Construct this shelter in the same manner as for other environments; however, pile snow around the sides for insulation.

Fallen Tree Shelter

To build this shelter, find a fallen tree and dig out the snow underneath it. The snow will not be deep under the tree. If you must remove branches from the inside, use them to line the floor.

Tree-Pit Shelter

Dig snow out from under a suitable large tree. It will not be as deep near the base of the tree. Use the cut branches to line the shelter. Use a ground sheet as overhead cover to prevent snow from falling off the tree into the shelter. If built properly, you can have 360-degree visibility.

FIRE

Fire is especially important in cold weather. It not only provides a means to prepare food, but also to get warm and to melt snow or ice for water. It also provides you with a significant psychological boost by making you feel a little more secure in your situation.

Use the techniques described earlier to build and light your fire. If you are in enemy territory, remember that the smoke, smell, and light from your fire may reveal your location. Light reflects from surrounding trees or rocks, making even indirect light a source of danger. Smoke tends to go straight up in cold, calm weather, making it a beacon during the day, but helping to conceal the smell at night. In warmer weather, especially in a wooded area, smoke tends to hug the ground, making it less visible in the day, but making its odor spread.

If you are in enemy territory, cut low tree boughs rather than the entire tree for firewood. Fallen trees are easily seen from the air.

All wood will burn, but some types of wood create more smoke than others. For instance, coniferous trees that contain resin and tar create more and darker smoke than deciduous trees.

There are few materials to use for fuel in the high mountainous regions of the arctic. You may find some grasses and moss, but very little. The lower the elevation, the more fuel available.

You may find some scrub willow and small, stunted spruce trees above the tree line. On sea ice, fuels are seemingly nonexistent. Driftwood or fats may be the only fuels available to a survivor on the barren coastlines in the arctic and sub-arctic regions.

Abundant fuels within the tree line are--

Spruce trees are common in the interior regions. As a conifer, spruce makes a lot of smoke when burned in the spring and summer months. However, it burns almost smoke-free in late fall and winter.

The tamarack tree is also a conifer. It is the only tree of the pine family that loses its needles in the fall. Without its needles, it looks like a dead spruce, but it has many knobby buds and cones on its bare branches. When burning, tamarack wood makes a lot of smoke and is excellent for signaling purposes.

Birch trees are deciduous and the wood burns hot and fast, as if soaked with oil or kerosene. Most birches grow near streams and lakes, but occasionally you will find a few on higher ground and away from water.

Willow and alder grow in arctic regions, normally in marsh areas or near lakes and streams. These woods burn hot and fast without much smoke.

Dried moss, grass, and scrub willow are other materials you can use for fuel.

These are usually plentiful near streams in tundras (open, treeless plains). By bundling or twisting grasses or other scrub vegetation to form a large, solid mass, you will have a slower burning, more productive fuel.

If fuel or oil is available from a wrecked vehicle or downed aircraft, use it for fuel. Leave the fuel in the tank for storage, drawing on the supply only as you need it. Oil congeals in extremely cold temperatures, therefore, drain it from the vehicle or aircraft while still warm if there is no danger of explosion or fire.

If you have no container, let the oil drain onto the snow or ice. Scoop up the fuel as you need it.

CAUTION

Do not expose flesh to petroleum, oil, and lubricants in extremely cold temperatures. The liquid state of these products is deceptive in that it can cause frostbite.

Some plastic products, such as MRE spoons, helmet visors, visor housings, aid foam rubber will ignite quickly from a burning match. They will also burn long enough to help start a fire. For example, a plastic spoon will burn for about 10 minutes.

In cold weather regions, there are some hazards in using fires, whether to keep warm or to cook. For example--

Fires have been known to burn underground, resurfacing nearby. Therefore, do not build a fire too close to a shelter.

In snow shelters, excessive heat will melt the insulating layer of snow that may also be your camouflage.

A fire inside a shelter lacking adequate ventilation can result in carbon monoxide poisoning.

A person trying to get warm or to dry clothes may become careless and burn or scorch his clothing and equipment.

Melting overhead snow may get you wet, bury you and your equipment, and possibly extinguish your fire.

In general, a small fire and some type of stove is the best combination for cooking purposes. A hobo stove is particularly suitable to the arctic. It is easy to make out of a tin can, and it conserves fuel.

A bed of hot coals provides the best cooking heat. Coals from a crisscross fire will settle uniformly. Make this type of fire by crisscrossing the firewood. A simple crane propped on a forked stick will hold a cooking container over a fire.

For heating purposes, a single candle provides enough heat to warm an enclosed shelter. A small fire about the size of a man's hand is ideal for use in enemy territory. It requires very little fuel, yet it generates considerable warmth and is hot enough to warm liquids.

WATER

There are many sources of water in the arctic and sub-arctic. Your location and the season of the year will determine where and how you obtain water.

Water sources in arctic and sub-arctic regions are more sanitary than in other regions due to the climatic and environmental conditions. However, always purify the water before drinking it.

During the summer months, the best natural sources of water are freshwater lakes, streams, ponds, rivers, and springs. Water from ponds or lakes may be slightly stagnant, but still usable. Running water in streams, rivers, and bubbling springs is usually fresh and suitable for drinking.

The brownish surface water found in a tundra during the summer is a good source of water. However, you may have to filter the water before purifying it.

You can melt freshwater ice and snow for water. Completely melt both before putting them in your mouth. Trying to melt ice or snow in your mouth takes away body heat and may cause internal cold injuries.

If on or near pack ice in the sea, you can use old sea ice to melt for water. In time, sea ice loses its salinity. You can identify this ice by its rounded corners and bluish color.

You can use body heat to melt snow. Place the snow in a water bag and place the bag between your layers of clothing. This is a slow process, but you can use it on the move or when you have no fire.

Note: Do not waste fuel to melt ice or snow when drinkable water is available from other sources.

When ice is available, melt it, rather than snow. One cup of ice yields more water than one cup of snow. Ice also takes less time to melt. You can melt ice or snow in a water bag, MRE ration bag, tin can, or improvised container by placing the container near a fire. Begin with a small amount of ice or snow in the container and, as it turns to water, add more ice or snow.

Another way to melt ice or snow is by putting it in a bag made from porous material and suspending the bag near the fire. Place a container under the bag to catch the water.

During cold weather, avoid drinking a lot of liquid before going to bed. Crawling out of a warm sleeping bag at night to relieve yourself means less rest and more exposure to the cold.

Once you have water, keep it next to you to prevent refreezing. Also, do not fill your canteen completely. Allowing the water to slosh around will help keep it from freezing.

FOOD

There are several sources of food in the arctic and subarctic regions. The type of food--fish, animal, fowl, or plant--and the ease in obtaining it depend on the time of the year and your location.

Fish

During the summer months, you can easily get fish and other water life from coastal waters, streams, rivers, and lakes.

The North Atlantic and North Pacific coastal waters are rich in seafood. You can easily find crawfish, snails, clams, oysters, and king crab. In areas where there is a great difference between the high and low tide water levels, you can easily find shellfish at low tide.

Dig in the sand on the tidal flats. Look in tidal pools and on offshore reefs. In areas where there is a small difference between the high- and low-tide water levels, storm waves often wash shellfish onto the beaches.

The eggs of the spiny sea urchin that lives in the waters around the Aleutian Islands and southern Alaska are excellent food. Look for the sea urchins in tidal pools. Break the shell by placing it between two stones. The eggs are bright yellow in color.

Most northern fish and fish eggs are edible. Exceptions are the meat of the arctic shark and the eggs of the sculpins.

The bivalves, such as clams and mussels, are usually more palatable than spiral-shelled seafood, such as snails.

WARNING

The black mussel, a common mollusk of the far north, may be poisonous in any season. Toxins sometimes found in the mussel's tissue are as dangerous as strychnine.

The sea cucumber is another edible sea animal. Inside its body are five long white muscles that taste much like clam meat.

In early summer, smelt spawn in the beach surf. Sometimes you can scoop them up with your hands.

You can often find herring eggs on the seaweed in midsummer. Kelp, the long ribbonlike seaweed, and other smaller seaweed that grow among offshore rocks are also edible.

Sea Ice Animals

You find polar bears in practically all arctic coastal regions, but rarely inland. Avoid them if possible. They are the most dangerous of all bears. They are tireless, clever hunters with good sight and an extraordinary sense of smell. If you must kill one for food, approach it cautiously. Aim for the brain; a bullet elsewhere will rarely kill one. Always cook polar bear meat before eating it.

CAUTION

Do not eat polar bear liver as it contains a toxic concentration of vitamin A.

Earless seal meat is some of the best meat available. You need considerable skill, however, to get close enough to an earless seal to kill it. In spring, seals often bask on the ice beside their breathing holes. They raise their heads about every 30 seconds, however, to look for their enemy, the polar bear.

To approach a seal, do as the Eskimos do--stay downwind from it, cautiously moving closer while it sleeps. If it moves, stop and imitate its movements by lying flat on the ice, raising your head up and down, and wriggling your body slightly.

Approach the seal with your body side-ways to it and your arms close to your body so that you look as much like another seal as possible. The ice at the edge of the breathing hole is usually smooth and at an incline, so the least movement of the seal may cause it to slide into the water.

Therefore, try to get within 22 to 45 meters of the seal and kill it instantly (aim for the brain). Try to reach the seal before it slips into the water. In winter, a dead seal will usually float, but it is difficult to retrieve from the water.

Keep the seal blubber and skin from coming into contact with any scratch or broken skin you may have. You could get "spekk-finger," that is, a reaction that causes the hands to become badly swollen.

Keep in mind that where there are seals, there are usually polar bears, and polar bears have stalked and killed seal hunters.

You can find porcupines in southern sub-arctic regions where there are trees. Porcupines feed on bark; if you find tree limbs stripped bare, you are likely to find porcupines in the area.

Ptarmigans, owls, Canadian jays, grouse, and ravens are the only birds that remain in the arctic during the winter. They are scarce north of the tree line. Ptarmigans and owls are as good for food as any game bird. Ravens are too thin to be worth the effort it takes to catch them.

Ptarmigans, which change color to blend with their surroundings, are hard to spot. Rock ptarmigans travel in pairs and you can easily approach them. Willow ptarmigans live among willow clumps in bottom-lands.

They gather in large flocks and you can easily snare them. During the summer months all arctic birds have a 2- to 3-week molting period during which they cannot fly and are easy to catch. Use one of the techniques described in Chapter 8 to catch them.

Skin and butcher game while it is still warm. If you do not have time to skin the game, at least remove its entrails, musk glands, and genitals before storing. If time allows, cut the meat into usable pieces and freeze each separately so that you can use the pieces as needed.

Leave the fat on all animals except seals. During the winter, game freezes quickly if left in the open. During the summer, you can store it in underground ice holes.

Plants

Although tundras support a variety of plants during the warm months, all are small, however, when compared to plants in warmer climates. For instance, the arctic willow and birch are shrubs rather than trees. The following is a list of some plant foods found in arctic and sub-arctic regions.

ARCTIC FOOD PLANTS

Arctic raspberry and blueberry

Arctic willow

Bearberry

Cranberry

Crowberry

Dandelion

Eskimo potato

Fireweed

Iceland moss

Marsh marigold

Reindeer moss

Rock tripe

Spatterdock

TRAVEL

As a survivor or an evader in an arctic or sub-arctic region, you will face many obstacles. Your location and the time of the year will determine the types of obstacles and the inherent dangers. You should--

Avoid traveling during a blizzard.

Take care when crossing thin ice. Distribute your weight by lying flat and crawling.

Cross streams when the water level is lowest. Normal freezing and thawing action may cause a stream level to vary as much as 2 to 2.5 meters per day. This variance may occur any time during the day, depending on the distance from a glacier, the temperature, and the terrain. Consider this variation in water level when selecting a campsite near a stream.

Consider the clear arctic air. It makes estimating distance difficult. You more frequently underestimate than overestimate distances.

Do not travel in "whiteout" conditions. The lack of contrasting colors makes it impossible to judge the nature of the terrain.

Always cross a snow bridge at right angles to the obstacle it crosses. Find the strongest part of the bridge by poking ahead of you with a pole or ice axe. Distribute your weight by crawling or by wearing snowshoes or skis.

Make camp early so that you have plenty of time to build a shelter.

Consider frozen or unfrozen rivers as avenues of travel. However, some rivers that appear frozen may have soft, open areas that make travel very difficult or may not allow walking, skiing, or sledding.

Use snowshoes if you are traveling over snow-covered terrain. Snow 30 or more centimeters deep makes traveling difficult. If you do not have snowshoes, make a pair using willow, strips of cloth, leather, or other suitable material.

It is almost impossible to travel in deep snow without snowshoes or skis. Traveling by foot leaves a well-marked trail for any pursuers to follow. If you must travel in deep snow, avoid snow-covered streams.

The snow, which acts as an insulator, may have prevented ice from forming over the water. In hilly terrain, avoid areas where avalanches appear possible.

Travel in the early morning in areas where there is danger of avalanches. On ridges, snow gathers on the lee side in overhanging piles called cornices. These often extend far out from the ridge and may break loose if stepped on.

WEATHER SIGNS

There are several good indicators of climatic changes.

Wind

You can determine wind direction by dropping a few leaves or grass or by watching the treetops. Once you determine the wind direction, you can predict the type of weather that is imminent. Rapidly shifting winds indicate an unsettled atmosphere and a likely change in the weather.

Clouds

Clouds come in a variety of shapes and patterns. A general knowledge of clouds and the atmospheric conditions they indicate can help you predict the weather.

Smoke

Smoke rising in a thin vertical column indicates fair weather. Low rising or "flattened out" smoke indicates stormy weather.

Birds and Insects

Birds and insects fly lower to the ground than normal in heavy, moisture-laden air. Such flight indicates that rain is likely. Most insect activity increases before a storm, but bee activity increases before fair weather.

Low-Pressure Front

Slow-moving or imperceptible winds and heavy, humid air often indicate a low-pressure front. Such a front promises bad weather that will probably linger for several days. You can "smell" and "hear" this front.

The sluggish, humid air makes wilderness odors more pronounced than during high-pressure conditions. In addition, sounds are sharper and carry farther in low-pressure than high-pressure conditions.

Chapter 16 Field-Expedient Direction Finding and Survival

In a survival situation, you will be extremely fortunate if you happen to have a map and compass. If you do have these two pieces of equipment, you will most likely be able to move toward help. If you are not proficient in using a map and compass, you must take the steps to gain this skill.

There are several methods by which you can determine direction by using the sun and the stars. These methods, however, will give you only a general direction. You can come up with a more nearly true direction if you know the terrain of the territory or country.

You must learn all you can about the terrain of the country or territory to which you or your unit may be sent, especially any prominent features or landmarks. This knowledge of the terrain together with using the methods explained below will let you come up with fairly true directions to help you navigate.

USING THE SUN AND SHADOWS

The earth's relationship to the sun can help you to determine direction on earth. The sun always rises in the east and sets in the west, but not exactly due east or due west. There is also some seasonal variation.

In the northern hemisphere, the sun will be due south when at its highest point in the sky, or when an object casts no appreciable shadow. In the southern hemisphere, this same noonday sun will mark due north. In the northern hemisphere, shadows will move clockwise.

Shadows will move counterclockwise in the southern hemisphere. With practice, you can use shadows to determine both direction and time of day. The shadow methods used for direction finding are the shadow-tip and watch methods.

Shadow-Tip Methods

In the first shadow-tip method, find a straight stick 1 meter long, and a level spot free of brush on which the stick will cast a definite shadow. This method is simple and accurate and consists of four steps:

Step 1. Place the stick or branch into the ground at a level spot where it will cast a distinctive shadow. Mark the shadow's tip with a stone, twig, or other means. This first shadow mark is always west-- everywhere on earth.

Step 2. Wait 10 to 15 minutes until the shadow tip moves a few centimeters. Mark the shadow tip's new position in the same way as the first.

Step 3. Draw a straight line through the two marks to obtain an approximate east-west line.

Step 4. Stand with the first mark (west) to your left and the second mark to your right--you are now facing north. This fact is true everywhere on earth.

An alternate method is more accurate but requires more time. Set up your shadow stick and mark the first shadow in the morning.

Use a piece of string to draw a clean arc through this mark and around the stick. At midday, the shadow will shrink and disappear. In the afternoon, it will lengthen again and at the point where it touches the arc, make a second mark. Draw a line through the two marks to get an accurate east-west line.

The Watch Method

You can also determine direction using a common or analog watch--one that has hands. The direction will be accurate if you are using true local time, without any changes for daylight savings time.

Remember, the further you are from the equator, the more accurate this method will be. If you only have a digital watch, you can overcome this obstacle. Quickly draw a watch on a circle of paper with the correct time on it and use it to determine your direction at that time.

In the northern hemisphere, hold the watch horizontal and point the hour hand at the sun. Bisect the angle between the hour hand and the 12 o'clock mark to get the north-south line. If there is any doubt as to which end of the line is north, remember that the sun rises in the east, sets in the west, and is due south at noon. The sun is in the east before noon and in the west after noon.

Note: If your watch is set on daylight savings time, use the midway point between the hour hand and 1 o'clock to determine the north-south line.

In the southern hemisphere, point the watch's 12 o'clock mark toward the sun and a midpoint halfway between 12 and the hour hand will give you the north-south line.

USING THE MOON

Because the moon has no light of its own, we can only see it when it reflects the sun's light. As it orbits the earth on its 28-day circuit, the shape of the reflected light varies according to its position. We say there is a new moon or no moon when it is on the opposite side of the earth from the sun.

Then, as it moves away from the earth's shadow, it begins to reflect light from its right side and waxes to become a full moon before waning, or losing shape, to appear as a sliver on the left side. You can use this information to identify direction.

If the moon rises before the sun has set, the illuminated side will be the west. If the moon rises after midnight, the illuminated side will be the east.

This obvious discovery provides us with a rough east-west reference during the night.

USING THE STARS

Your location in the Northern or Southern Hemisphere determines which constellation you use to determine your north or south direction.

The Northern Sky

The main constellations to learn are the Ursa Major, also known as the Big Dipper or the Plow, and Cassiopeia. Neither of these constellations ever sets. They are always visible on a clear night. Use them to locate Polaris, also known as the polestar or the North Star.

The North Star forms part of the Little Dipper handle and can be confused with the Big Dipper. Prevent confusion by using both the Big Dipper and Cassiopeia together. The Big Dipper and Cassiopeia are always directly opposite each. other and rotate counterclockwise around Polaris, with Polaris in the center.

The Big Dipper is a seven star constellation in the shape of a dipper. The two stars forming the outer lip of this dipper are the "pointer stars" because they point to the North Star. Mentally draw a line from the outer bottom star to the outer top star of the Big Dipper's bucket. Extend this line about five times the distance between the pointer stars. You will find the North Star along this line.

Cassiopeia has five stars that form a shape like a "W" on its side. The North Star is straight out from Cassiopeia's center star.

After locating the North Star, locate the North Pole or true north by drawing an imaginary line directly to the earth.

The Southern Sky

Because there is no star bright enough to be easily recognized near the south celestial pole, a constellation known as the Southern Cross is used as a signpost to the South. The Southern Cross or Crux has five stars. Its four brightest stars form a cross that tilts to one side. The two stars that make up the cross's long axis are the pointer stars.

To determine south, imagine a distance five times the distance between these stars and the point where this imaginary line ends is in the general direction of south. Look down to the horizon from this imaginary point and select a landmark to steer by. In a static survival situation, you can fix this location in daylight if you drive stakes in the ground at night to point the way.

MAKING IMPROVISED COMPASSES

You can construct improvised compasses using a piece of ferrous metal that can be needle shaped or a flat double-edged razor blade and a piece of nonmetallic string or long hair from which to suspend it. You can magnetize or polarize the metal by slowly stroking it in one direction on a piece of silk or carefully through your hair using deliberate strokes.

You can also polarize metal by stroking it repeatedly at one end with a magnet. Always rub in one direction only. If you have a battery and some electric wire, you can polarize the metal electrically. The wire should be insulated. If not insulated, wrap the metal object in a single, thin strip of paper to prevent contact.

The battery must be a minimum of 2 volts. Form a coil with the electric wire and touch its ends to the battery's terminals. Repeatedly insert one end of the metal object in and out of the coil. The needle will become an electromagnet. When suspended from a piece of nonmetallic string, or floated on a small piece of wood in water, it will align itself with a north-south line.

You can construct a more elaborate improvised compass using a sewing needle or thin metallic object, a nonmetallic container (for example, a plastic dip container), its lid with the center cut out and waterproofed, and the silver tip from a pen. To construct this compass, take an ordinary sewing needle and break in half.

One half will form your direction pointer and the other will act as the pivot point. Push the portion used as the pivot point through the bottom center of your container; this portion should be flush on the bottom and not interfere with the lid. Attach the center of the other portion (the pointer) of the needle on the pen's silver tip using glue, tree sap, or melted plastic. Magnetize one end of the pointer and rest it on the pivot point.

OTHER MEANS OF DETERMINING DIRECTION

The old saying about using moss on a tree to indicate north is not accurate because moss grows completely around some trees. Actually, growth is more lush on the side of the tree facing the south in the Northern Hemisphere and vice versa in the Southern Hemisphere.

If there are several felled trees around for comparison, look at the stumps. Growth is more vigorous on the side toward the equator and the tree growth rings will be more widely spaced. On the other hand, the tree growth rings will be closer together on the side toward the poles.

Wind direction may be helpful in some instances where there are prevailing directions and you know what they are.

Recognizing the differences between vegetation and moisture patterns on north- and south-facing slopes can aid in determining direction. In the northern hemisphere, north-facing slopes receive less sun than south-facing slopes and are therefore cooler and damper.

In the summer, north-facing slopes retain patches of snow. In the winter, the trees and open areas on south-facing slopes are the first to lose their snow, and ground snowpack is shallower.

SURVIVAL MOVEMENT IN HOSTILE AREAS

The "rescue at any cost" philosophy of previous conflicts is not likely to be possible in future conflicts. Our potential adversaries have made great progress in air defense measures and radio direction finding (RDF) techniques.

We must assume that U.S. military forces trapped behind enemy lines in future conflicts may not experience quick recovery by friendly elements. Soldiers may have to move for extended times and distances to places less threatening to the recovery forces. The soldier will not likely know the type of recovery to expect.

Each situation and the available resources determine the type of recovery possible. Since no one can be absolutely sure until the recovery effort begins, soldiers facing a potential cutoff from friendly forces should be familiar with all the possible types of recovery, their related problems, and their responsibilities to the recovery effort. Preparation and training can improve the chances of success.

PHASES OF PLANNING

Preparation is a requirement for all missions. When planning, you must consider how to avoid capture and return to your unit. Contingency plans must be prepared in conjunction with unit standing operating procedures (SOPs). Courses of action you or your unit will take must also be considered.

Contingency Plan of Action (CPA)

Intelligence sections can help prepare personnel for contingency actions through information supplied in area studies, SERE (survival, evasion, resistance, and escape) contingency guides, threat briefings, current intelligence reports, and current contact and authentication procedures.

Pre-mission preparation includes the completion of a CPA. The study and research needed to develop the CPA will make you aware of the current situation in your mission area. Your CPA will let recovery forces know your probable actions should you have to move to avoid capture.

Start preparing even before pre-mission planning. Many parts of the CPA are SOP for your unit. Include the CPA in your training. Planning starts in your daily training.

The CPA is your entire plan for your return to friendly control. It consists of five paragraphs written in the operation order format. You can take most of paragraph 1, Situation, with you on the mission. Appendix H contains the CPA format. It also indicates what portion of the CPA you can take with you.

A comprehensive CPA is a valuable asset to the soldier trapped behind enemy lines who must try to avoid capture. To complete paragraph 1, know your unit's assigned area or concentrate on potential mission areas of the world. Many open or closed sources contain the information you need to complete a CPA.

Open sources may include newspapers, magazines, country or area handbooks, area studies, television, radio, persons familiar with the area, and libraries. Closed sources may include area studies, area assessments, SERE contingency guides, various classified field manuals, and intelligence reports.

Prepare your CPA in three phases. During your normal training, prepare paragraph 1, Situation. Prepare paragraphs 2, 3, 4, and 5 during your pre-mission planning. After deployment into an area, continually update your CPA based on mission changes and intelligence updates.

The CPA is a guide. You may add or delete certain portions based on the mission. The CPA may be a recovery force's only means of determining your location and intentions after you start to move. It is an essential tool for your survival and return to friendly control.

Standing Operating Procedures

Unit SOPs are valuable tools your unit has that will help your planning. When faced with a dangerous situation requiring immediate action, it is not the time to discuss options; it is the time to act. Many of the techniques used during small unit movement can be carried over to fit requirements for moving and returning to friendly control. Items from the SOP should include, but are not limited to--

Movement team size (three to four persons per team).

Team communications (technical and nontechnical).

Essential equipment.

Actions at danger areas.

Signaling techniques.

Immediate action drills.

Linkup procedures.

Helicopter recovery devices and procedures.

Security procedures during movement and at hide sites.

Rally points.

Rehearsals work effectively for reinforcing these SOP skills and also provide opportunities for evaluation and improvement.

Notification to Move and Avoid Capture

An isolated unit has several general courses of action it can take to avoid the capture of the group or individuals. These courses of action are not courses the commander can choose instead of his original mission. He cannot arbitrarily abandon the assigned mission.

Rather, he may adopt these courses of action after completing his mission when his unit cannot complete its assigned mission (because of combat power losses) or when he receives orders to extract his unit from its current position. If such actions are not possible, the commander may decide to have the unit try to move to avoid capture and return to friendly control.

In either case, as long as there is communication with higher headquarters, that headquarters will make the decision.

If the unit commander loses contact with higher headquarters, he must make the decision to move or wait. He bases his decision on many factors, including the mission, rations and ammunition on hand, casualties, the chance of relief by friendly forces, and the tactical situation.

The commander of an isolated unit faces other questions. What course of action will inflict maximum damage on the enemy? What course of action will assist in completing the higher headquarters' overall mission?

Movement teams conduct the execution portion of the plan when notified by higher headquarters or, if there is no contact with higher headquarters, when the highest ranking survivor decides that the situation requires the unit to try to escape capture or destruction.

Movement team leaders receive their notification through pre-briefed signals. Once the signal to try to avoid capture is given, it must be passed rapidly to all personnel. Notify higher headquarters, if possible.

If unable to communicate with higher headquarters, leaders must recognize that organized resistance has ended, and that organizational control has ceased. Command and control is now at the movement team or individual level and is returned to higher organizational control only after reaching friendly lines.

EXECUTION

Upon notification to avoid capture, all movement team members will try to link up at the initial movement point. This point is where team members rally and actually begin their movement. Tentatively select the initial movement point during your planning phase through a map recon.

Once on the ground, the team verifies this location or selects a better one. All team members must know its location. The initial movement point should be easy to locate and occupy for a minimum amount of time.

Once the team has rallied at the initial movement point, it must--

Give first aid.

Inventory its equipment (decide what to abandon, destroy, or take along).

Apply camouflage.

Make sure everyone knows the tentative hide locations.

Ensure everyone knows the primary and alternate routes and rally points en route to the hide locations.

Always maintain security.

Split the team into smaller elements. The ideal element should have two to three members; however, it could include more depending on team equipment and experience.

The movement portion of returning to friendly control is the most dangerous as you are now most vulnerable. It is usually better to move at night because of the concealment darkness offers. Exceptions to such movement would be when moving through hazardous terrain or dense vegetation (for example, jungle or mountainous terrain). When moving, avoid the following even if it takes more time and energy to bypass:

Obstacles and barriers.

Roads and trails.

Inhabited areas.

Waterways and bridges.

Natural lines of drift.

Man-made structures.

All civilian and military personnel.

Movement in enemy-held territory is a very slow and deliberate process. The slower you move and the more careful you are, the better. Your best security will be using your senses. Use your eyes and ears to detect people before they detect you.

Make frequent listening halts. In daylight, observe a section of your route before you move along it. The distance you travel before you hide will depend on the enemy situation, your health, the terrain, the availability of cover and concealment for hiding, and the amount of darkness left.

Once you have moved into the area in which you want to hide (hide area), select a hide site. Keep the following formula in mind when selecting a hide site: BLISS.

B - Blends in with the surroundings.

L - Low in silhouette.

I - Irregular in shape.

S - Small in size.

S - Secluded.

Avoid the use of existing buildings or shelters. Usually, your best option will be to crawl into the thickest vegetation you can find. Construct any type of shelter within the hide area only in cold weather and desert environments. If you build a shelter, follow the BLISS formula.

Hide Site Activities

After you have located your hide site, do not move straight into it. Use a button hook or other deceptive technique to move to a position outside of the hide site. Conduct a listening halt before moving individually into the hide site. Be careful not to disturb or cut any vegetation.

Once you have occupied the hide site, limit your activities to maintaining security, resting, camouflaging, and planning your next moves.

Maintain your security through visual scanning and listening. Upon detection of the enemy, the security personnel alert all personnel, even if the team's plan is to stay hidden and not move upon sighting the enemy. Take this action so that everyone is aware of the danger and ready to react.

If any team member leaves the team, give him a five-point contingency plan. Take such steps especially when a recon team or a work party is out of the hole-up or hide site.

It is extremely important to stay healthy and alert when trying to avoid capture. Take every opportunity to rest, but do not sacrifice security. Rotate security so that all members of your movement team can rest. Treat all injuries, no matter how minor. Loss of your health will mean loss of your ability to continue to avoid capture.

Camouflage is an important aspect of both moving and securing a hide site. Always use a buddy system to ensure that camouflage is complete. Ensure that team members blend with the hide site. Use natural or man-made materials. If you add any additional camouflage material to the hide site, do not cut vegetation in the immediate area.

Plan your next actions while at the hide site. Start your planning process immediately upon occupying the hide site. Inform all team members of their current location and designate an alternate hide site location. Once this is done, start planning for the team's next movement.

Planning the team's movement begins with a map recon. Choose the next hide area first. Then choose a primary and an alternate route to the hide area. In choosing the routes, do not use straight lines.

Use one or two radical changes in direction. Pick the routes that offer the best cover and concealment, the fewest obstacles, and the least likelihood of contact with humans. There should be locations along the route where the team can get water. To aid team navigation, use azimuths, distances, checkpoints or steering marks, and corridors.

Plan rally points and rendezvous points at intervals along the route.

Other planning considerations may fall under what the team already has in the team SOP. Examples are immediate action drills, actions on sighting the enemy, and hand-and-arm signals.

Once planning is complete, ensure that everyone knows and memorizes the entire plan. The team members should know the distances and azimuths for the entire route to the next hide area. They should study the map and know the various terrain they will be moving across so that they can move without using the map.

Do not occupy a hide site for more than 24 hours. In most situations, hide during the day and move at night. Limit your actions in the hide site to those discussed above.

Once in the hide site, restrict all movement to less than 45 centimeters above the ground. Do not build fires or prepare food. Smoke and food odors will reveal your location. Before leaving the hide site, sterilize it to prevent tracking.

Hole-Up Areas

After moving and hiding for several days, usually three or four, you or the movement team will have to move into a hole-up area. This is an area where you can rest, recuperate, and get and prepare food.

Choose an area near a water source. You then have a place to get water, to place fishing devices, and to trap game. Since waterways are a line of communication, locate your hide site well away from the water.

The hole-up area should offer plenty of cover and concealment for movement in and around the area. Always maintain security while in the hole-up area. Always man the hole-up area.

Actions in the hole-up area are the same as in hide site, except that you can move away from the hole-up area to get and prepare food. Actions in the hole-up area include--

Selecting and occupying the next hide site (remember you are still in a dangerous situation; this is not a friendly area).

Reconnoitering the area for resources and potential concealed movement routes to the alternate hide site.

Gathering food (nuts, berries, vegetables). When moving around the area for food, maintain security and avoid leaving tracks or other signs. When setting traps and snares, keep them well-camouflaged and in areas where people are not likely to discover them. Remember, the local population sometimes heavily travels trails near water sources.

Getting water from sources within the hide area. Be careful not to leave tracks of signs along the banks of water sources when getting water. Moving on hard rocks or logs along the banks to get water will reduce the signs you leave.

Setting clandestine fishing devices, such as stakeouts, below the surface of the water to avoid detection.

Locating a fire site well away from the hide site. Use this site to prepare food or boil water. Camouflage and sterilize the fire site after each use. Be careful that smoke and light from the fire does not compromise the hole-up area.

While in the hole-up area, security is still your primary concern. Designate team members to perform specific tasks. To limit movement around the area, you may have a two-man team perform more than one task. For example, the team getting water could also set the fishing devices. Do not occupy the hole-up area longer than 72 hours.

RETURN TO FRIENDLY CONTROL

Establishing contact with friendly lines or patrols is the most crucial part of movement and return to friendly control. All your patience, planning, and hardships will be in vain if you do not exercise caution when contacting friendly frontline forces.

Friendly patrols have killed personnel operating behind enemy lines because they did not make contact properly. Most of the casualties could have been avoided if caution had been exercised and a few simple procedures followed. The normal tendency is to throw caution to the winds when in sight of friendly forces. You must overcome this tendency and understand that linkup is a very sensitive situation.

Border Crossings

If you have made your way to a friendly or neutral country, use the following procedures to cross the border and link up with friendly forces on the other side:

Occupy a hide site on the near side of the border and send a team out to reconnoiter the potential crossing site.

Surveil the crossing site for at least 24 hours, depending on the enemy situation.

Make a sketch of the site, taking note of terrain, obstacles, guard routines and rotations, and any sensor devices or trip wires. Once the recon is complete, the team moves to the hide site, briefs the rest of the team, and plans to cross the border at night.

After crossing the border, set up a hide site on the far side of the border and try to locate friendly positions. Do not reveal your presence.

Depending on the size of your movement team, have two men surveil the potential linkup site with friendly forces until satisfied that the personnel are indeed friendly.

Make contact with the friendly forces during daylight. Personnel chosen to make contact should be unarmed, have no equipment, and have positive identification readily available. The person who actually makes the linkup should be someone who looks least like the enemy.

During the actual contact, have only one person make the contact. The other person provides the security and observes the linkup area from a safe distance. The observer should be far enough away so that he can warn the rest of the movement team if something goes wrong.

Wait until the party he is contacting looks in his direction so that he does not surprise the contact. He stands up from behind cover, with hands overhead and states that he is an American. After this, he follows any instructions given him. He avoids answering any tactical questions and does not give any indication that there are other team members.

Reveal that there are other personnel with him only after verifying his identity and satisfying himself he has made contact with friendly forces.

Language problems or difficulties confirming identities may arise. The movement team should maintain security, be patient, and have a contingency plan.

Note: If you are moving to a neutral country, you are surrendering to that power and become a detained person.

Linkup at the FEBA/FLOT

If caught between friendly and enemy forces and there is heavy fighting in the area, you may choose to hide and let the friendly lines pass over you. If overrun by friendly forces, you may try to link up from their rear during daylight hours. If overrun by enemy forces, you may move further to the enemy rear, try to move to the forward edge of the battle area (FEBA)/forward line of own troops (FLOT) during a lull in the fighting, or move to another area along the front.

The actual linkup will be done as for linkup during a border crossing. The only difference is that you must be more careful on the initial contact.

Frontline personnel are more likely to shoot first and ask questions later, especially in areas of heavy fighting. You should be near or behind cover before trying to make contact.

Linkup With Friendly Patrols

If friendly lines are a circular perimeter or an isolated camp, for example, any direction you approach from will be considered enemy territory. You do not have the option of moving behind the lines and trying to link up. This move makes the linkup extremely dangerous.

One option you have is to place the perimeter under observation and wait for a friendly patrol to move out in your direction, providing a chance for a linkup. You may also occupy a position outside of the perimeter and call out to get the attention of the friendly forces. Ideally, display anything that is white while making contact.

If nothing else is available, use any article of clothing. The idea is to draw attention while staying behind cover. Once you have drawn attention to your signal and called out, follow instructions given to you.

Be constantly on the alert for friendly patrols because these provide a means for return to friendly control. Find a concealed position that allows you maximum visual coverage of the area.

Try to memorize every terrain feature so that, if necessary, you can infiltrate to friendly positions under the cover of darkness. Remember, trying to infiltrate in darkness is extremely dangerous.

Because of the missions of combat and recon patrols and where they are operating, making contact can be dangerous. If you decide not to make contact, you can observe their route and approach friendly lines at about the same location. Such observation will enable you to avoid mines and booby traps.

Once you have spotted a patrol, remain in position and, if possible, allow the patrol to move toward you. When the patrol is 25 to 50 meters from your position, signal them and call out a greeting that is clearly and unmistakably of American origin.

If you have nothing white, an article of clothing will suffice to draw attention. If the distance is greater than 50 meters, a recon patrol may avoid contact and bypass your position. If the distance is less than 25 meters, a patrol member may react instantly by firing a fatal shot.

It is crucial, at the time of contact, that there is enough light for the patrol to identify you as an American.

Whatever linkup technique you decide to use, use extreme caution. From the perspective of the friendly patrol or friendly personnel occupying a perimeter, you are hostile until they make positive identification.

CAMOUFLAGE

In a survival situation, especially in a hostile environment, you may find it necessary to camouflage yourself, your equipment, and your movement. It may mean the difference between survival and capture by the enemy. Camouflage and movement techniques, such as stalking, will also help you get animals or game for food using primitive weapons and skills.

PERSONAL CAMOUFLAGE

When camouflaging yourself, consider that certain shapes are particular to humans. The enemy will look for these shapes. The shape of a hat, helmet, or black boots can give you away. Even animals know and run from the shape of a human silhouette.

Break up your outline by placing small amounts of vegetation from the surrounding area in your uniform, equipment, and headgear. Try to reduce any shine from skin or equipment. Blend in with the surrounding colors and simulate the texture of your surroundings.

Shape and Outline

Change the outline of weapons and equipment by tying vegetation or strips of cloth onto them. Make sure the added camouflage does not hinder the equipment's operation. When hiding, cover yourself and your equipment with leaves, grass, or other local debris. Conceal any signaling devices you have prepared, but keep them ready for use.

Color and Texture

Each area of the world and each climatic condition (arctic/winter, temperate/jungle, or swamp/desert) has color patterns and textures that are natural for that area. While color is self-explanatory, texture defines the surface characteristics of something when looking at it.

For example, surface textures may be smooth, rough, rocky, leafy, or many other possible combinations. Use color and texture together to camouflage yourself effectively. It makes little sense to cover yourself with dead, brown vegetation in the middle of a large grassy field. Similarly, it would be useless to camouflage yourself with green grass in the middle of a desert or rocky area.

To hide and camouflage movement in any specific area of the world, you must take on the color and texture of the immediate surroundings. Use natural or man-made materials to camouflage yourself. Camouflage paint, charcoal from burned paper or wood, mud, grass, leaves, strips of cloth or burlap, pine boughs, and camouflaged uniforms are a few examples.

Cover all areas of exposed skin, including face, hands, neck, and ears. Use camouflage paint, charcoal, or mud to camouflage yourself. Cover with a darker color areas that stick out more and catch more light (forehead, nose, cheekbones, chin, and ears).

Cover other areas, particularly recessed or shaded areas (around the eyes and under the chin), with lighter colors. Be sure to use an irregular pattern.

Attach vegetation from the area or strips of cloth of the proper color to clothing and equipment. If you use vegetation, replace it as it wilts.

As you move through an area, be alert to the color changes and modify your camouflage colors as necessary.

Shine

As skin gets oily, it becomes shiny. Equipment with worn off paint is also shiny. Even painted objects, if smooth, may shine. Glass objects such as mirrors, glasses, binoculars, and telescopes shine.

You must cover these glass objects when not in use. Anything that shines automatically attracts attention and will give away your location.

Whenever possible, wash oily skin and reapply camouflage. Skin oil will wash off camouflage, so reapply it frequently. If you must wear glasses, camouflage them by applying a thin layer of dust to the outside of the lenses. This layer of dust will reduce the reflection of light.

Cover shiny spots on equipment by painting, covering with mud, or wrapping with cloth or tape. Pay particular attention to covering boot eyelets, buckles on equipment, watches and jewelry, zippers, and uniform insignia. Carry a signal mirror in its designed pouch or in a pocket with the mirror portion facing your body.

Shadow

When hiding or traveling, stay in the deepest part of the shadows. The outer edges of the shadows are lighter and the deeper parts are darker. Remember, if you are in an area where there is plenty of vegetation, keep as much vegetation between you and a potential enemy as possible.

This action will make it very hard for the enemy to see you as the vegetation will partially mask you from his view. Forcing an enemy to look through many layers of masking vegetation will fatigue his eyes very quickly.

When traveling, especially in built-up areas at night, be aware of where you cast your shadow. It may extend out around the comer of a building and give away your position.

Also, if you are in a dark shadow and there is a light source to one side, an enemy on the other side can see your silhouette against the light.

Movement

Movement, especially fast movement, attracts attention. If at all possible, avoid movement in the presence of an enemy. If capture appears imminent in your present location and you must move, move away slowly, making as little noise as possible.

By moving slowly in a survival situation, you decrease the chance of detection and conserve energy that you may need for long-term survival or long-distance evasion.

When moving past obstacles, avoid going over them. If you must climb over an obstacle, keep your body level with its top to avoid silhouetting yourself.

Do not silhouette yourself against the skyline when crossing hills or ridges. When you are moving, you will have difficulty detecting the movement of others. Stop frequently, listen, and look around slowly to detect signs of hostile movement.

Noise

Noise attracts attention, especially if there is a sequence of loud noises such as several snapping twigs. If possible, avoid making any noise at all. Slow down your pace as much as necessary to avoid making noise when moving around or away from possible threats.

Use background noises to cover the noise of your movement. Sounds of aircraft, trucks, generators, strong winds, and people talking will cover some or all of the sounds produced by your movement. Rain will mask a lot of movement noise, but it also reduces your ability to detect potential enemy noise.

Scent

Whether hunting animals or avoiding the enemy, it is always wise to camouflage the scent associated with humans. Start by washing yourself and your clothes without using soap. This washing method removes soap and body odors. Avoiding strong smelling foods, such as garlic, helps reduce body odors. Do not use tobacco products, candy, gum, or cosmetics.

You can use aromatic herbs or plants to wash yourself and your clothing, to rub on your body and clothing, or to chew on to camouflage your breath.

Pine needles, mint, or any similar aromatic plant will help camouflage your scent from both animals and humans. Standing in smoke from a fire can help mask your scent from animals. While animals are afraid of fresh smoke from a fire, older smoke scents are normal smells after forest fires and do not scare them.

While traveling, use your sense of smell to help you find or avoid humans. Pay attention to smells associated with humans, such as fire, cigarettes, gasoline, oil, soap, and food.

Such smells may alert you to their presence long before you can see or hear them, depending on wind speed and direction. Note the wind's direction and, when possible, approach from or skirt around on the downwind side when nearing humans or animals.

METHODS OF STALKING

Sometimes you need to move, undetected, to or from a location. You need more than just camouflage to make these moves successfully. The ability to stalk or move without making any sudden quick movement or loud noise is essential to avoiding detection.

You must practice stalking if it is to be effective. Use the following techniques when practicing.

Upright Stalking

Take steps about half your normal stride when stalking in the upright position. Such strides help you to maintain your balance. You should be able to stop at any point in that movement and hold that position as long as necessary. Curl the toes up out of the way when stepping down so the outside edge of the ball of the foot touches the ground.

Feel for sticks and twigs that may snap when you place your weight on them. If you start to step on one, lift your foot and move it. After making contact with the outside edge of the ball of your foot, roll to the inside ball of your foot, place your heel down, followed by your toes.

Then gradually shift your weight forward to the front foot. Lift the back foot to about knee height and start the process over again.

Keep your hands and arms close to your body and avoid waving them about or hitting vegetation. When moving in a crouch, you gain extra support by placing your hands on your knees. One step usually takes 1 minute to complete, but the time it takes will depend on the situation.

Crawling

Crawl on your hands and knees when the vegetation is too low to allow you to walk upright without being seen. Move one limb at a time and be sure to set it down softly, feeling for anything that may snap and make noise. Be careful that your toes and heels do not catch on vegetation.

Prone Staking

To stalk in the prone position, you do a low, modified push-up on your hands and toes, moving yourself forward slightly, and then lowering yourself again slowly. Avoid dragging and scraping along the ground as this makes excessive noise and leaves large trails for trackers to follow.

Animal Stalking

Before stalking an animal, select the best route. If the animal is moving, you will need an intercepting route. Pick a route that puts objects between you and the animal to conceal your movement from it.

By positioning yourself in this way, you will be able to move faster, until you pass that object. Some objects, such as large rocks and trees, may totally conceal you, and others, such as small bushes and grass, may only partially conceal you. Pick the route that offers the best concealment and requires the least amount of effort.

Keep your eyes on the animal and stop when it looks your way or turns its ears your way, especially if it suspects your presence. As you get close, squint your eyes slightly to conceal both the light-dark contrast of the whites of the eyes and any shine from your eyes. Keep your mouth closed so that the animal does not see the whiteness or shine of your teeth.

CONTACT WITH PEOPLE

Some of the best and most frequently given advice, when dealing with local peoples, is for the survivor to accept, respect, and adapt to their ways. Thus, "when in Rome, do as the Romans do." This is excellent advice, but there are several considerations involved in putting this advice into practice.

CONTACT WITH LOCAL PEOPLE

You must give serious consideration to dealing with the local people. Do they have a primitive culture? Are they farmers, fishermen, friendly people, or enemy? As a survivor, "cross-cultural communication" can vary radically from area to area and from people to people.

It may mean interaction with people of an extremely primitive culture or contact with people who have a relatively modem culture. A culture is identified by standards of behavior that its members consider proper and acceptable but may or may not conform to your idea of what is proper.

No matter who these people are, you can expect they will have laws, social and economic values, and political and religious beliefs that may be radically different from yours. Before deploying into your area of operations, study these different cultural aspects. Prior study and preparation will help you make or avoid contact if you have to deal with the local population.

People will be friendly, unfriendly, or they will choose to ignore you. Their attitude may be unknown. If the people are known to be friendly, try to keep them friendly through your courtesy and respect for their religion, politics, social customs, habits, and all other aspects of their culture.

If the people are known to be enemies or are unknowns, make every effort to avoid any contact and leave no sign of your presence. A basic knowledge of the daily habits of the local people will be essential in this attempt. If after careful observation you determine that an unknown people are friendly, you may contact them if you absolutely need their help.

Usually, you have little to fear and much to gain from cautious and respectful contact with local people of friendly or neutral countries. If you become familiar with the local customs, display common decency, and most important, show respect for their customs, you should be able to avoid trouble and possibly gain needed help.

To make contact, wait until only one person is near and, if possible, let that person make the initial approach. Most people will be willing to help a survivor who appears to be in need. However, local political attitudes, instruction, or propaganda efforts may change the attitudes of otherwise friendly people.

Conversely, in unfriendly countries, many people, especially in remote areas, may feel animosity toward their politicians and may be more friendly toward a survivor.

The key to successful contact with local peoples is to be friendly, courteous, and patient. Displaying fear, showing weapons, and making sudden or threatening movements can cause a local person to fear you. Such actions can prompt a hostile response.

When attempting a contact, smile as often as you can. Many local peoples are shy and seem unapproachable, or they may ignore you. Approach them slowly and do not rush your contact.

THE SURVIVOR'S BEHAVIOR

Use salt, tobacco, silver money, and similar items discreetly when trading with local people. Paper money is well-known worldwide. Do not overpay; it may lead to embarrassment and even danger. Always treat people with respect. Do not bully them or laugh at them.

Using sign language or acting out needs or questions can be very effective. Many people are used to such language and communicate using nonverbal sign language. Try to learn a few words and phrases of the local language in and around your potential area of operations.

Trying to speak someone's language is one of the best ways to show respect for his culture. Since English is widely used, some of the local people may understand a few words of English.

Some areas may be taboo. They range from religious or sacred places to diseased or danger areas. In some areas, certain animals must not be killed. Learn the rules and follow them.

Watch and learn as much as possible. Such actions will help to strengthen relations and provide new knowledge and skills that may be very important later. Seek advice on local hazards and find out from friendly people where the hostile people are.

Always remember that people frequently insist that other peoples are hostile, simply because they do not understand different cultures and distant peoples. The people they can usually trust are their immediate neighbors--much the same as in our own neighborhood.

Frequently, local people, like ourselves, will suffer from contagious diseases. Build a separate shelter, if possible, and avoid physical contact without giving the impression of doing so.

Personally prepare your food and drink, if you can do so without giving offense. Frequently, the local people will accept the use of "personal or religious custom" as an explanation for isolationist behavior.

Barter, or trading, is common in more primitive societies. Hard coin is usually good, whether for its exchange value or as jewelry or trinkets. In isolated areas, matches, tobacco, salt, razor blades, empty containers, or cloth may be worth more than any form of money.

Be very cautious when touching people. Many people consider "touching" taboo and such actions may be dangerous. Avoid sexual contact.

Hospitality among some people is such a strong cultural trait that they may seriously reduce their own supplies to feed a stranger. Accept what they offer and share it equally with all present. Eat in the same way they eat and, most important, try to eat all they offer.

If you make any promises, keep them. Respect personal property and local customs and manners, even if they seem odd. Make some kind of payment for food, supplies, and so forth. Respect privacy. Do not enter a house unless invited.

CHANGES TO POLITICAL ALLEGIANCE

In today's world of fast-paced international politics, political attitudes and commitments within nations are subject to rapid change. The population of many countries, especially politically hostile countries, must not be considered friendly just because they do not demonstrate open hostility. Unless briefed to the contrary; avoid all contact with such people.

Chapter 17 Interrogation

The Non-Coercive Counterintelligence
Interrogation

General Remarks

The term non-coercive is used above to denote
methods of interrogation that are not based upon the
coercion of an unwilling subject through the
employment of superior force originating outside
himself. However, the non-coercive interrogation is
not conducted without pressure. On the contrary,
the goal is to generate maximum pressure, or at
least as much as is needed to induce compliance.
The difference is that the pressure is generated
inside the interrogatee. His resistance is sapped, his
urge to yield is fortified, until in the end he defeats
himself.

Manipulating the subject psychologically until he
becomes compliant, without applying external
methods of forcing him to submit, sounds harder
than it is. The initial advantage lies with the
interrogator. From the outset, he knows a great deal
more about the source than the source knows about
him. And he can create and amplify an effect of
omniscience in a number of ways. For example, he
can show the interrogatee a thick file bearing his
own name. Even if the file contains little or nothing
but blank paper, the air of familiarity with which the
interrogator refers to the subject's background can

convince some sources that all is known and that resistance is futile.

If the interrogatee is under detention, the interrogator can also manipulate his environment. Merely by cutting off all other human contacts, "the interrogator monopolizes the social environment of the source." He exercises the powers of an all-powerful parent, determining when the source will be sent to bed, when and what he will eat, whether he will be rewarded for good behavior or punished for being bad. The interrogator can and does make the subject's world not only unlike the world to which he had been accustomed but also strange in itself - a world in which familiar patterns of time, space, and sensory perception are overthrown.

He can shift the environment abruptly. For example, a source who refuses to talk at all can be placed in unpleasant solitary confinement for a time. Then a friendly soul treats him to an unexpected walk in the woods. Experiencing relief and exhilaration, the subject will usually find it impossible not to respond to innocuous comments on the weather and the flowers. These are expanded to include reminiscences, and soon a precedent of verbal exchange has been established. Both the Germans and the Chinese have used this trick effectively.

The interrogator also chooses the emotional key or keys in which the interrogation or any part of it will be played.

The Structure of the Interrogation

A counterintelligence interrogation consists of four parts: the opening, the reconnaissance, the detailed questioning and the conclusion.

1. The Opening

Most resistant interrogatees block off access to significant counterintelligence in their possession for one or more of four reasons. The first is a specific negative reaction to the interrogator. Poor initial handling or a fundamental antipathy can make a source uncooperative even if he has nothing significant or damaging to conceal. The second cause is that some sources are resistant "by nature" - i.e. by early conditioning - to any compliance with authority. The third is that the subject believes that the information sought will be damaging or incriminating for him personally that cooperation with the interrogator will have consequences more painful for him than the results of non-cooperation.

The fourth is ideological resistance. The source has identified himself with a cause, a political movement or organization, or an opposition intelligence service. Regardless of his attitude toward the interrogator, his own personality, and his fears for the future, the person who is deeply devoted to a hostile cause will ordinarily prove strongly resistant under interrogation.

A principal goal during the opening phase is to confirm the personality assessment obtained through screening and to allow the interrogator to gain a deeper understanding of the source as an individual. Unless time is crucial, the interrogator should not become impatient if the interrogatee wanders from the purposes of the interrogation and reverts to personal concerns. Significant facts not produced during screening may be revealed. The screening report itself is brought to life, the type becomes an individual, as the subject talks.

And sometimes seemingly rambling monologues about personal matters are preludes to significant admissions. Some people cannot bring themselves to provide information that puts them in an unfavorable light until, through a lengthy prefatory rationalization, they feel that they have set the stage that the interrogator will now understand why they acted as they did. If face-saving is necessary to the interrogatee it will be a waste of time to try to force him to cut the preliminaries short and get down to cases. In his view, he is dealing with the important topic, the why. He will be offended and may become wholly uncooperative if faced with insistent demands for the naked what.

There is another advantage in letting the subject talk freely and even ramblingly in the first stage of interrogation. The interrogator is free to observe. Human beings communicate a great deal by non-verbal means. Skilled interrogators, for example, listen closely to voices and learn a great deal from them. An interrogation is not merely a verbal performance; it is a vocal performance, and the voice projects tension, fear, a dislike of certain topics, and other useful pieces of information.

It is also helpful to watch the subject's mouth, which is as a rule much more revealing than his eyes. Gestures and postures also tell a story. If a subject normally gesticulates broadly at times and is at other times physically relaxed but at some point sits stiffly motionless, his posture is likely to be the physical image of his mental tension. The interrogator should make a mental note of the topic that caused such a reaction.

One textbook on interrogation lists the following physical indicators of emotions and recommends that interrogators note them, not as conclusive proofs but as assessment aids:

(1) A ruddy or flushed face is an indication of anger or embarrassment but not necessarily of guilt.

(2) A "cold sweat" is a strong sign of fear and shock.

(3) A pale face indicates fear and usually shows that the interrogator is hitting close to the mark.

(4) A dry mouth denotes nervousness.

(5) Nervous tension is also shown by wringing a handkerchief or clenching the hands tightly.

(6) Emotional strain or tension may cause a pumping of the heart which becomes visible in the pulse and throat.

(7) A slight gasp, holding the breath, or an unsteady voice may betray the subject.

(8) Fidgeting may take many forms, all of which are good indications of nervousness.

(9) A man under emotional strain or nervous tension will involuntarily draw his elbows to his sides. It is a protective defense mechanism.

(10) The movement of the foot when one leg is crossed over the knee of the other can serve as an indicator. The circulation of the blood to the lower leg is partially cut off, thereby causing a slight lift or movement of the free foot with each heart beat. This becomes more pronounced and observable as the pulse rate increases.

Pauses are also significant. Whenever a person is talking about a subject of consequence to himself, he goes through a process of advance self-monitoring, performed at lightning speed. This self-monitoring is more intense if the person is talking to a stranger and especially intense if he is answering the stranger's questions. Its purpose is to keep from the questioner any guilty information or information that would be damaging to the speaker's self-esteem. Where questions or answers get close to sensitive areas, the pre-scanning is likely to create mental blocks. These in turn produce unnatural pauses, meaningless sounds designed to give the speaker more time, or other interruptions. It is not easy to distinguish between innocent blocks -- things held back for reasons of personal prestige -- and guilty blocks -- things the interrogator needs to know. But the successful establishment of rapport will tend to eliminate innocent blocks, or at least to keep them to a minimum.

The establishment of rapport is the second principal purpose of the opening phase of the interrogation. Sometimes the interrogator knows in advance, as a result of screening, that the subject will be uncooperative. At other times the probability of resistance is established without screening: detected hostile agents, for example, usually have not only the will to resist but also the means, through a cover story or other explanation. But the anticipation of withholding increases rather than diminishes, the value of rapport. In other words, a lack of rapport may cause an interrogatee to withhold information that he would otherwise provide freely, whereas the existence of rapport may induce an interrogatee who is initially determined to withhold to change his attitude.

Therefore the interrogator must not become hostile if confronted with initial hostility, or in any other way confirm such negative attitudes as he may encounter at the outset. During this first phase his attitude should remain business-like but also quietly (not ostentatiously) friendly and welcoming. Such opening remarks by subjects as, "I know what you so-and-so's are after, and I can tell you right now that you're not going to get it from me" are best handled by an unperturbed "Why don't you tell me what has made you angry?"

At this stage the interrogator should avoid being drawn into conflict, no matter how provocatory may be the attitude or language of the interrogatee. If he meets truculence with neither insincere protestations that he is the subject's "pal" nor an equal anger but rather a calm interest in what has aroused the subject, the interrogator has gained two advantages right at the start. He has established the superiority that he will need later, as the questioning develops, and he has increased the chances of establishing rapport.

How long the opening phase continues depends upon how long it takes to establish rapport or to determine that voluntary cooperation is unobtainable. It may be literally a matter of seconds, or it may be a drawn-out, up-hill battle. Even though the cost in time and patience is sometimes high, the effort to make the subject feel that his questioner is a sympathetic figure should not be abandoned until all reasonable resources have been exhausted (unless, of course, the interrogation does not merit much time). Otherwise, the chances are that the interrogation will not produce optimum results. In fact, it is likely to be a failure, and the interrogator should not be dissuaded from the effort to establish rapport by an inward conviction that no man in his right mind would incriminate himself by providing the kind of information that is sought.

The history of interrogation is full of confessions and other self-incriminations that were in essence the result of a substitution of the interrogation world for the world outside. In other words, as the sights and sounds of an outside world fade away, its significance for the interrogatee tends to do likewise. That world is replaced by the interrogation room, its two occupants, and the dynamic relationship between them. As interrogation goes on, the subject tends increasingly to divulge or withhold in accordance with the values of the interrogation world rather than those of the outside world (unless the periods of questioning are only brief interruptions in his normal life). In this small world of two inhabitants a clash of personalities -- as distinct from a conflict of purposes -- assumes exaggerated force, like a tornado in a wind-tunnel.

The self-esteem of the interrogatee and of the interrogator becomes involved, and the interrogatee fights to keep his secrets from his opponent for subjective reasons, because he is grimly determined not to be the loser, the inferior. If on the other hand the interrogator establishes rapport, the subject may withhold because of other reasons, but his resistance often lacks the bitter, last-ditch intensity that results if the contest becomes personalized.

The interrogator who senses or determines in the opening phase that what he is hearing is a legend should resist the first, natural impulse to demonstrate its falsity. In some interrogatees the ego-demands, the need to save face, are so intertwined with preservation of the cover story that calling the man a liar will merely intensify resistance. It is better to leave an avenue of escape, a loophole which permits the source to correct his story without looking foolish.

If it is decided, much later in the interrogation, to confront the interrogatee with proof of lying, the following related advice about legal cross-examination may prove helpful.

"Much depends upon the sequence in which one conducts the cross-examination of a dishonest witness. You should never hazard the important question until you have laid the foundation for it in such a way that, when confronted with the fact, the witness can neither deny nor explain it. One often sees the most damaging documentary evidence, in the forms of letters or affidavits, fall absolutely flat as betrayers of falsehood, merely because of the unskillful way in which they are handled. If you have in your possession a letter written by the witness, in which he takes an opposite position on some part of the case to the one he has just sworn to, avoid the common error of showing the witness the letter for identification, and then reading it to him with the inquiry, 'What have you to say to that?'

During the reading of his letter the witness will be collecting his thoughts and getting ready his explanations in anticipation of the question that is to follow, and the effect of the damaging letter will be lost.... The correct method of using such a letter is to lead the witness quietly into repeating the statements he has made in his direct testimony, and which his letter contradicts. Then read it off to him. The witness has no explanation. He has stated the fact, there is nothing to qualify."

2. The Reconnaissance

If the interrogatee is cooperative at the outset or if rapport is established during the opening phase and the source becomes cooperative, the reconnaissance stage is needless; the interrogator proceeds directly to detailed questioning. But if the interrogatee is withholding, a period of exploration is necessary. Assumptions have normally been made already as to what he is withholding: that he is a fabricator, or an RIS agent, or something else he deems it important to conceal. Or the assumption may be that he had knowledge of such activities carried out by someone else. At any rate, the purpose of the reconnaissance is to provide a quick testing of the assumption and, more importantly, to probe the causes, extent, and intensity of resistance.

During the opening phase the interrogator will have charted the probable areas of resistance by noting those topics which caused emotional or physical reactions, speech blocks, or other indicators. He

330

now begins to probe these areas. Every experienced interrogator has noted that if an interrogatee is withholding, his anxiety increases as the questioning nears the mark. The safer the topic, the more voluble the source. But as the questions make him increasingly uncomfortable, the interrogatee becomes less communicative or perhaps even hostile.

During the opening phase the interrogator has gone along with this protective mechanism. Now, however, he keeps coming back to each area of sensitivity until he has determined the location of each and the intensity of the defenses. If resistance is slight, mere persistence may overcome it; and detailed questioning may follow immediately. But if resistance is strong, a new topic should be introduced, and detailed questioning reserved for the third stage.

Two dangers are especially likely to appear during the reconnaissance. Up to this point the interrogator has not continued a line of questioning when resistance was encountered. Now, however, he does so, and rapport may be strained. Some interrogatees will take this change personally and tend to personalize the conflict. The interrogator should resist this tendency. If he succumbs to it, and becomes engaged in a battle of wits, he may not be able to accomplish the task at hand. The second temptation to avoid is the natural inclination to resort prematurely to ruses or coercive techniques in order to settle the matter then and there. The basic purpose of the reconnaissance is to determine the kind and degree of pressure that will be needed in the third stage. The interrogator should reserve his fire-power until he knows what he is up against.

3. The Detailed Questioning

a. If rapport is established and if the interrogatee has nothing significant to hide, detailed questioning presents only routine problems. The major routine considerations are the following:

The interrogator must know exactly what he wants to know. He should have on paper or firmly in mind all the questions to which he seeks answers. It usually happens that the source has a relatively large body of information that has little or no intelligence value and only a small collection of nuggets. He will naturally tend to talk about what he knows best. The interrogator should not show quick impatience, but neither should he allow the results to get out of focus. The determinant remains what we need, not what the interrogatee can most readily provide.

At the same time it is necessary to make every effort to keep the subject from learning through the interrogation process precisely where our informational gaps lie. This principle is especially important if the interrogatee is following his normal life, going home each evening and appearing only once or twice a week for questioning, or if his bona fides remain in doubt. Under almost all circumstances, however, a clear revelation of our interests and knowledge should be avoided. It is usually a poor practice to hand to even the most cooperative interrogatee an orderly list of questions and ask him to write the answers. (This stricture does not apply to the writing of autobiographies or on informational matters not a subject of controversy with the source.) Some time is normally spent on matters of little or no intelligence interest for purposes of concealment.

The interrogator can abet the process by making occasional notes -- or pretending to do so -- on items that seem important to the interrogatee but are not of intelligence value. From this point of view an interrogation can be deemed successful if a source who is actually a hostile agent can report to the opposition only the general fields of our interest but cannot pinpoint specifics without including misleading information.

It is sound practice to write up each interrogation report on the day of questioning or, at least, before the next session, so that defects can be promptly remedied and gaps or contradictions noted in time.

It is also a good expedient to have the interrogatee make notes of topics that should be covered, which occur to him while discussing the immediate matters at issue. The act of recording the stray item or thought on paper fixes it in the interrogatee's mind. Usually topics popping up in the course of an interrogation are forgotten if not noted; they tend to disrupt the interrogation plan if covered by way of digression on the spot.

Debriefing questions should usually be couched to provoke a positive answer and should be specific. The questioner should not accept a blanket negative without probing. For example, the question "Do you know anything about Plant X?" is likelier to draw a negative answer then "Do you have any friends who work at Plant X?" or "Can you describe its exterior?"

It is important to determine whether the subject's knowledge of any topic was acquired at first hand, learned indirectly, or represents merely an assumption. If the information was obtained indirectly, the identities of sub-sources and related information about the channel are needed. If statements rest on assumptions, the facts upon which the conclusions are based are necessary to evaluation.

As detailed questioning proceeds, addition biographic data will be revealed. Such items should be entered into the record, but it is normally preferable not to diverge from an impersonal topic in order to follow a biographic lead. Such leads can be taken up later unless they raise new doubts about bona fides.

As detailed interrogation continues, and especially at the half-way mark, the interrogator's desire to complete the task may cause him to be increasingly business-like or even brusque. He may tend to curtail or drop the usual inquiries about the subject's well-being with which he opened earlier sessions. He may feel like dealing more and more abruptly with reminiscences or digressions. His interest has shifted from the interrogatee himself, who jut a while ago was an interesting person, to the task of getting at what he knows. But if rapport has been established, the interrogatee will be quick to sense and resent this change of attitude. This point is particularly important if the interrogatee is a defector faced with bewildering changes and in a highly emotional state. Any interrogatee has his ups and downs, times when he is tired or half-ill, times when his personal problems have left his nerves frayed.

The peculiar intimacy of the interrogation situation and the very fact that the interrogator has deliberately fostered rapport will often lead the subject to talk about his doubts, fears, and other personal reactions. The interrogator should neither cut off this flow abruptly nor show impatience unless it takes up an inordinate amount of time or unless it seems likely that all the talking about personal matters is being used deliberately as a smoke screen to keep the interrogator from doing his job. If the interrogatee is believed cooperative, then from the beginning to the end of the process he should feel that the interrogator's interest in him has remained constant. Unless the interrogation is soon over, the interrogatee's attitude toward his questioner is not likely to remain constant. He will feel more and more drawn to the questioner or increasingly antagonistic. As a rule, the best way for the interrogator to keep the relationship on an even keel is to maintain the same quiet, relaxed, and open-minded attitude from start to finish.

Detailed interrogation ends only when (1) all useful counterintelligence information has been obtained; (2) diminishing returns and more pressing commitments compel a cessation; or (3) the base, station, admits full or partial defeat. Termination for any reason other than the first is only temporary. It is a profound mistake to write off a successfully resistant interrogatee or one whose questioning was ended before his potential was exhausted. KUBARK must keep track of such persons, because people and circumstances change. Until the source dies or tells us everything that he knows that is pertinent to our purposes, his interrogation may be interrupted, perhaps for years -- but it has not been completed.

The Conclusion

The end of an interrogation is not the end of the interrogator's responsibilities. From the beginning of planning to the end of questioning it has been necessary to understand and guard against the various troubles that a vengeful ex-source can cause. As was pointed out earlier, KUBARK's lack of executive authority abroad and its operational need for facelessness make it peculiarly vulnerable to attack in the courts or the press. The best defense against such attacks is prevention, through enlistment or enforcement of compliance. However real cooperation is achieved, its existence seems to act as a deterrent to later hostility. The initially resistant subject may become cooperative because of a partial identification with the interrogator and his interests, or the source may make such an identification because of his cooperation. In either event, he is unlikely to cause serious trouble in the future. Real difficulties are more frequently created by interrogatees who have succeeded in withholding.

Techniques of Non-Coercive Interrogation of Resistant Sources

If source resistance is encountered during screening or during the opening or reconnaissance phases of the interrogation, non-coercive methods of sapping opposition and strengthening the tendency to yield and to cooperate may be applied. Although these methods appear here in an approximate order of increasing pressure, it should not be inferred that each is to be tried until the key fits the lock. On the contrary, a large part of the skill and the success of the experienced interrogator lies in his ability to match method to source. The use of unsuccessful techniques will of itself increase the interrogatee's will and ability to resist.

This principle also affects the decision to employ coercive techniques and governs the choice of these methods. If in the opinion of the interrogator a totally resistant source has the skill and determination to withstand any con-coercive method or combination of methods, it is better to avoid them completely.

The effectiveness of most of the non-coercive techniques depends upon their unsettling effect. The interrogation situation is in itself disturbing to most people encountering it for the first time. The aim is to enhance this effect, to disrupt radically the familiar emotional and psychological associations of the subject. When this aim is achieved, resistance is seriously impaired. There is an interval -- which may be extremely brief -- of suspended animation, a kind of psychological shock or paralysis. It is caused by a traumatic or sub-traumatic experience which explodes, as it were, the world that is familiar to the subject as well as his image of himself within that world. Experienced interrogators recognize this effect when it appears and know that at this moment the source is far more open to suggestion, far likelier to comply, than he was just before he experienced the shock.

Another effect frequently produced by non-coercive (as well as coercive) methods is the evocation within the interrogatee of feelings of guilt. Most persons have areas of guilt in their emotional topographies, and an interrogator can often chart these areas just by noting refusals to follow certain lines of questioning. Whether the sense of guilt has real or imaginary causes does not affect the result of intensification of guilt feelings. Making a person feel more and more guilty normally increases both his anxiety and his urge to cooperate as a means of escape.

In brief, the techniques that follow should match the personality of the individual interrogatee, and their effectiveness is intensified by good timing and rapid exploitation of the moment of shock. (A few of the following items are drawn from Sheehan.) (32)

Going Next Door

Occasionally the information needed from a recalcitrant interrogatee is obtainable from a willing source. The interrogator should decide whether a confession is essential to his purpose or whether information which may be held by others as well as the unwilling source is really his goal. The labor of extracting the truth from unwilling interrogatees should be undertaken only if the same information is not more easily obtainable elsewhere or if operational considerations require self-incrimination.

Nobody Loves You

An interrogatee who is withholding items of no grave consequence to himself may sometimes be persuaded to talk by the simple tactic of pointing out that to date all of the information about his case has come from persons other than himself. The interrogator wants to be fair. He recognizes that some of the denouncers may have been biased or malicious. In any case, there is bound to be some slanting of the facts unless the interrogatee redresses the balance. The source owes it to himself to be sure that the interrogator hears both sides of the story.

The All-Seeing Eye (or Confession is Good for the Soul)

The interrogator who already knows part of the story explains to the source that the purpose of the questioning is not to gain information; the interrogator knows everything already. His real purpose is to test the sincerity (reliability, honor, etc.) of the source. The interrogator then asks a few questions to which he knows the answers. If the subject lies, he is informed firmly and dispassionately that he has lied. By skilled manipulation of the known, the questioner can convince a naive subject that all his secrets are out and that further resistance would be not only pointless but dangerous. If this technique does not work very quickly, it must be dropped before the interrogatee learns the true limits of the questioner's knowledge.

The Informer

Detention makes a number of tricks possible. One of these, planting an informant as the source's cellmate, is so well-known, especially in Communist countries, that its usefulness is impaired if not destroyed. Less well known is the trick of planting two informants in the cell. One of them, A, tries now and then to pry a little information from the source; B remains quiet. At the proper time, and during A's absence, B warns the source not to tell A anything because B suspects him of being an informant planted by the authorities.

Suspicion against a single cellmate may sometimes be broken down if he shows the source a hidden microphone that he has "found" and suggests that they talk only in whispers at the other end of the room.

News from Home

Allowing an interrogatee to receive carefully selected letters from home can contribute to effects desired by the interrogator. Allowing the source to write letters, especially if he can be led to believe that they will be smuggled out without the knowledge of the authorities, may produce information which is difficult to extract by direct questioning.

The Witness

If others have accused the interrogatee of spying for a hostile service or of other activity which he denies, there is a temptation to confront the recalcitrant source with his accuser or accusers. But a quick confrontation has two weaknesses: it is likely to intensify the stubbornness of denials, and it spoils the chance to use more subtle methods.

341

One of these is to place the interrogatee in an outer office and escort past him, and into the inner office, an accuser whom he knows personally or, in fact, any person -- even one who is friendly to the source and uncooperative with the interrogators -- who is believed to know something about whatever the interrogatee is concealing. It is also essential that the interrogatee know or suspect that the witness may be in possession of the incriminating information. The witness is whisked past the interrogatee; the two are not allowed to speak to each other. A guard and a stenographer remain in the outer office with the interrogatee. After about an hour the interrogator who has been questioning the interrogatee in past sessions opens the door and asks the stenographer to come in, with steno pad and pencils. After a time she re-emerges and types material from her pad, making several carbons. She pauses, points at the interrogatee, and asks the guard how his name is spelled. She may also ask the interrogatee directly for the proper spelling of a street, a prison, the name of a Communist intelligence officer, or any other factor closely linked to the activity of which he is accused. She takes her completed work into the inner office, comes back out, and telephones a request that someone come up to act as legal witness. Another man appears and enters the inner office. The person cast in the informer's role may have been let out a back door at the beginning of these proceedings; or if cooperative, he may continue his role. In either event, a couple of interrogators, with or without the "informer", now emerge from the inner office. In contrast to their earlier demeanor, they are now relaxed and smiling. The interrogator in charge says to the guard, "O.K., Tom, take him back. We don't need him any more." Even if the interrogatee now insists on telling his side of the story, he is told to relax, because the interrogator will get around to him tomorrow or the next day.

A session with the witness may be recorded. If the witness denounces the interrogatee there is no problem. If he does not, the interrogator makes an effort to draw him out about a hostile agent recently convicted in court or otherwise known to the witness. During the next interrogation session with the source, a part of the taped denunciation can be played back to him if necessary. Or the witnesses' remarks about the known spy, edited as necessary, can be so played back that the interrogatee is persuaded that he is the subject of the remarks.

Cooperative witnesses may be coached to exaggerate so that if a recording is played for the interrogatee or a confrontation is arranged, the source -- for example, a suspected courier -- finds the witness overstating his importance. The witness claims that the interrogatee is only incidentally a courier, that actually he is the head of an RIS kidnapping gang. The interrogator pretends amazement and says into the recorder, "I thought he was only a courier; and if he had told us the truth, I planned to let him go. But this is much more serious. On the basis of charges like these I'll have to hand him over to the local police for trial." On hearing these remarks, the interrogatee may confess the truth about the lesser guilt in order to avoid heavier punishment. If he continues to withhold, the interrogator may take his side by stating, "You know, I'm not at all convinced that so-and-so told a straight story. I feel, personally, that he was exaggerating a great deal. Wasn't he? What's the true story?"

Joint Suspects

If two or more interrogation sources are suspected of joint complicity in acts directed against U.S. security, they should be separated immediately. If time permits, it may be a good idea (depending upon the psychological assessment of both) to postpone interrogation for about a week. Any anxious inquiries from either can be met by a knowing grin and some such reply as, "We'll get to you in due time. There's no hurry now." If documents, witnesses, or other sources yield information about interrogatee A, such remarks as "B says it was in Smolensk that you denounced so-and-so to the secret police. Is that right? Was it in 1937?" help to establish in A's mind the impression that B is talking.

If the interrogator is quite certain of the facts in the case but cannot secure an admission from either A or B, a written confession may be prepared and A's signature may be reproduced on it. (It is helpful if B can recognize A's signature, but not essential.) The confession contains the salient facts, but they are distorted; the confession shows that A is attempting to throw the entire responsibility upon B. Edited tape recordings which sound as though A had denounced B may also be used for the purpose, separately or in conjunction with the written "confession." If A is feeling a little ill or dispirited, he can also be led past a window or otherwise shown to B without creating a chance for conversation; B is likely to interpret A's hang-dog look as evidence of confession and denunciation. (It is important that in all such gambits, A be the weaker of the two, emotionally and psychologically.) B then reads (or hears) A's "confession." If B persists in withholding, the interrogator should dismiss him promptly, saying that A's signed confession is sufficient for the purpose and that it does not matter whether B corroborates it or not. At the following session with B, the interrogator selects some minor matter, not substantively damaging to B but nevertheless exaggerated, and says, "I'm not sure A was really fair to you here. Would you care to tell me your side of the story?" If B rises to this bait, the interrogator moves on to areas of greater significance.

The outer-and-inner office routine may also be employed. A, the weaker, is brought into the inner office, and the door is left slightly ajar or the transom open. B is later brought into the outer office by a guard and placed where he can hear, though not too clearly. The interrogator begins routine questioning of A, speaking rather softly and inducing A to follow suit. Another person in the inner office, acting by prearrangement, then quietly leads A out through another door. Any noises of departure are covered by the interrogator, who rattles the ash tray or moves a table or large chair. As soon as the second door is closed again and A is out of earshot, the interrogator resumes his questioning. His voice grows louder and angrier. He tells A to speak up, that he can hardly hear him. He grows abusive, reaches a climax, and then says, "Well, that's better. Why didn't you say so in the first place?" The rest of the monologue is designed to give B the impression that A has now started to tell the truth. Suddenly the interrogator pops his head through the doorway and is angry on seeing B and the guard. "You jerk!" he says to the guard, "What are you doing here?" He rides down the guard's mumbled attempt to explain the mistake, shouting, "Get him out of here! I'll take care of you later!"

When, in the judgment of the interrogator, B is fairly well convinced that A has broken down and told his story, the interrogator may elect to say to B, "Now that A has come clean with us, I'd like to let him go. But I hate to release one of you before the other; you ought to get out at the same time. A seems to be pretty angry with you -- feels that you got him into this jam. He might even go back to your Soviet case officer and say that you haven't returned because you agreed to stay here and work for us. Wouldn't it be better for you if I set you both free together? Wouldn't it be better to tell me your side of the story?"

Ivan Is a Dope

It may be useful to point out to a hostile agent that the cover story was ill-contrived, that the other service botched the job, that it is typical of the other service to ignore the welfare of its agents. The interrogator may personalize this pitch by explaining that he has been impressed by the agent's courage and intelligence. He sells the agent the idea that the interrogator, not his old service, represents a true friend, who understands him and will look after his welfare.

Joint Interrogators

The commonest of the joint interrogator techniques is the Mutt-and-Jeff routine: the brutal, angry, domineering type contrasted with the friendly, quiet type. This routine works best with women, teenagers, and timid men. If the interrogator who has done the bulk of the questioning up to this point has established a measure of rapport, he should play the friendly role. If rapport is absent, and especially if antagonism has developed, the principal interrogator may take the other part. The angry interrogator speaks loudly from the beginning; and unless the interrogatee clearly indicates that he is now ready to tell his story, the angry interrogator shouts down his answers and cuts him off. He thumps the table. The quiet interrogator should not watch the show unmoved but give subtle indications that he too is somewhat afraid of his colleague. The angry interrogator accuses the subject of other offenses, any offenses, especially those that are heinous or demeaning. He makes it plain that he personally considers the interrogatee the vilest person on earth. During the harangue the friendly, quiet interrogator breaks in to say, "Wait a minute, Jim. Take it easy."

The angry interrogator shouts back, "Shut up! I'm handling this. I've broken crumb-bums before, and I'll break this one, wide open." He expresses his disgust by spitting on the floor or holding his nose or any gross gesture. Finally, red-faced and furious, he says, "I'm going to take a break, have a couple of stiff drinks. But I'll be back at two -- and you, you bum, you better be ready to talk." When the door slams behind him, the second interrogator tells the subject how sorry he is, how he hates to work with a man like that but has no choice, how if maybe brutes like that would keep quiet and give a man a fair chance to tell his side of the story, etc., etc.

An interrogator working alone can also use the Mutt-and-Jeff technique. After a number of tense and hostile sessions the interrogatee is ushered into a different or refurnished room with comfortable furniture, cigarettes, etc. The interrogator invites him to sit down and explains his regret that the source's former stubbornness forced the interrogator to use such tactics. Now everything will be different. The interrogator talks man-to-man. An American POW, debriefed on his interrogation by a hostile service that used this approach, has described the result: "Well, I went in and there was a man, an officer he was... -- he asked me to sit down and was very friendly.... It was very terrific. I, well, I almost felt like I had a friend sitting there. I had to stop every now and then and realize that this man wasn't a friend of mine.... I also felt as though I couldn't be rude to him.... It was much more difficult for me to -- well, I almost felt I had as much responsibility to talk to him and reason and justification as I have to talk to you right now."

Another joint technique casts both interrogators in friendly roles. But whereas the interrogator in charge is sincere, the second interrogator's manner and voice convey the impression that he is merely pretending sympathy in order to trap the interrogated. He slips in a few trick questions of the "When-did-you-stop-beating-your-wife?" category. The interrogator in charge warns his colleague to desist. When he repeats the tactics, the interrogator in charge says, with a slight show of anger, "We're not here to trap people but to get at the truth. I suggest that you leave now. I'll handle this."

It is usually unproductive to cast both interrogators in hostile roles.

Language

If the recalcitrant subject speaks more than one language, it is better to question him in the tongue with which he is least familiar as long as the purpose of interrogation is to obtain a confession. After the interrogatee admits hostile intent or activity, a switch to the better-known language will facilitate follow-up.

An abrupt switch of languages may trick a resistant source. If an interrogatee has withstood a barrage of questions in German or Korean, for example, a sudden shift to "Who is your case officer?" in Russian may trigger the answer before the source can stop himself.

An interrogator quite at home in the language being used may nevertheless elect to use an interpreter if the interrogatee does not know the language to be used between the interrogator and interpreter and also does not know that the interrogator knows his own tongue. The principal advantage here is that hearing everything twice helps the interrogator to note voice, expression, gestures, and other indicators more attentively. This gambit is obviously unsuitable for any form of rapid-fire questioning, and in any case it has the disadvantage of allowing the subject to pull himself together after each query. It should be used only with an interpreter who has been trained in the technique.

It is of basic importance that the interrogator not using an interpreter be adept in the language selected for use. If he is not, if slips of grammar or a strong accent mar his speech, the resistant source will usually feel fortified. Almost all people have been conditioned to relate verbal skill to intelligence, education, social status, etc. Errors or mispronunciations also permit the interrogatee to misunderstand or feign misunderstanding and thus gain time. He may also resort to polysyllabic obfuscations upon realizing the limitations of the interrogator's vocabulary.

Spinoza and Mortimer Snerd

If there is reason to suspect that a withholding source possesses useful counterintelligence information but has not had access to the upper reaches of the target organizations, the policy and command level, continued questioning about lofty topics that the source knows nothing about may pave the way for the extraction of information at lower levels. The interrogatee is asked about KGB policy, for example: the relation of the service to its government, its liaison arrangements, etc., etc. His complaints that he knows nothing of such matters are met by flat insistence that he does know, he would have to know, that even the most stupid men in his position know. Communist interrogators who used this tactic against American POW's coupled it with punishment for "don't know" responses -- typically by forcing the prisoner to stand at attention until he gave some positive response. After the process had been continued long enough, the source was asked a question to which he did know the answer. Numbers of Americans have mentioned "...the tremendous feeling of relief you get when he finally asks you something you can answer." One said, "I know it seems strange now, but I was positively grateful to them when they switched to a topic I knew something about."

The Wolf in Sheep's Clothing

It has been suggested that a successfully withholding source might be tricked into compliance if led to believe that he is dealing with the opposition. The success of the ruse depends upon a successful imitation of the opposition. A case officer previously unknown to the source and skilled in the appropriate language talks with the source under such circumstances that the latter is convinced that he is dealing with the opposition. The source is debriefed on what he has told the Americans and what he has not told them. The trick is likelier to succeed if the interrogatee has not been in confinement but a staged "escape," engineered by a stool-pigeon, might achieve the same end. Usually the trick is so complicated and risky that its employment is not recommended.

Alice in Wonderland

The aim of the Alice in Wonderland or confusion technique is to confound the expectations and conditioned reactions of the interrogatee. He is accustomed to a world that makes some sense, at least to him: a world of continuity and logic, a predictable world. He clings to this world to reinforce his identity and powers of resistance.

The confusion technique is designed not only to obliterate the familiar but to replace it with the weird. Although this method can be employed by a single interrogator, it is better adapted to use by two or three. When the subject enters the room, the first interrogator asks a doubletalk question -- one which seems straightforward but is essentially nonsensical. Whether the interrogatee tries to answer or not, the second interrogator follows up (interrupting any attempted response) with a wholly unrelated and equally illogical query. Sometimes two or more questions are asked simultaneously. Pitch, tone, and volume of the interrogators' voices are unrelated to the import of the questions. No pattern of questions and answers is permitted to develop, nor do the questions themselves relate logically to each other. In this strange atmosphere the subject finds that the pattern of speech and thought which he has learned to consider normal have been replaced by an eerie meaninglessness. The interrogatee may start laughing or refuse to take the situation seriously. But as the process continues, day after day if necessary, the subject begins to try to make sense of the situation, which becomes mentally intolerable. Now he is likely to make significant admissions, or even to pour out his story, just to stop the flow of babble which assails him. This technique may be especially effective with the orderly, obstinate type.

Regression

There are a number of non-coercive techniques for inducing regression, All depend upon the interrogator's control of the environment and, as always, a proper matching of method to source. Some interrogatees can be repressed by persistent manipulation of time, by retarding and advancing clocks and serving meals at odd times -- ten minutes or ten hours after the last food was given. Day and night are jumbled. Interrogation sessions are similarly unpatterned the subject may be brought back for more questioning just a few minutes after being dismissed for the night. Half-hearted efforts to cooperate can be ignored, and conversely he can be rewarded for non-cooperation. (For example, a successfully resisting source may become distraught if given some reward for the "valuable contribution" that he has made.)

The Alice in Wonderland technique can reinforce the effect. Two or more interrogators, questioning as a team and in relays (and thoroughly jumbling the timing of both methods) can ask questions which make it impossible for the interrogatee to give sensible, significant answers. A subject who is cut off from the world he knows seeks to recreate it, in some measure, in the new and strange environment. He may try to keep track of time, to live in the familiar past, to cling to old concepts of loyalty, to establish -- with one or more interrogators -- interpersonal relations resembling those that he has had earlier with other people, and to build other bridges back to the known. Thwarting his attempts to do so is likely to drive him deeper and deeper into himself, until he is no longer able to control his responses in adult fashion.

The placebo technique is also used to induce regression The interrogatee is given a placebo (a harmless sugar pill). Later he is told that he has imbibed a drug, a truth serum, which will make him want to talk and which will also prevent his lying. The subject's desire to find an excuse for the compliance that represents his sole avenue of escape from his distressing predicament may make him want to believe that he has been drugged and that no one could blame him for telling his story now. Gottschelk observes, "Individuals under increased stress are more likely to respond to placebos."

Orne has discussed an extension of the placebo concept in explaining what he terms the "magic room" technique. "An example... would be... the prisoner who is given a hypnotic suggestion that his hand is growing warm. However, in this instance, the prisoner's hand actually does become warm, a problem easily resolved by the use of a concealed diathermy machine. Or it might be suggested... that... a cigarette will taste bitter. Here again, he could be given a cigarette prepared to have a slight but noticeably bitter taste."

In discussing states of heightened suggestibility (which are not, however, states of trance) Orne says, "Both hypnosis and some of the drugs inducing hypnoidal states are popularly viewed as situations where the individual is no longer master of his own fate and therefore not responsible for his actions. It seems possible then that the hypnotic situation, as distinguished from hypnosis itself, might be used to relieve the individual of a feeling of responsibility for his own actions and thus lead him to reveal information."

In other words, a psychologically immature source, or one who has been regressed, could adopt an implication or suggestion that he has been drugged, hypnotized, or otherwise rendered incapable of resistance, even if he recognizes at some level that the suggestion is untrue, because of his strong desire to escape the stress of the situation by capitulating. These techniques provide the source with the rationalization that he needs.

Whether regression occurs spontaneously under detention or interrogation, and whether it is induced by a coercive or non-coercive technique, it should not be allowed to continue past the point necessary to obtain compliance. Severe techniques of regression are best employed in the presence of a psychiatrist, to insure full reversal later. As soon as he can, the interrogator presents the subject with the way out, the face-saving reason for escaping from his painful dilemma by yielding. Now the interrogator becomes fatherly. Whether the excuse is that others have already confessed ("all the other boys are doing it"), that the interrogatee had a chance to redeem himself ("you're really a good boy at heart"), or that he can't help himself ("they made you do it"), the effective rationalization, the one the source will jump at, is likely to be elementary. It is an adult's version of the excuses of childhood.

The Polygraph

The polygraph can be used for purposes other than the evaluation of veracity. For example, it may be used as an adjunct in testing the range of languages spoken by an interrogatee or his sophistication in intelligence matters, for rapid screening to determine broad areas of knowledgeability, and as an aid in the psychological assessment of sources. Its primary function in a counterintelligence interrogation, however, is to provide a further means of testing for deception or withholding.

A resistant source suspected of association with a hostile clandestine organization should be tested polygraphically at least once. Several examinations may be needed. As a general rule, the polygraph should not be employed as a measure of last resort. More reliable readings will be obtained if the instrument is used before the subject has been placed under intense pressure, whether such pressure is coercive or not. Sufficient information for the purpose is normally available after screening and one or two interrogation sessions.

Although the polygraph has been a valuable aid, no interrogator should feel that it can carry his responsibility for him.

The best results are obtained when the CI interrogator and the polygraph operator work closely together in laying the groundwork for technical examination. The operator needs all available information about the personality of the source, as well as the operational background and reasons for suspicion. The CI interrogator in turn can cooperate more effectively and can fit the results of technical examination more accurately into the totality of his findings if he has a basic comprehension of the instrument and its workings.

The following discussion is based upon R.C. Davis' "Physiological Responses as a Means of Evaluating Information." Although improvements appear to be in the offing, the instrument in widespread use today measures breathing, systolic blood pressure, and galvanic skin response (GSR). "One drawback in the use of respiration as an indicator," according to Davis, "is its susceptibility to voluntary control." Moreover, if the source "knows that changes in breathing will disturb all physiologic variables under control of the autonomic division of the nervous system, and possibly even some others, a certain amount of cooperation or a certain degree of ignorance is required for lie detection by physiologic methods to work." In general, "... breathing during deception is shallower and slower than in truth telling... the inhibition of breathing seems rather characteristic of anticipation of a stimulus."

The measurement of systolic blood pressure provides a reading on a phenomenon not usually subject to voluntary control. The pressure "... will typically rise by a few millimeters of mercury in response to a question, whether it is answered truthfully or not. The evidence is that the rise will generally be greater when (the subject) is lying." However, discrimination between truth-telling and lying on the basis of both breathing and blood pressure "... is poor (almost nil) in the early part of the sitting and improves to a high point later."

The galvanic skin response is one of the most easily triggered reactions, but recovery after the reaction is slow, and "... in a routine examination the next question is likely to be introduced before recovery is complete. Partly because of this fact there is an adapting trend in the GSR with stimuli repeated every few minutes the response gets smaller, other things being equal."

Davis examines three theories regarding the polygraph. The conditional response theory holds that the subject reacts to questions that strike sensitive areas, regardless of whether he is telling the truth or not. Experimentation has not substantiated this theory. The theory of conflict presumes that a large physiologic disturbance occurs when the subject is caught between his habitual inclination to tell the truth and his strong desire not to divulge a certain set of facts. Davis suggests that if this concept is valid, it holds only if the conflict is intense.

The threat-of-punishment theory maintains that a large physiologic response accompanies lying because the subject fears the consequence of failing to deceive. "In common language it might be said that he fails to deceive the machine operator for the very reason that he fears he will fail. The 'fear' would be the very reaction detected." This third theory is more widely held than the other two. Interrogators should note the inference that a resistant source who does not fear that detection of lying will result in a punishment of which he is afraid would not, according to this theory, produce significant responses.

Graphology

The validity of graphological techniques for the analysis of the personalities of resistant interrogatees has not been established. There is some evidence that graphology is a useful aid in the early detection of cancer and of certain mental illnesses. If the interrogator or his unit decides to have a source's handwriting analyzed, the samples should be submitted to Headquarters as soon as possible, because the analysis is more useful in the preliminary assessment of the source than in the later interrogation. Graphology does have the advantage of being one of the very few techniques not requiring the assistance or even the awareness of the interrogatee. As with any other aid, the interrogator is free to determine for himself whether the analysis provides him with new and valid insights, confirms other observations, is not helpful, or is misleading.

Coercive Counterintelligence Interrogation
of Resistant Sources

The Theory of Coercion

Coercive procedures are designed not only to exploit the resistant source's internal conflicts and induce him to wrestle with himself but also to bring a superior outside force to bear upon the subject's resistance. Non-coercive methods are not likely to succeed if their selection and use is not predicated upon an accurate psychological assessment of the source. In contrast, the same coercive method may succeed against persons who are very unlike each other. The changes of success rise steeply, nevertheless, if the coercive technique is matched to the source's personality. Individuals react differently even to such seemingly non-discriminatory stimuli as drugs. Moreover, it is a waste of time and energy to apply strong pressures on a hit-or-miss basis if a tap on the psychological jugular will produce compliance.

All coercive techniques are designed to induce regression. As Hinkle notes in "The Physiological State of the Interrogation Subject as it Affects Brain Function", the result of external pressures of sufficient intensity is the loss of those defenses most recently acquired by civilized man: "... the capacity to carry out the highest creative activities, to meet new, challenging, and complex situations, to deal with trying interpersonal relations, and to cope with repeated frustrations. Relatively small degrees of homeostatic derangement, fatigue, pain, sleep loss, or anxiety may impair these functions." As a result, "most people who are exposed to coercive procedures will talk and usually reveal some information that they might not have revealed otherwise."

One subjective reaction often evoked by coercion is a feeling of guilt. Meltzer observes, "In some lengthy interrogations, the interrogator may, by virtue of his role as the sole supplier of satisfaction and punishment, assume the stature and importance of a parental figure in the prisoner's feeling and thinking. Although there may be intense hatred for the interrogator, it is not unusual for warm feelings also to develop. This ambivalence is the basis for guilt reactions, and if the interrogator nourishes these feelings, the guilt may be strong enough to influence the prisoner's behavior.... Guilt makes compliance more likely...."

Farber says that the response to coercion typically contains "... at least three important elements: debility, dependency, and dread." Prisoners "... have reduced viability, are helplessly dependent on their captors for the satisfaction of their many basic needs, and experience the emotional and motivational reactions of intense fear and anxiety.... Among the [American] POW's pressured by the Chinese Communists, the DDD syndrome in its full-blown form constituted a state of discomfort that was well-nigh intolerable." If the debility-dependency-dread state is unduly prolonged, however, the arrestee may sink into a defensive apathy from which it is hard to arouse him.

Psychologists and others who write about physical or psychological duress frequently object that under sufficient pressure subjects usually yield but that their ability to recall and communicate information accurately is as impaired as the will to resist. This pragmatic objection has somewhat the same validity for a counterintelligence interrogation as for any other. But there is one significant difference.

Confession is a necessary prelude to the CI interrogation of a hitherto unresponsive or concealing source. And the use of coercive techniques will rarely or never confuse an interrogatee so completely that he does not know whether his own confession is true or false. He does not need full mastery of all his powers of resistance and discrimination to know whether he is a spy or not. Only subjects who have reached a point where they are under delusions are likely to make false confessions that they believe. Once a true confession is obtained, the classic cautions apply.

The pressures are lifted, at least enough so that the subject can provide counterintelligence information as accurately as possible. In fact, the relief granted the subject at this time fits neatly into the interrogation plan. He is told that the changed treatment is a reward for truthfulness and an evidence that friendly handling will continue as long as he cooperates.

The profound moral objection to applying duress past the point of irreversible psychological damage has been stated. Judging the validity of other ethical arguments about coercion exceeds the scope of this paper. What is fully clear, however, is that controlled coercive manipulation of an interrogatee may impair his ability to make fine distinctions but will not alter his ability to answer correctly such gross questions as "Are you a Soviet agent? What is your assignment now? Who is your present case officer?"

When an interrogator senses that the subject's resistance is wavering, that his desire to yield is growing stronger than his wish to continue his resistance, the time has come to provide him with the acceptable rationalization: a face-saving reason or excuse for compliance. Novice interrogators may be tempted to seize upon the initial yielding triumphantly and to personalize the victory. Such a temptation must be rejected immediately. An interrogation is not a game played by two people, one to become the winner and the other the loser. It is simply a method of obtaining correct and useful information. Therefore the interrogator should intensify the subject's desire to cease struggling by showing him how he can do so without seeming to abandon principle, self-protection, or other initial causes of resistance. If, instead of providing the right rationalization at the right time, the interrogator seizes gloatingly upon the subject's wavering, opposition will stiffen again.

The following are the principal coercive techniques of interrogation: arrest, detention, deprivation of sensory stimuli through solitary confinement or similar methods, threats and fear, debility, pain, heightened suggestibility and hypnosis, narcosis, and induced regression. This section also discusses the detection of malingering by interrogatees and the provision of appropriate rationalizations for capitulating and cooperating.

C. Arrest

The manner and timing of arrest can contribute substantially to the interrogator's purposes. "What we aim to do is to ensure that the manner of arrest achieves, if possible, surprise, and the maximum amount of mental discomfort in order to catch the suspect off balance and to deprive him of the initiative. One should therefore arrest him at a moment when he least expects it and when his mental and physical resistance is at its lowest. The ideal time at which to arrest a person is in the early hours of the morning because surprise is achieved then, and because a person's resistance physiologically as well as psychologically is at its lowest.... If a person cannot be arrested in the early hours..., then the next best time is in the evening....

Detention

If, through the cooperation of a liaison service or by unilateral means, arrangements have been made for the confinement of a resistant source, the circumstances of detention are arranged to enhance within the subject his feelings of being cut off from the known and the reassuring, and of being plunged into the strange. Usually his own clothes are immediately taken away, because familiar clothing reinforces identity and thus the capacity for resistance. (Prisons give close hair cuts and issue prison garb for the same reason.) If the interrogatee is especially proud or neat, it may be useful to give him an outfit that is one or two sizes too large and to fail to provide a belt, so that he must hold his pants up.

The point is that man's sense of identity depends upon a continuity in his surroundings, habits, appearance, actions, relations with others, etc. Detention permits the interrogator to cut through these links and throw the interrogatee back upon his own unaided internal resources.

Little is gained if confinement merely replaces one routine with another. Prisoners who lead monotonously unvaried lives "... cease to care about their utterances, dress, and cleanliness. They become dulled, apathetic, and depressed." And apathy can be a very effective defense against interrogation. Control of the source's environment permits the interrogator to determine his diet, sleep pattern, and other fundamentals. Manipulating these into irregularities, so that the subject becomes disorientated, is very likely to create feelings of fear and helplessness. Hinkle points out, "People who enter prison with attitudes of foreboding, apprehension, and helplessness generally do less well than those who enter with assurance and a conviction that they can deal with anything that they may encounter.... Some people who are afraid of losing sleep, or who do not wish to lose sleep, soon succumb to sleep loss...."

In short, the prisoner should not be provided a routine to which he can adapt and from which he can draw some comfort -- or at least a sense of his own identity. Everyone has read of prisoners who were reluctant to leave their cells after prolonged incarceration. Little is known about the duration of confinement calculated to make a subject shift from anxiety, coupled with a desire for sensory stimuli and human companionship, to a passive, apathetic acceptance of isolation and an ultimate pleasure in this negative state. Undoubtedly the rate of change is determined almost entirely by the psychological characteristics of the individual. In any event, it is advisable to keep the subject upset by constant disruptions of patterns.

For this reason, it is useful to determine whether the interrogattee has been jailed before, how often, under what circumstances, for how long, and whether he was subjected to earlier interrogation. Familiarity with confinement and even with isolation reduces the effect.

Deprivation of Sensory Stimuli

The chief effect of arrest and detention, and particularly of solitary confinement, is to deprive the subject of many or most of the sights, sounds, tastes, smells, and tactile sensations to which he has grown accustomed. John C. Lilly examined eighteen autobiographical accounts written by polar explorers and solitary seafarers. He found "... that isolation per se acts on most persons as a powerful stress.... In all cases of survivors of isolation at sea or in the polar night, it was the first exposure which caused the greatest fears and hence the greatest danger of giving way to symptoms; previous experience is a powerful aid in going ahead, despite the symptoms. "The symptoms most commonly produced by isolation are superstition, intense love of any other living thing, perceiving inanimate objects as alive, hallucinations, and delusions."

The apparent reason for these effects is that a person cut off from external stimuli turns his awareness inward, upon himself, and then projects the contents of his own unconscious outwards, so that he endows his faceless environment with his own attributes, fears, and forgotten memories. Lilly notes, "It is obvious that inner factors in the mind tend to be projected outward, that some of the mind's activity which is usually reality-bound now becomes free to turn to fantasy and ultimately to hallucination and delusion."

A number of experiments conducted at McGill University, the National Institute of Mental Health, and other sites have attempted to come as close as possible to the elimination of sensory stimuli, or to masking remaining stimuli, chiefly sounds, by a stronger but wholly monotonous overlay. The results of these experiments have little applicability to interrogation because the circumstances are dissimilar. Some of the findings point toward hypotheses that seem relevant to interrogation, but conditions like those of detention for purposes of counterintelligence interrogation have not been duplicated for experimentation.

At the National Institute of Mental Health two subjects were "... suspended with the body and all but the top of the head immersed in a tank containing slowly flowing water at 34.5 [degrees] C (94.5 [degrees] F)...." Both subjects wore black-out masks, which enclosed the whole head but allowed breathing and nothing else. The sound level was extremely low; the subject heard only his own breathing and some faint sounds of water from the piping. Neither subject stayed in the tank longer than three hours. Both passed quickly from normally directed thinking through a tension resulting from unsatisfied hunger for sensory stimuli and concentration upon the few available sensations to private reveries and fantasies and eventually to visual imagery somewhat resembling hallucinations.

"In our experiments, we notice that after immersion the day apparently is started over, i. e., the subject feels as if he has risen from bed afresh; this effect persists, and the subject finds he is out of step with the clock for the rest of the day."

Drs. Wexler, Mendelson, Leiderman, and Solomon conducted a somewhat similar experiment on seventeen paid volunteers. These subjects were "... placed in a tank-type respirator with a specially built mattress.... The vents of the respirator were left open, so that the subject breathed for himself. His arms and legs were enclosed in comfortable but rigid cylinders to inhibit movement and tactile contact. The subject lay on his back and was unable to see any part of his body. The motor of the respirator was run constantly, producing a dull, repetitive auditory stimulus. The room admitted no natural light, and artificial light was minimal and constant." (42) Although the established time limit was 36 hours and though all physical needs were taken care of, only 6 of the 17 completed the stint. The other eleven soon asked for release. Four of these terminated the experiment because of anxiety and panic; seven did so because of physical discomfort. The results confirmed earlier findings that (1) the deprivation of sensory stimuli induces stress; (2) the stress becomes unbearable for most subjects; (3) the subject has a growing need for physical and social stimuli; and (4) some subjects progressively lose touch with reality, focus inwardly, and produce delusions, hallucinations, and other pathological effects.

In summarizing some scientific reporting on sensory and perceptual deprivation, Kubzansky offers the following observations:

"Three studies suggest that the more well-adjusted or 'normal' the subject is, the more he is affected by deprivation of sensory stimuli. Neurotic and psychotic subjects are either comparatively unaffected or show decreases in anxiety, hallucinations, etc."

These findings suggest - but by no means prove - the following theories about solitary confinement and isolation:

1. The more completely the place of confinement eliminates sensory stimuli, the more rapidly and deeply will the interrogatee be affected. Results produced only after weeks or months of imprisonment in an ordinary cell can be duplicated in hours or days in a cell which has no light (or weak artificial light which never varies), which is sound-proofed, in which odors are eliminated, etc. An environment still more subject to control, such as water-tank or iron lung, is even more effective.

2. An early effect of such an environment is anxiety. How soon it appears and how strong it is depends upon the psychological characteristics of the individual.

3. The interrogator can benefit from the subject's anxiety. As the interrogator becomes linked in the

subject's mind with the reward of lessened anxiety, human contact, and meaningful activity, and thus with providing relief for growing discomfort, the questioner assumes a benevolent role.

4. The deprivation of stimuli induces regression by depriving the subject's mind of contact with an outer world and thus forcing it in upon itself. At the same time, the calculated provision of stimuli during interrogation tends to make the regressed subject view the interrogator as a father-figure. The result, normally, is a strengthening of the subject's tendencies toward compliance.

Threats and Fear

The threat of coercion usually weakens or destroys resistance more effectively than coercion itself. The threat to inflict pain, for example, can trigger fears more damaging than the immediate sensation of pain. In fact, most people underestimate their capacity to withstand pain. The same principle holds for other fears: sustained long enough, a strong fear of anything vague or unknown induces regression, whereas the materialization of the fear, the infliction of some form of punishment, is likely to come as a relief. The subject finds that he can hold out, and his resistances are strengthened. "In general, direct physical brutality creates only resentment, hostility, and further defiance."

The effectiveness of a threat depends not only on what sort of person the interrogatee is and whether he believes that his questioner can and will carry the threat out but also on the interrogator's reasons for threatening. If the interrogator threatens because he is angry, the subject frequently senses the fear of failure underlying the anger and is strengthened in his own resolve to resist. Threats delivered coldly are more effective than those shouted in rage. It is especially important that a threat not be uttered in response to the interrogatee's own expressions of hostility. These, if ignored, can induce feelings of guilt, whereas retorts in kind relieve the subject's feelings.

Another reason why threats induce compliance not evoked by the inflection of duress is that the threat grants the interrogatee time for compliance. It is not enough that a resistant source should placed under the tension of fear; he must also discern an acceptable escape route. Biderman observes, "Not only can the shame or guilt of defeat in the encounter with the interrogator be involved, but also the more fundamental injunction to protect one's self-autonomy or 'will'.... A simple defense against threats to the self from the anticipation of being forced to comply is, of course, to comply 'deliberately' or 'voluntarily'.... To the extent that the foregoing interpretation holds, the more intensely motivated the [interrogatee] is to resist, the more intense is the pressure toward early compliance from such anxieties, for the greater is the threat to self-esteem which is involved in contemplating the possibility of being 'forced to' comply...." In brief, the threat is like all other coercive techniques in being most effective when so used as to foster regression and when joined with a suggested way out of the dilemma, a rationalization acceptable to the interrogatee.

The threat of death has often been found to be worse than useless. It "has the highest position in law as a defense, but in many interrogation situations it is a highly ineffective threat. Many prisoners, in fact, have refused to yield in the face of such threats who have subsequently been 'broken' by other procedures." The principal reason is that the ultimate threat is likely to induce sheer hopelessness if the interrogatee does not believe that it is a trick; he feels that he is as likely to be condemned after compliance as before. The threat of death is also ineffective when used against hard-headed types who realize that silencing them forever would defeat the interrogator's purpose. If the threat is recognized as a bluff, it will not only fail but also pave the way to failure for later coercive ruses used by the interrogator.

Debility

No report of scientific investigation of the effect of debility upon the interrogatee's powers of resistance has been discovered. For centuries interrogators have employed various methods of inducing physical weakness: prolonged constraint; prolonged exertion; extremes of heat, cold, or moisture; and deprivation or drastic reduction of food or sleep. Apparently the assumption is that lowering the source's physiological resistance will lower his psychological capacity for opposition. If this notion were valid, however, it might reasonably be expected that those subjects who are physically weakest at the beginning of an interrogation would be the quickest to capitulate, a concept not supported by experience.

The available evidence suggests that resistance is sapped principally by psychological rather than physical pressures. The threat of debility - for example, a brief deprivation of food - may induce much more anxiety than prolonged hunger, which will result after a while in apathy and, perhaps, eventual delusions or hallucinations. In brief, it appears probable that the techniques of inducing debility become counter-productive at an early stage. The discomfort, tension, and restless search for an avenue of escape are followed by withdrawal symptoms, a turning away from external stimuli, and a sluggish unresponsiveness.

Another objection to the deliberate inducing of debility is that prolonged exertion, loss of sleep, etc., themselves become patterns to which the subject adjusts through apathy. The interrogator should use his power over the resistant subject's physical environment to disrupt patterns of response, not to create them. Meals and sleep granted irregularly, in more than abundance or less than adequacy, the shifts occurring on no discernible time pattern, will normally disorient an interrogatee and sap his will to resist more effectively than a sustained deprivation leading to debility.

Pain

Everyone is aware that people react very differently to pain. The reason, apparently, is not a physical difference in the intensity of the sensation itself. Lawrence E. Hinkle observes, "The sensation of pain seems to be roughly equal in all men, that is to say, all people have approximately the same threshold at which they begin to feel pain, and when carefully graded stimuli are applied to them, their estimates of severity are approximately the same.... Yet... when men are very highly motivated... they have been known to carry out rather complex tasks while enduring the most intense pain." He also states, "In general, it appears that whatever may be the role of the constitutional endowment in determining the reaction to pain, it is a much less important determinant than is the attitude of the man who experiences the pain."

The wide range of individual reactions to pain may be partially explicable in terms of early conditioning. The person whose first encounters with pain were frightening and intense may be more violently affected by its later infliction than one whose original experiences were mild. Or the reverse may be true, and the man whose childhood familiarized him with pain may dread it less, and react less, than one whose distress is heightened by fear of the unknown. The individual remains the determinant.

It has been plausibly suggested that, whereas pain inflicted on a person from outside himself may actually focus or intensify his will to resist, his resistance is likelier to be sapped by pain which he seems to inflict upon himself. "In the simple torture situation the contest is one between the individual and his tormentor (.... and he can frequently endure). When the individual is told to stand at attention for long periods, an intervening factor is introduced. The immediate source of pain is not the interrogator but the victim himself. The motivational strength of the individual is likely to exhaust itself in this internal encounter.... As long as the subject remains standing, he is attributing to his captor the power to do something worse to him, but there is actually no showdown of the ability of the interrogator to do so."

Interrogatees who are withholding but who feel qualms of guilt and a secret desire to yield are likely to become intractable if made to endure pain. The reason is that they can then interpret the pain as punishment and hence as expiation. There are also persons who enjoy pain and its anticipation and who will keep back information that they might otherwise divulge if they are given reason to expect that withholding will result in the punishment that they want. Persons of considerable moral or intellectual stature often find in pain inflicted by others a confirmation of the belief that they are in the hands of inferiors, and their resolve not to submit is strengthened.

Intense pain is quite likely to produce false confessions, concocted as a means of escaping from distress. A time-consuming delay results, while investigation is conducted and the admissions are proven untrue. During this respite the interrogatee can pull himself together. He may even use the time to think up new, more complex "admissions" that take still longer to disprove. KUBARK is especially vulnerable to such tactics because the interrogation is conducted for the sake of information and not for police purposes.

If an interrogatee is caused to suffer pain rather late in the interrogation process and after other tactics have failed, he is almost certain to conclude that the interrogator is becoming desperate. He may then decide that if he can just hold out against this final assault, he will win the struggle and his freedom. And he is likely to be right. Interrogatees who have withstood pain are more difficult to handle by other methods. The effect has been not to repress the subject but to restore his confidence and maturity.

Heightened Suggestibility and Hypnosis

In recent years a number of hypotheses about hypnosis have been advanced by psychologists and others in the guise of proven principles. Among these are the flat assertions that a person cannot be hypnotized against his will; that while hypnotized

378

he cannot be induced to divulge information that he wants urgently to conceal; and that he will not undertake, in trance or through post-hypnotic suggestion, actions to which he would normally have serious moral or ethical objections. If these and related contentions were proven valid, hypnosis would have scant value for the interrogator.

But despite the fact that hypnosis has been an object of scientific inquiry for a very long time, none of these theories has yet been tested adequately. Each of them is in conflict with some observations of fact. In any event, an interrogation handbook cannot and need not include a lengthy discussion of hypnosis. The case officer or interrogator needs to know enough about the subject to understand the circumstances under which hypnosis can be a useful tool, so that he can request expert assistance appropriately.

Operational personnel, including interrogators, who chance to have some lay experience or skill in hypnotism should not themselves use hypnotic techniques for interrogation or other operational purposes. There are two reasons for this position. The first is that hypnotism used as an operational tool by a practitioner who is not a psychologist, psychiatrist, or M.D. can produce irreversible psychological damage. The lay practitioner does not know enough to use the technique safely. The second reason is that an unsuccessful attempt to hypnotize a subject for purposes of interrogation, or a successful attempt not adequately covered by post-hypnotic amnesia or other protection, can easily lead to lurid and embarrassing publicity or legal charges.

Hypnosis is frequently called a state of heightened suggestibility, but the phrase is a description rather than a definition. Merton M. Gill and Margaret Brenman state, "The psychoanalytic theory of hypnosis clearly implies, where it does not explicitly state, that hypnosis is a form of regression." And they add, "...induction [of hypnosis] is the process of bringing about a regression, while the hypnotic state is the established regression." It is suggested that the interrogator will find this definition the most useful. The problem of overcoming the resistance of an uncooperative interrogatee is essentially a problem of inducing regression to a level at which the resistance can no longer be sustained. Hypnosis is one way of regressing people.

Martin T. Orne has written at some length about hypnosis and interrogation. Almost all of his conclusions are tentatively negative. Concerning the role played by the will or attitude of the interrogates, Orne says, "Although the crucial experiment has not yet been done, there is little or no evidence to indicate that trance can be induced against a person's wishes." He adds, "...the actual occurrence of the trance state is related to the wish of the subject to enter hypnosis." And he also observes, "...whether a subject will or will not enter trance depends upon his relationship with the hyponotist rather than upon the technical procedure of trance induction."

These views are probably representative of those of many psychologists, but they are not definitive. As Orne himself later points out, the interrogatee "... could be given a hypnotic drug with appropriate verbal suggestions to talk about a given topic. Eventually enough of the drug would be given to cause a short period of unconsciousness. When the subject wakes, the interrogator could then read from his 'notes' of the hypnotic interview the information presumably told him." (Orne had previously pointed out that this technique requires that the interrogator possess significant information about the subject without the subject's knowledge.) "It can readily be seen how this... maneuver... would facilitate the elicitation of information in subsequent interviews." Techniques of inducing trance in resistant subjects through preliminary administration of so-called silent drugs (drugs which the subject does not know he has taken) or through other non-routine methods of induction are still under investigation. Until more facts are known, the question of whether a resister can be hypnotized involuntarily must go unanswered.

Orne also holds that even if a resister can be hypnotized, his resistance does not cease. He postulates "... that only in rare interrogation subjects would a sufficiently deep trance be obtainable to even attempt to induce the subject to discuss material which he is unwilling to discuss in the waking state. The kind of information which can be obtained in these rare instances is still an unanswered question." He adds that it is doubtful that a subject in trance could be made to reveal information which he wished to safeguard. But here too Orne seems somewhat too cautious or pessimistic. Once an interrogatee is in a hypnotic trance, his understanding of reality becomes subject to manipulation. For example, a KUBARK interrogator could tell a suspect double agent in trance that the KGB is conducting the questioning, and thus invert the whole frame of reference. In other words, Orne is probably right in holding that most recalcitrant subjects will continue effective resistance as long as the frame of reference is undisturbed. But once the subject is tricked into believing that he is talking to friend rather than foe, or that divulging the truth is the best way to serve his own purposes, his resistance will be replaced by cooperation. The value of hypnotic trance is not that it permits the interrogator to impose his will but rather that it can be used to convince the interrogatee that there is no valid reason not to be forthcoming.

A third objection raised by Orne and others is that material elicited during trance is not reliable. Orne says, "... it has been shown that the accuracy of such information... would not be guaranteed since subjects in hypnosis are fully capable of lying." Again, the observation is correct; no known manipulative method guarantees veracity. But if hypnosis is employed not as an immediate instrument for digging out the truth but rather as a way of making the subject want to align himself with his interrogators, the objection evaporates.

Hypnosis offers one advantage not inherent in other interrogation techniques or aids: the post-hypnotic suggestion. Under favorable circumstances it should be possible to administer a silent drug to a resistant source, persuade him as the drug takes effect that he is slipping into a hypnotic trance, place him under actual hypnosis as consciousness is returning, shift his frame of reference so that his reasons for resistance become reasons for cooperating, interrogate him, and conclude the session by implanting the suggestion that when he emerges from trance he will not remember anything about what has happened.

This sketchy outline of possible uses of hypnosis in the interrogation of resistant sources has no higher goal than to remind operational personnel that the technique may provide the answer to a problem not otherwise soluble. To repeat: hypnosis is distinctly not a do-it-yourself project. Therefore the interrogator, base, or center that is considering its use must anticipate the timing sufficiently not only to secure the obligatory headquarters permission but also to allow for an expert's travel time and briefing.

Narcosis

Just as the threat of pain may more effectively induce compliance than its infliction, so an interrogatee's mistaken belief that he has been drugged may make him a more useful interrogation subject than he would be under narcosis. Louis A. Gottschalk cites a group of studies as indicating "that 30 to 50 per cent of individuals are placebo reactors, that is, respond with symptomatic relief to taking an inert substance." In the interrogation situation, moreover, the effectiveness of a placebo may be enhanced because of its ability to placate the conscience. The subject's primary source of resistance to confession or divulgence may be pride, patriotism, personal loyalty to superiors, or fear of retribution if he is returned to their hands. Under such circumstances his natural desire to escape from stress by complying with the interrogator's wishes may become decisive if he is provided an acceptable rationalization for compliance. "I was drugged" is one of the best excuses.

Drugs are no more the answer to the interrogator's prayer than the polygraph, hypnosis, or other aids. Studies and reports "dealing with the validity of material extracted from reluctant informants... indicate that there is no drug which can force every informant to report all the information he has. Not only may the inveterate criminal psychopath lie under the influence of drugs which have been tested, but the relatively normal and well-adjusted individual may also successfully disguise factual data." Gottschalk reinforces the latter observation in mentioning an experiment involving drugs which indicated that "the more normal, well-integrated individuals could lie better than the guilt-ridden, neurotic subjects."

Nevertheless, drugs can be effective in overcoming resistance not dissolved by other techniques. As has already been noted, the so-called silent drug (a pharmacologically potent substance given to a person unaware of its administration) can make possible the induction of hypnotic trance in a previously unwilling subject. Gottschalk says, "The judicious choice of a drug with minimal side effects, its matching to the subject's personality, careful gauging of dosage, and a sense of timing... [make] silent administration a hard-to-equal ally for the hypnotist intent on producing self-fulfilling and inescapable suggestions... the drug effects should prove... compelling to the subject since the perceived sensations originate entirely within himself."

Particularly important is the reference to matching the drug to the personality of the interrogatee. The effect of most drugs depends more upon the personality of the subject than upon the physical characteristics of the drugs themselves. If the approval of Headquarters has been obtained and if a doctor is at hand for administration, one of the most important of the interrogator's functions is providing the doctor with a full and accurate description of the psychological make-up of the interrogatee, to facilitate the best possible choice of a drug.

Persons burdened with feelings of shame or guilt are likely to unburden themselves when drugged, especially if these feelings have been reinforced by the interrogator. And like the placebo, the drug provides an excellent rationalization of helplessness for the interrogatee who wants to yield but has hitherto been unable to violate his own values or loyalties.

Like other coercive media, drugs may affect the content of what an interrogatee divulges. Gottschalk notes that certain drugs "may give rise to psychotic manifestations such as hallucinations, illusions, delusions, or disorientation", so that "the verbal material obtained cannot always be considered valid." For this reason drugs (and the other aids discussed in this section) should not be used persistently to facilitate the interrogative debriefing that follows capitulation. Their function is to cause capitulation, to aid in the shift from resistance to cooperation. Once this shift has been accomplished, coercive techniques should be abandoned both for moral reasons and because they are unnecessary and even counter-productive.

This discussion does not include a list of drugs that have been employed for interrogation purposes or a discussion of their properties because these are medical considerations within the province of a doctor rather than an interogator.

The Detection of Malingering

The detection of malingering is obviously not an interrogation technique, coercive or otherwise. But the history of interrogation is studded with the stories of persons who have attempted, often successfully, to evade the mounting pressures of interrogation by feigning physical or mental illness. KUBARK interrogators may encounter seemingly sick or irrational interrogatees at times and places which make it difficult or next-to-impossible to summon medical or other professional assistance. Because a few tips may make it possible for the interrogator to distinguish between the malingerer and the person who is genuinely ill, and because both illness and malingering are sometimes produced by coercive interrogation, a brief discussion of the topic has been included here.

Most persons who feign a mental or physical illness do not know enough about it to deceive the well-informed. Malcolm L. Meltzer says, "The detection of malingering depends to a great extent on the simulator's failure to understand adequately the characteristics of the role he is feigning.... Often he presents symptoms which are exceedingly rare, existing mainly in the fancy of the layman. One such symptom is the delusion of misidentification, characterized by the... belief that he is some powerful or historic personage. This symptom is very unusual in true psychosis, but is used by a number of simulators. In schizophrenia, the onset tends to be gradual, delusions do not spring up full-blown over night; in simulated disorders, the onset is usually fast and delusions may be readily available. The feigned psychosis often contains many contradictory and inconsistent symptoms, rarely existing together. The malingerer tends to go to extremes in his portrayal of his symptoms; he exaggerates, over dramatizes, grimaces, shouts, is overly bizarre, and calls attention to himself in other ways....

"Another characteristic of the malingerer is that he will usually seek to evade or postpone examination. A study of the behavior of lie-detector subjects, for example, showed that persons later 'proven guilty' showed certain similarities of behavior. The guilty persons were reluctant to take the test, and they tried in various ways to postpone or delay it. They often appeared highly anxious and sometimes took a hostile attitude toward the test and the examiner. Evasive tactics sometimes appeared, such as sighing, yawning, moving about, all of which foil the examiner by obscuring the recording. Before the examination, they felt it necessary to explain why their responses might mislead the examiner into thinking they were lying. Thus the procedure of subjecting a suspected malingerer to a lie-detector test might evoke behavior which would reinforce the suspicion of fraud."

Meltzer also notes that malingerers who are not professional psychologists can usually be exposed through Rorschach tests.

An important element in malingering is the frame of mind of the examiner. A person pretending madness awakens in a professional examiner not only suspicion but also a desire to expose the fraud, whereas a well person who pretends to be concealing mental illness and who permits only a minor symptom or two to peep through is much likelier to create in the expert a desire to expose the hidden sickness.

Meltzer observes that simulated mutism and amnesia can usually be distinguished from the true states by narcoanalysis. The reason, however, is the reverse of the popular misconception. Under the influence of appropriate drugs the malingerer will persist in not speaking or in not remembering, whereas the symptoms of the genuinely afflicted will temporarily disappear. Another technique is to pretend to take the deception seriously, express grave concern, and tell the "patient" that the only remedy for his illness is a series of electric shock treatments or a frontal lobotomy.

Conclusion

A brief summary of the foregoing may help to pull the major concepts of coercive interrogation together:

1. The principal coercive techniques are arrest, detention, the deprivation of sensory stimuli, threats and fear, debility, pain, heightened suggestibility and hypnosis, and drugs.

2. If a coercive technique is to be used, or if two or more are to be employed jointly, they should be chosen for their effect upon the individual and carefully selected to match his personality.

3. The usual effect of coercion is regression. The interrogatee's mature defenses crumbles as he becomes more childlike. During the process of regression the subject may experience feelings of guilt, and it is usually useful to intensify these.

4. When regression has proceeded far enough so that the subject's desire to yield begins to overbalance his resistance, the interrogator should supply a face-saving rationalization. Like the coercive technique, the rationalization must be carefully chosen to fit the subject's personality.

5. The pressures of duress should be slackened or lifted after compliance has been obtained, so that the interrogatee's voluntary cooperation will not be impeded.

No mention has been made of what is frequently the last step in an interrogation conducted by a Communist service: the attempted conversion.

In the Western view the goal of the questioning is information; once a sufficient degree of cooperation has been obtained to permit the interrogator access to the information he seeks, he is not ordinarily concerned with the attitudes of the source.

Under some circumstances, however, this pragmatic indifference can be short-sighted. If the interrogatee remains semi-hostile or remorseful after a successful interrogation has ended, less time may be required to complete his conversion (and conceivably to create an enduring asset) than might be needed to deal with his antagonism if he is merely squeezed and forgotten.

Chapter 18 Execution

The life of the Partisan is a life of death, and most frequently their own. With every waking moment the Partisan is acutely aware that at any time their lives may be lost due to combat or capture.

The most frequent method upon the battlefields of the world for executing Partisans is by Firing Squad, and as we have previously discussed this type of execution most often occurs after torture and interrogation.

For certain 'High Profile' Partisans however they may be confronted with being executed for their 'crimes' by the State, and if this be the case here are exampled the most commonly excepted execution methods currently used by the United States:

FIRING SQUAD

Procedure: Shooting can be carried out by a single executioner who fires from short range at the back of the head or neck as in China. The traditional firing squad is made up of three to six shooters per prisoner who stand or kneel opposite the condemned who is usually tied to a chair or to a stake.

Normally the shooters aim at the chest, since this is easier to hit than the head, causing rupture of the heart, great vessels, and lungs so that the condemned person dies of hemorrhage and shock. It is not unusual for the officer in charge to have to give the prisoner a pistol shot to the head to finish them off after the initial volley has failed to kill them.

The Utah statute authorizing execution by firing squad only provides: "If the judgment of death is to be carried out by shooting, the executive director of the department or his designee shall select a five-person firing squad of peace officers." At the appropriate time, the condemned offender is led to the execution area or chamber, which is used for both lethal injection and firing squad executions.

The offender is placed in a specially designed chair which has a pan beneath it to catch and conceal blood and other fluids. Restraints are applied to the offender's arms, legs, chest and head. A head restraint is applied loosely around the offender's neck to hold his neck and head in an upright position. The offender is dressed in a dark blue outfit with a white cloth circle attached by Velcro to the area over the offender's heart.

Behind the offender are sandbags to absorb the volley and prevent ricochets. Approximately 20 feet directly in front of the offender is a wall. This wall has firing ports for each member of the firing squad. The weapons used are 30_30 caliber rifles. No special ammunition is used.

Following the offender's statement, a hood is placed over the offender's head. The warden leaves the room. The firing squad members stand in the firing position. They support their rifles on the platform rests. With their rifle barrels in the firing ports, the team members sight through open sights on the white cloth circle on the offender's chest.

On the command to fire, the squad fires simultaneously. One squad member has a blank charge in his weapon but no member knows which member is designated to receive this blank charge.

History: In recent history only two inmates have been executed by firing squad, both in Utah: Gary Gilmore (1977) and John Albert Taylor (1996). While the method was popular with the military in times of war, there has been one such execution since the Civil War: Private Eddie Slovak in WWII.

HANGING

Procedure: Prior to any execution, the gallows area trap door and release mechanisms are inspected for proper operation. The rope, which is of manila hemp of at least 3/4"and not more than 1 1/4"in diameter and approximately 30 feet in length, is soaked and then stretched while drying to eliminate any spring, stiffness, or tendency to coil.

The hangman's knot, which is tied pursuant to military regulations, is treated with wax, soap, or clear oil, to ensure that the rope slides smoothly through the knot. The end of the rope which does not contain the noose is tied to a grommet in the ceiling and then is tied off to a metal T-shaped bracket, which takes the force delivered by the offender's drop.

Additionally, prior to an execution, the condemned offender's file is reviewed to determine if there are any unusual characteristics the offender possesses that might warrant deviation from field instructions on hanging. A physical examination and measuring process is conducted to assure almost instant death and a minimum of bruising.

If careful measuring and planning is not done, strangulation, obstructed blood flow, or beheading could result. At the appropriate time on execution day, the inmate, in restraints, is escorted to the gallows area and is placed standing over a hinged trap door from which the offender will be dropped. Following the offender's last statement, a hood is placed over the offender's head. Restraints are also applied.

If the offender refuses to stand or cannot stand, he is placed on a collapse board. A determination of the proper amount of the drop of the condemned offender through the trap door is calculated using a standard military execution chart for hanging.

The "drop" must be based on the prisoner's weight, to deliver 1260 foot_pounds of force to the neck. The noose is then placed snugly around the convict's neck, behind his or her left ear, which will cause the neck to snap. The trap door then opens, and the convict drops.

If properly done, death is caused by dislocation of the third and fourth cervical vertebrae, or by asphyxiation. A button mechanically releases the trap door and escorts then move to the lower floor location to assist in the removal of the offender's body.

History: Hanging is the oldest method of execution in the United States, but fell into disfavor in the 20th century after many botched attempts, and was replaced by electrocution as the most common method. There have been only 3 executions by hanging since 1977: Westley Dodd (WA 1993), Charles Campbell (WA 1994), and Billy Bailey (DE 1998).

LETHAL GAS

Procedure: State statutes typically and simply provide: "The punishment of death must be inflicted by the administration of a lethal gas."

The execution protocol for most jurisdictions authorizes the use of a steel airtight execution chamber, equipped with a chair and attached restraints. The inmate is restrained at his chest, waist, arms, and ankles, and wears a mask during the execution.

The chair is equipped with a metal container beneath the seat. Cyanide pellets are placed in this container. A metal canister is on the floor under the container filled with a sulfuric acid solution. There are three executioners, and each executioner turns one key.

When the three keys are turned, an electric switch causes the bottom of the cyanide container to open allowing the cyanide to fall into the sulfuric acid solution, producing a lethal gas.

Unconsciousness can occur within a few seconds if the prisoner takes a deep breath. However, if he or she holds their breath death can take much longer, and the prisoner usually goes into wild convulsions. A heart monitor attached to the inmate is read in the control room, and after the warden pronounces the inmate dead, ammonia is pumped into the execution chamber to neutralize the gas.

Exhaust fans then remove the inert fumes from the chamber into two scrubbers that contain water and serve as a neutralizing agent. The neutralizing process takes approximately 30 minutes from the time the offender's death is determined. Death is estimated to usually occur within 6 to 18 minutes of the lethal gas emissions.

The most common problems encountered are the obvious agony suffered by the inmate and the length of time to cause death.

History: The use of a gas chamber for execution was inspired by the use of poisonous gas in World War I, as well as the popularity of the gas oven as a means of suicide. Nevada became the first state to adopt execution by lethal gas in 1924 and carried out the first execution in 1924. Since then it has served as the means of carrying out the death sentence 31 times. Lethal gas was seen as an improvement over other forms of execution, because it was less violent and did not disfigure or mutilate the body. The last execution by lethal gas took place in Arizona in 1999.

ELECTROCUTION

Procedure: State statutes typically provide: "The sentence shall be executed by causing to pass through the body of the convict a current of electricity of sufficient intensity to cause death, and the application and continuance of such current through the body of such convict shall continue until such convict is dead."

The execution protocol for most jurisdictions authorizes the use of a wooden chair with restraints and connections to an electric current. The offender enters the execution chamber and is placed in the electric chair. The chair is constructed of oak and is set on a rubber matting and bolted to a concrete floor. Lap, chest, arm, and forearm straps are secured. A leg piece (anklet) is laced to the offender's right calf and a sponge and electrode is attached. The headgear consists of a metal headpiece covered with a leather hood which conceals the offender's face. The metal part of the headpiece consists of a copper wire mesh screen to which the electrode is brazened. A wet sponge is placed between the electrode and the offender's scalp.

The safety switch is closed. The circuit breaker is engaged. The execution control panel is activated. The automatic cycle begins with the programmed 2,300 volts (9.5 amps) for eight seconds, followed by 1,000 volts (4 amps) for 22 seconds, followed by 2,300 volts (9.5 amps) for eight seconds.

When the cycle is complete, the equipment is disconnected and the manual circuit behind the chair is disengaged. If the offender is not pronounced dead, the execution cycle is then repeated.

The most common problems encountered include burning of varying degrees to parts of the body, and a failure of the procedures to cause death without repeated shocks. Witness accounts of many botched executions over the years have caused electrocution to be replaced with lethal injection as the most common method of execution.

History: In 1888, New York became the first state to adopt electrocution as its method of execution. William Kemmler was the first man executed by electrocution in 1890. See, In re Kemmler, 136 U.S. 436 (1890). The last state to adopt electrocution as a method of execution was in 1949. From 1930-1980 it was clearly the most common method of execution in the United States.

LETHAL INJECTION

Procedure: State statutes typically provide: "The punishment of death must be inflicted by continuous, intravenous administration of a lethal quantity of an ultrashort-acting barbiturate in combination with a chemical paralytic agent until death is pronounced by a licensed physician according to accepted standards of medical practice."

The execution protocol for most jurisdictions authorizes the use of a combination of three drugs. The first, sodium thiopental or sodium pentothal, is a barbiturate that renders the prisoner unconscious. The second, pancuronium bromide, is a muscle relaxant that paralyzes the diaphragm and lungs. The third, potassium chloride, causes cardiac arrest. Each chemical is lethal in the amounts administered.

The inmate is escorted into the execution chamber and is strapped onto a gurney with ankle and wrist restraints. The inmate is connected to a cardiac monitor which is connected to a printer outside the execution chamber.

An IV is started in two usable veins, one in each arm, and a flow of normal saline solution is

400

administered at a slow rate. One line is held in reserve in case of a blockage or malfunction in the other.

At the warden's signal, 5.0 grams of sodium pentothal (in 20 cc of diluent) is administered, then the line is flushed with sterile normal saline solution. This is followed by 50 cc of pancuronium bromide, a saline flush, and finally, 50 cc of potassium chloride.

The most common problem encountered is collapsing veins and the inability to properly insert the IV. Some states allow for a Thorazine or sedative injection to facilitate IV insertion.

History: Lethal injection had first been proposed as a means of execution in 1888 when New York considered it but ultimately opted for electrocution. In 1977, Oklahoma became the first state to adopt lethal injection. Texas performed the first execution by lethal injection in 1982 with the execution of Charlie Brooks.

Epilogue

There is no one book that is able to provide you with all the necessary skills and information you would need to survive as a Partisan, but what we've provided you here in this book with is the basis upon which to build that knowledge.

That is all we, or anyone can do for you.

The rest of what you need to know, and do, in order to survive depends upon your own individual circumstances and means.

But, whatever your circumstances and means are there is no excuse for not beginning your preparations...now, today!

History has long shown that the survivors of any conflict, or disaster, are those that were prepared, and not just prepared with food, water, clothing and shelter, but prepared of mind. And the preparation of your mind for surviving what you have never faced before is perhaps the largest battle you will have to fight.

The armies of the world are our standing testament to that no matter how well a soldier may be trained, no matter how finely their skills are honed, when it comes to battle they may still break, and frequently do.

There is no more shocking assault to a human being than death, either in the taking of life or in simply the seeing of it. There are no movie or television fictional accounts of death that are able to prepare one for actually seeing the effects of war and disaster upon a human body. There is likewise no training or preparation that is able to acclimate you to the taking of a human life.

But these are issues to which you must prepare yourself mentally, for when it comes time for you to defend yourself, or your family, the time for thinking will be past and the time for doing will be upon you in but the blink of an eye.

But the history of our human race also shows that ordinary people do survive the assault of death upon their minds and senses, but to also forever changing you these experiences will also do.

When that time comes when you have to take a human life in war as a Partisan, you must also be prepared for the eventuality that you will have to execute your enemy. A Partisan by his or her very nature is not equipped to provide medical treatment for wounded enemies, and that is but one of the many thoughts you will have to train yourself for.

A wounded enemy left behind is also a potential threat to your life, and the lives of others who may be depending upon you. The illusions of justice and fair play in the life of a Partisan are just that, illusions.

In your actions against your enemies you must also be prepared for the fact that innocent people will die by your actions, and again you as a Partisan must reconcile yourself to this fact of war.

You must always remember that as a Partisan you are not only feared by your enemy, you are also hated, and if captured you can fully expect the harshest and most vile treatment your enemy is able to do to you....and do not think this lightly, they will savage your mind and your body, and those of anyone associated with you, with the utmost savagery.

Therefore, you must be prepared to not let yourself fall into the hands of your enemies, even if that means the taking of your own life. For those very few Partisans who throughout history have survived their capture, torture and imprisonment by their enemies the overwhelming numbers of them if given the choice to make over would have ended their lives themselves.

Is this something you can do? Can you reconcile the taking of your own life for the protection of your fellow Partisans and the saving yourself a fate worse than death with your beliefs? Think hard, very hard about this!

The fear of your enemy is also something that you must deal with beforehand, for in your enemy's propaganda they will seek to convince you that all resistance against them is utterly futile. But it isn't!

And the battlefields of the world today prove this conclusively.

In the nation of Iraq, and against the most mighty military force the world has ever known, the United States, the Partisans of that conflict still prevail. For like all Partisans before them they realize the myths that underlie superior forces...and which also your enemy will do everything in their power to keep you from knowing.

And the greatest of these myths of superior forces is that they are able to be everywhere all the time.

Far from being able to be everywhere all the time, the enemy you will face as a Partisan is a structured monolith that is governed by hierarchal structure that reduces their battlefield effectiveness.

That is not to discount the vastly superior number of forces and weapons firepower they are able to bring to bear against you, but is simply a fact that in order to wield their full force against a Partisan is a tradeoff between superior numbers and time.

And that is the Partisans most effective tool against his enemy, time. The time and speed in which a Partisan is able to attack and then retreat from battle is his greatest asset, never forget this.

The hierarchal structure of the enemy you will be facing will never be able to react to the speed of the Partisan without prior knowledge of a planned attack. That is why it is your most important battlefield lesson is to never strike your enemy at their strengths, but at their weaknesses.

And the greatest weakness your enemy has is the moral of its ordinary soldiers, who are the prime targets the Partisan must always seek out and destroy, their lives if possible, their moral to fight if not.

History has shown that Partisan operations to kill and destroy high profile enemy officers, or high profile targets, are not worth the efforts in either time or lives of Partisans expended. So remember the Partisan must also use his abilities to strike fear and not targets.

With this in mind, the first objective of the Partisan is to deny to their enemy a sense of freedom of movement or safety. This is most commonly accomplished by Partisan snipers who will randomly target enemy soldiers in the areas where they are operating.

The greatest fear of your enemy's soldiers is that of being attacked by a sniper, and the effective use of Partisan snipers greatly reduces the mobility of the enemy they are facing.

Other than the use of snipers the Partisan must always be prepared to take advantage when an unforeseen opportunity to kill an enemy presents itself. This could be an enemy vehicle that has broken down or a small group of enemy soldiers that are sitting at a café having coffee.

Remember, the more effective that Partisans are the less effective will be the enemy they are facing, and who will be forced to constantly retreat into their main bases for mutual protection by their greater numbers.

The vastly superior technology of the enemy the Partisan faces is another myth you must dispel. This is not to minimize the power of the technology you will be facing but rather to put it into battle perspective.

The greatest power upon the modern battlefield facing the Partisan is the speed at which your enemy is able to communicate with each other. The most effective way for the Partisan to defeat this advantage is to never plan their battles to last more than a few minutes. Attack and disperse. Attack and disperse. Don't forget this!

Remember, the success of a Partisan attack is not measured in the numbers of enemy soldiers killed or wounded but is instead in their demoralization. This is accomplished by denying to the enemy any semblance of safety or security. Every waking moment of your enemy must be filled with fear of the Partisans.

As repugnant as this may be to you as a human being you must also be prepared to mutilate the dead bodies of your enemies. The most historical of this is in the beheading of a captured enemy soldier and putting it on display where other enemy forces will see it.

Remember, you as a Partisan are not going to defeat your enemy by superior force but you can take away from them their will to fight. With every opportunity that presents itself you must also seek to find those ways and methods which will keep your enemy in a constant state of fear.

A Partisan must also be prepared to not allow any of his fellow countrymen to collaborate with the enemy. An enemy occupying force will always seek to provide economic benefit to the civilian population they are seeking to control, and this must always be denied to them.

For those of your fellow citizens that accept employment by the enemy forces they should be killed as an example to others of what will happen should they collaborate with the enemy.

The Partisan use of civilians working with the enemy for intelligence purposes should never be considered either. The reason for this is your enemies ability to spot those civilians and the damage their information can cause to your Partisan group should they be captured and tortured.

By not allowing your civilian population to have free contact with the enemy this also increases your enemies sense of alienation and a likewise decrease in their moral.

The recent historical examples of the United States against Vietnam, the Soviet Union against Afghanistan, and today's present example of the United States against Iraq are examples that you as Partisan should learn from. For in each of these wars the ultimate victory was achieved by the Partisan forces against a vastly superior and technologically advanced military force.

And the victory of these Partisan forces was achieved only by the complete demoralization of their enemy.

Everything you are reading here is ruthless and should go against the common sensibilities of all normal people, but war is ruthless....it is not normal, and upon entering its vile door the world that you are now accustomed to ceases to exist.

If you are not prepared to accept this then your choices are to either become a collaborator with the enemy or to become a refugee, if that is even possible.

To collaborate with the enemy is the worst of your options because it puts you into an impossible situation where you will not be protected by either the enemy forces or your own countrymen.

In being a refugee your chances of survival are greatly enhanced, but again, this is supposing that this option exists for you. Your best chances for surviving as a refugee are to have seen the conflict coming and to have left your country before hostilities have begun. [see Sorcha Faal's book Picking Up The Pieces]

The definition of a Partisan by the enemy you will be facing will also include anyone who assists you. From the youngest child, to the oldest grandmother, all are considered to be Partisan targets by your enemy.

For as the fear and destruction of moral you as a Partisan will be causing to your enemy, they will also be attempting to do to you.

Their ability to accomplish the terrorization of Partisans lies in their vastly superior firepower and weapons. Where the Partisan will utilize snipers, your enemy will utilize mass destruction.

You kill one of their soldiers; they bomb one of your villages. You destroy one of their vehicles; they launch a helicopter assault upon a town party. You blow up one of their outposts; they fire rockets at a school full of your town's children.

Since your enemy will also be in control of your country's propaganda media they will call their attacks 'accidents', or 'collateral damage'. The

Partisans they will call 'terrorists', 'cold blooded killers'.

But to whatever label your enemy puts upon you always remember, you are fighting for your freedom, they are fighting for your enslavement.

So, is your freedom...the freedom of your countrymen, worth the horrific life you would live as a Partisan? Only you are able to answer that question.

But, should you choose the path of the Partisan you will not be walking alone, for beside you will be the ghosts of all the Freedom Fighters who have taken up arms against tyrannical invaders since mankind began.

Likewise though, do not be disillusioned as to the life a Partisan lives, for it is one of death and destruction on a scale no human beings can ever prepare themselves for.

Perhaps the greatest examples of Partisans in the world's history remain those of the early 18th century American Colonies, and included such famous Partisans as: George Washington, Thomas Paine, Thomas Jefferson, Benjamin Franklin and John Adams.

And it is worth finishing the Partisan Handbook by quoting from this men, for one day, and perhaps sooner than you realize, this book may be the only thing that you possess as you lie in the burned out rubble of a building in your own town awaiting a battle that may be your last.

So, from those who had walked before you, perhaps in that dark hour you may soon be facing their words can give you both wisdom and courage.

Arbitrary power is most easily established on the ruins of liberty abused to licentiousness.
George Washington

As Mankind becomes more liberal, they will be more apt to allow that all those who conduct themselves as worthy members of the community are equally entitled to the protections of civil government. I hope ever to see America among the foremost nations of justice and liberality.
George Washington

Associate yourself with men of good quality if you esteem your own reputation. It is better be alone than in bad company.
George Washington

Bad seed is a robbery of the worst kind: for your pocket-book not only suffers by it, but your preparations are lost and a season passes away unimproved.
George Washington

412

Be courteous to all, but intimate with few, and let those few be well tried before you give them your confidence.
George Washington

Discipline is the soul of an army. It makes small numbers formidable; procures success to the weak, and esteem to all.
George Washington

Few men have virtue to withstand the highest bidder.
George Washington

Friendship is a plant of slow growth and must undergo and withstand the shocks of adversity before it is entitled to the appellation.
George Washington

Happiness and moral duty are inseparably connected.
George Washington

How soon we forget history... Government is not reason. Government is not eloquence. It is force. And, like fire, it is a dangerous servant and a fearful master.
George Washington

I have no other view than to promote the public good, and am unambitious of honors not founded in the approbation of my Country.
George Washington

I hope I shall possess firmness and virtue enough to maintain what I consider the most enviable of all titles, the character of an honest man.
George Washington

I know of no pursuit in which more real and important services can be rendered to any country than by improving its agriculture, its breed of useful animals, and other branches of a husbandman's cares.
George Washington

I walk on untrodden ground. There is scarcely any part of my conduct which may not hereafter be drawn into precedent.
George Washington

If the freedom of speech is taken away then dumb and silent we may be led, like sheep to the slaughter.
George Washington

If we desire to avoid insult, we must be able to repel it; if we desire to secure peace, one of the most powerful instruments of our rising prosperity, it must be known, that we are at all times ready for War.
George Washington

It is far better to be alone, than to be in bad company.
George Washington

It is our true policy to steer clear of entangling alliances with any portion of the foreign world.
George Washington

It is the child of avarice, the brother of iniquity, and the father of mischief.
George Washington

It may be laid down as a primary position, and the basis of our system, that every Citizen who enjoys the protection of a Free Government, owes not only a proportion of his property, but even of his personal services to the defense of it.
George Washington

It will be found an unjust and unwise jealousy to deprive a man of his natural liberty upon the supposition he may abuse it.
George Washington

Labor to keep alive in your breast that little spark of celestial fire, called conscience.
George Washington

Lenience will operate with greater force, in some instances than rigor. It is therefore my first wish to have all of my conduct distinguished by it.
George Washington

Let us raise a standard to which the wise and honest can repair; the rest is in the hands of God.
George Washington

Let us with caution indulge the supposition that morality can be maintained without religion. Reason and experience both forbid us to expect that national morality can prevail in exclusion of religious principle.
George Washington

Let your Discourse with Men of Business be Short and Comprehensive.
George Washington

Let your heart feel for the afflictions and distress of everyone, and let your hand give in proportion to your purse.
George Washington

Liberty, when it begins to take root, is a plant of rapid growth.
George Washington

Mankind, when left to themselves, are unfit for their own government.
George Washington

My first wish is to see this plague of mankind, war, banished from the earth.
George Washington

My manner of living is plain and I do not mean to be put out of it. A glass of wine and a bit of mutton are always ready.
George Washington

My mother was the most beautiful woman I ever saw. All I am I owe to my mother. I attribute all my success in life to the moral, intellectual and physical education I received from her.
George Washington

My observation is that whenever one person is found adequate to the discharge of a duty... it is worse executed by two persons, and scarcely done at all if three or more are employed therein.
George Washington

Observe good faith and justice toward all nations. Cultivate peace and harmony with all.
George Washington

Over grown military establishments are under any form of government inauspicious to liberty, and are to be regarded as particularly hostile to republican liberty.
George Washington

The constitution vests the power of declaring war in Congress; therefore no offensive expedition of importance can be undertaken until after they shall have deliberated upon the subject and authorized such a measure.
George Washington

The foolish and wicked practice of profane cursing and swearing is a vice so mean and low that every person of sense and character detests and despises it.
George Washington

The marvel of all history is the patience with which men and women submit to burdens unnecessarily laid upon them by their governments.
George Washington

The time is near at hand which must determine whether Americans are to be free men or slaves.
George Washington

The tumultuous populace of large cities are ever to be dreaded. Their indiscriminate violence prostrates for the time all public authority, and its consequences are sometimes extensive and terrible.
George Washington

The very atmosphere of firearms anywhere and everywhere restrains evil interference - they deserve a place of honor with all that's good.
George Washington

To be prepared for war is one of the most effective means of preserving peace.
George Washington

True friendship is a plant of slow growth, and must undergo and withstand the shocks of adversity, before it is entitled to the appellation.
George Washington

War - An act of violence whose object is to constrain the enemy, to accomplish our will.
George Washington

We should not look back unless it is to derive useful lessons from past errors, and for the purpose of profiting by dearly bought experience.
George Washington

When firearms go, all goes. We need them every hour.
George Washington

When we assumed the Soldier, we did not lay aside the Citizen.
George Washington

Worry is the interest paid by those who borrow trouble.
George Washington

A bad cause will never be supported by bad means and bad men.
Thomas Paine

A long habit of not thinking a thing wrong gives it a superficial appearance of being right.
Thomas Paine

A thing moderately good is not so good as it ought to be. Moderation in temper is always a virtue; but moderation in principle is always a vice.
Thomas Paine

An army of principles can penetrate where an army of soldiers cannot.
Thomas Paine

Arms discourage and keep the invader and plunderer in awe, and preserve order in the world as well as property... Horrid mischief would ensue were the law-abiding deprived of the use of them.
Thomas Paine

Belief in a cruel God makes a cruel man.
Thomas Paine

But such is the irresistible nature of truth, that all it asks, and all it wants is the liberty of appearing.
Thomas Paine

Character is much easier kept than recovered.
Thomas Paine

Every science has for its basis a system of principles as fixed and unalterable as those by which the universe is regulated and governed. Man cannot make principles; he can only discover them.
Thomas Paine

From such beginnings of governments, what could be expected, but a continual system of war and extortion?
Thomas Paine

Government, even in its best state, is but a necessary evil; in its worst state, an intolerable one.
Thomas Paine

He that would make his own liberty secure, must guard even his enemy from opposition; for if he violates this duty he establishes a precedent that will reach himself.
Thomas Paine

Human nature is not of itself vicious.
Thomas Paine

I believe in the equality of man; and I believe that religious duties consist in doing justice, loving mercy, and endeavoring to make our fellow-creatures happy.
Thomas Paine

I do not believe in the creed professed by the Jewish Church, by the Roman Church, by the Greek Church, by the Turkish Church, by the Protestant Church, nor by any church that I know of. My own mind is my own church.
Thomas Paine

I love the man that can smile in trouble, that can gather strength from distress, and grow brave by reflection. 'Tis the business of little minds to shrink, but he whose heart is firm, and whose conscience approves his conduct, will pursue his principles unto death.
Thomas Paine

If there must be trouble, let it be in my day, that my child may have peace.
Thomas Paine

If we do not hang together, we shall surely hang separately.
Thomas Paine

It is necessary to the happiness of man that he be mentally faithful to himself. Infidelity does not consist in believing, or in disbelieving, it consists in professing to believe what he does not believe.
Thomas Paine

It is not a field of a few acres of ground, but a cause, that we are defending, and whether we defeat the enemy in one battle, or by degrees, the consequences will be the same.
Thomas Paine

It is the direction and not the magnitude which is to be taken into consideration.
Thomas Paine

Lead, follow, or get out of the way.
Thomas Paine

My country is the world, and my religion is to do good.
Thomas Paine

My mind is my own church.
Thomas Paine

Reason obeys itself; and ignorance submits to whatever is dictated to it.
Thomas Paine

Reputation is what men and women think of us; character is what God and angels know of us.
Thomas Paine

Society in every state is a blessing, but government, even in its best stage, is but a necessary evil; in its worst state an intolerable one.
Thomas Paine

That government is best which governs least.
Thomas Paine

That which we obtain too easily, we esteem too lightly.
Thomas Paine

The abilities of man must fall short on one side or the other, like too scanty a blanket when you are abed. If you pull it upon your shoulders, your feet

are left bare; if you thrust it down to your feet, your shoulders are uncovered.
Thomas Paine

The greatest remedy for anger is delay.
Thomas Paine

The harder the conflict, the more glorious the triumph.
Thomas Paine

The instant formal government is abolished, society begins to act. A general association takes place, and common interest produces common security.
Thomas Paine

The most formidable weapon against errors of every kind is reason.
Thomas Paine

The Vatican is a dagger in the heart of Italy.
Thomas Paine

The whole religious complexion of the modern world is due to the absence from Jerusalem of a lunatic asylum.
Thomas Paine

The World is my country, all mankind are my brethren, and to do good is my religion.
Thomas Paine

There are two distinct classes of what are called thoughts: those that we produce in ourselves by reflection and the act of thinking and those that bolt into the mind of their own accord.
Thomas Paine

These are times that try men's souls. The summer soldier and the sunshine patriot will, in this crisis, shrink from the service of their country; but he that stands now, deserves the love and thanks of man and woman.
Thomas Paine

Those who expect to reap the blessings of freedom must, like men, undergo the fatigue of supporting it.
Thomas Paine

Time makes more converts than reason.
Thomas Paine

'Tis the business of little minds to shrink; but he whose heart is firm, and whose conscience approves his conduct, will pursue his principles unto death.
Thomas Paine

Titles are but nicknames, and every nickname is a title.
Thomas Paine

To establish any mode to abolish war, however advantageous it might be to Nations, would be to take from such Government the most lucrative of its branches.
Thomas Paine

To say that any people are not fit for freedom, is to make poverty their choice, and to say they had rather be loaded with taxes than not.
Thomas Paine

Virtues are acquired through endeavor, Which rests wholly upon yourself. So, to praise others for their virtues Can but encourage one's own efforts.
Thomas Paine

War involves in its progress such a train of unforeseen and unsupposed circumstances that no human wisdom can calculate the end. It has but one thing certain, and that is to increase taxes.
Thomas Paine

We can only reason from what is; we can reason on actualities, but not on possibilities.
Thomas Paine

We have it in our power to begin the world over again.
Thomas Paine

What we obtain too cheap, we esteem too lightly; it is dearness only that gives everything its value.
Thomas Paine

When men yield up the privilege of thinking, the last shadow of liberty quits the horizon.
Thomas Paine

When we are planning for posterity, we ought to remember that virtue is not hereditary.
Thomas Paine

A Bill of Rights is what the people are entitled to against every government, and what no just government should refuse, or rest on inference.
Thomas Jefferson

A coward is much more exposed to quarrels than a man of spirit.
Thomas Jefferson

A democracy is nothing more than mob rule, where fifty-one percent of the people may take away the rights of the other forty-nine.
Thomas Jefferson

A superintending power to maintain the Universe in its course and order.
Thomas Jefferson

A wise and frugal government, which shall leave men free to regulate their own pursuits of industry and improvement, and shall not take from the mouth of labor and bread it has earned - this is the sum of good government.
Thomas Jefferson

Advertisements contain the only truths to be relied on in a newspaper.
Thomas Jefferson

All tyranny needs to gain a foothold is for people of good conscience to remain silent.
Thomas Jefferson

All, too, will bear in mind this sacred principle, that though the will of the majority is in all cases to prevail, that will to be rightful must be reasonable; that the minority possess their equal rights, which equal law must protect, and to violate would be oppression.
Thomas Jefferson

Always take hold of things by the smooth handle.
Thomas Jefferson

An association of men who will not quarrel with one another is a thing which has never yet existed, from the greatest confederacy of nations down to a town meeting or a vestry.
Thomas Jefferson

An enemy generally says and believes what he wishes.
Thomas Jefferson

At last now you can be what the old cannot recall and the young long for in dreams, yet still include them all.
Thomas Jefferson

Banking establishments are more dangerous than standing armies.
Thomas Jefferson

Bodily decay is gloomy in prospect, but of all human contemplations the most abhorrent is body without mind.
Thomas Jefferson

But friendship is precious, not only in the shade, but in the sunshine of life, and thanks to a benevolent arrangement the greater part of life is sunshine.
Thomas Jefferson

Commerce with all nations, alliance with none, should be our motto.
Thomas Jefferson

Conquest is not in our principles. It is inconsistent with our government.
Thomas Jefferson

Delay is preferable to error.
Thomas Jefferson

Dependence begets subservience and venality, suffocates the germ of virtue, and prepares fit tools for the designs of ambition.
Thomas Jefferson

Determine never to be idle. No person will have occasion to complain of the want of time who never

loses any. It is wonderful how much may be done if we are always doing.
Thomas Jefferson

Do not bite at the bait of pleasure, till you know there is no hook beneath it.
Thomas Jefferson

Do you want to know who you are? Don't ask. Act! Action will delineate and define you.
Thomas Jefferson

Don't talk about what you have done or what you are going to do.
Thomas Jefferson

Educate and inform the whole mass of the people... They are the only sure reliance for the preservation of our liberty.
Thomas Jefferson

Enlighten the people generally, and tyranny and oppressions of body and mind will vanish like evil spirits at the dawn of day.
Thomas Jefferson

Errors of opinion may be tolerated where reason is left free to combat it.
Thomas Jefferson

Every citizen should be a soldier. This was the case with the Greeks and Romans, and must be that of every free state.
Thomas Jefferson

Every generation needs a new revolution.
Thomas Jefferson

Experience demands that man is the only animal which devours his own kind, for I can apply no milder term to the general prey of the rich on the poor.
Thomas Jefferson

Experience hath shewn, that even under the best forms of government those entrusted with power have, in time, and by slow operations, perverted it into tyranny.
Thomas Jefferson

Fix reason firmly in her seat, and call to her tribunal every fact, every opinion. Question with boldness even the existence of a God; because, if there be one, he must more approve of the homage of reason, than that of blindfolded fear.
Thomas Jefferson

For a people who are free, and who mean to remain so, a well-organized and armed militia is their best security.
Thomas Jefferson

For here we are not afraid to follow truth wherever it may lead.
Thomas Jefferson

Force is the vital principle and immediate parent of despotism.
Thomas Jefferson

Friendship is but another name for an alliance with the follies and the misfortunes of others. Our own share of miseries is sufficient: why enter then as volunteers into those of another?
Thomas Jefferson

Great innovations should not be forced on slender majorities.
Thomas Jefferson

Happiness is not being pained in body or troubled in mind.
Thomas Jefferson

He who knows nothing is closer to the truth than he whose mind is filled with falsehoods and errors.
Thomas Jefferson

History, in general, only informs us of what bad government is.
Thomas Jefferson

Honesty is the first chapter in the book of wisdom.
Thomas Jefferson

How much have cost us the evils that never happened!
Thomas Jefferson

How much pain they have cost us, the evils which have never happened.
Thomas Jefferson

I abhor war and view it as the greatest scourge of mankind.
Thomas Jefferson

I am an Epicurean. I consider the genuine (not the imputed) doctrines of Epicurus as containing everything rational in moral philosophy which Greek and Roman leave to us.
Thomas Jefferson

I am mortified to be told that, in the United States of America, the sale of a book can become a subject of inquiry, and of criminal inquiry too.
Thomas Jefferson

I believe that banking institutions are more dangerous to our liberties than standing armies. Already they have raised up a monied aristocracy that has set the government at defiance. The issuing power should be taken from the banks and restored to the people to whom it properly belongs.
Thomas Jefferson

I believe that every human mind feels pleasure in doing good to another.
Thomas Jefferson

I cannot live without books.
Thomas Jefferson

I do not find in orthodox Christianity one redeeming feature.
Thomas Jefferson

I do not take a single newspaper, nor read one a month, and I feel myself infinitely the happier for it.
Thomas Jefferson

I find that the harder I work, the more luck I seem to have.
Thomas Jefferson

I have no ambition to govern men; it is a painful and thankless office.
Thomas Jefferson

I have recently been examining all the known superstitions of the world, and do not find in our particular superstition (Christianity) one redeeming feature. They are all alike founded on fables and mythology.
Thomas Jefferson

I have sworn upon the alter of God, eternal hostility against every form of tyranny over the mind of man.
Thomas Jefferson

I hope our wisdom will grow with our power, and teach us, that the less we use our power the greater it will be.
Thomas Jefferson

I hope we shall crush in its birth the aristocracy of our monied corporations which dare already to challenge our government to a trial by strength, and bid defiance to the laws of our country.
Thomas Jefferson

I know of no safe depository of the ultimate powers of the society but the people themselves; and if we think them not enlightened enough to exercise their control with a wholesome discretion, the remedy is not to take it from them but to inform their discretion.
Thomas Jefferson

I like the dreams of the future better than the history of the past.
Thomas Jefferson

I own that I am not a friend to a very energetic government. It is always oppressive.
Thomas Jefferson

I predict future happiness for Americans if they can prevent the government from wasting the labors of the people under the pretense of taking care of them.
Thomas Jefferson

I sincerely believe that banking establishments are more dangerous than standing armies, and that the principle of spending money to be paid by posterity, under the name of funding, is but swindling futurity on a large scale.
Thomas Jefferson

I think with the Romans, that the general of today should be a soldier tomorrow if necessary.
Thomas Jefferson

I tremble for my country when I reflect that God is just; that his justice cannot sleep forever.
Thomas Jefferson

I was bold in the pursuit of knowledge, never fearing to follow truth and reason to whatever results they led, and bearding every authority which stood in their way.
Thomas Jefferson

I would rather be exposed to the inconveniences attending too much liberty than those attending too small a degree of it.
Thomas Jefferson

I'm a great believer in luck and I find the harder I work, the more I have of it.
Thomas Jefferson

If a nation expects to be ignorant and free, in a state of civilization, it expects what never was and never will be.
Thomas Jefferson

If God is just, I tremble for my country.
Thomas Jefferson

If the present Congress errs in too much talking, how can it be otherwise in a body to which the people send one hundred and fifty lawyers, whose trade it is to question everything, yield nothing, and talk by the hour?
Thomas Jefferson

If there is one principle more deeply rooted in the mind of every American, it is that we should have nothing to do with conquest.
Thomas Jefferson

Ignorance is preferable to error, and he is less remote from the truth who believes nothing than he who believes what is wrong.
Thomas Jefferson

In every country and every age, the priest had been hostile to Liberty.
Thomas Jefferson

In matters of style, swim with the current; in matters of principle, stand like a rock.
Thomas Jefferson

In truth, politeness is artificial good humor, it covers the natural want of it, and ends by rendering habitual a substitute nearly equivalent to the real virtue.
Thomas Jefferson

It behooves every man who values liberty of conscience for himself, to resist invasions of it in the case of others: or their case may, by change of circumstances, become his own.
Thomas Jefferson

It does me no injury for my neighbor to say there are twenty gods or no God.
Thomas Jefferson

It is always better to have no ideas than false ones; to believe nothing, than to believe what is wrong.
Thomas Jefferson

It is error alone which needs the support of government. Truth can stand by itself.
Thomas Jefferson

It is in our lives and not our words that our religion must be read.
Thomas Jefferson

It is incumbent on every generation to pay its own debts as it goes. A principle which if acted on would save one-half the wars of the world.
Thomas Jefferson

It is more dangerous that even a guilty person should be punished without the forms of law than that he should escape.
Thomas Jefferson

It is neither wealth nor splendor; but tranquility and occupation which give you happiness.
Thomas Jefferson

It is our duty still to endeavor to avoid war; but if it shall actually take place, no matter by whom brought on, we must defend ourselves. If our house be on fire, without inquiring whether it was fired from within or without, we must try to extinguish it.
Thomas Jefferson

Leave all the afternoon for exercise and recreation, which are as necessary as reading. I will rather say more necessary because health is worth more than learning.
Thomas Jefferson

Liberty is to the collective body, what health is to every individual body. Without health no pleasure can be tasted by man; without liberty, no happiness can be enjoyed by society.
Thomas Jefferson

Mankind are more disposed to suffer, while evils are sufferable, than to right themselves by abolishing the forms to which they are accustomed.
Thomas Jefferson

Merchants have no country. The mere spot they stand on does not constitute so strong an attachment as that from which they draw their gains.
Thomas Jefferson

Money, not morality, is the principle commerce of civilized nations.
Thomas Jefferson

My only fear is that I may live too long. This would be a subject of dread to me.
Thomas Jefferson

My reading of history convinces me that most bad government results from too much government.
Thomas Jefferson

My theory has always been, that if we are to dream, the flatteries of hope are as cheap, and pleasanter, than the gloom of despair.
Thomas Jefferson

Nations of eternal war [expend] all their energies... in the destruction of the labor, property, and lives of their people.
Thomas Jefferson

Never put off till tomorrow what you can do today.
Thomas Jefferson

Never spend your money before you have earned it.
Thomas Jefferson

No duty the Executive had to perform was so trying as to put the right man in the right place.
Thomas Jefferson

No free man shall ever be debarred the use of arms.
Thomas Jefferson

No man will ever carry out of the Presidency the reputation which carried him into it.
Thomas Jefferson

No occupation is so delightful to me as the culture of the earth, and no culture comparable to that of the garden.
Thomas Jefferson

Nothing can stop the man with the right mental attitude from achieving his goal; nothing on earth can help the man with the wrong mental attitude.
Thomas Jefferson

Nothing gives one person so much advantage over another as to remain always cool and unruffled under all circumstances.
Thomas Jefferson

One man with courage is a majority.
Thomas Jefferson

Only aim to do your duty, and mankind will give you credit where you fail.
Thomas Jefferson

Our country is now taking so steady a course as to show by what road it will pass to destruction, to wit: by consolidation of power first, and then corruption, its necessary consequence.
Thomas Jefferson

Our greatest happiness does not depend on the condition of life in which chance has placed us, but is always the result of a good conscience, good health, occupation, and freedom in all just pursuits.
Thomas Jefferson

Peace and abstinence from European interferences are our objects, and so will continue while the present order of things in America remain uninterrupted.
Thomas Jefferson

Peace and friendship with all mankind is our wisest policy, and I wish we may be permitted to pursue it.
Thomas Jefferson

Peace, commerce and honest friendship with all nations; entangling alliances with none.
Thomas Jefferson

Politics is such a torment that I advise everyone I love not to mix with it.
Thomas Jefferson

Question with boldness even the existence of a God; because, if there be one, he must more approve of the homage of reason, than that of blind-folded fear.
Thomas Jefferson

Resort is had to ridicule only when reason is against us.
Thomas Jefferson

Rightful liberty is unobstructed action according to our will within limits drawn around us by the equal rights of others. I do not add 'within the limits of the law' because law is often but the tyrant's will, and always so when it violates the rights of the individual.
Thomas Jefferson

So confident am I in the intentions, as well as wisdom, of the government, that I shall always be satisfied that what is not done, either cannot, or ought not to be done.
Thomas Jefferson

Sometimes it is said that man cannot be trusted with the government of himself. Can he, then be trusted with the government of others? Or have we found angels in the form of kings to govern him? Let history answer this question.
Thomas Jefferson

Speeches that are measured by the hour will die with the hour.
Thomas Jefferson

Taste cannot be controlled by law.
Thomas Jefferson

That government is best which governs the least, because its people discipline themselves.
Thomas Jefferson

That government is the strongest of which every man feels himself a part.
Thomas Jefferson

The advertisement is the most truthful part of a newspaper.
Thomas Jefferson

The boisterous sea of liberty is never without a wave.
Thomas Jefferson

The care of human life and happiness, and not their destruction, is the first and only object of good government.
Thomas Jefferson

The Creator has not thought proper to mark those in the forehead who are of stuff to make good generals. We are first, therefore, to seek them blindfold, and then let them learn the trade at the expense of great losses.
Thomas Jefferson

The democracy will cease to exist when you take away from those who are willing to work and give to those who would not.
Thomas Jefferson

The earth belongs to the living, not to the dead.
Thomas Jefferson

The glow of one warm thought is to me worth more than money.
Thomas Jefferson

The God who gave us life, gave us liberty at the same time.
Thomas Jefferson

The good opinion of mankind, like the lever of Archimedes, with the given fulcrum, moves the world.
Thomas Jefferson

The legitimate powers of government extend to such acts only as they are injurious to others.
Thomas Jefferson

The man who reads nothing at all is better educated than the man who reads nothing but newspapers.
Thomas Jefferson

The most successful war seldom pays for its losses.
Thomas Jefferson

The most valuable of all talents is that of never using two words when one will do.
Thomas Jefferson

The natural cause of the human mind is certainly from credulity to skepticism.
Thomas Jefferson

The natural progress of things is for liberty to yield and government to gain ground.
Thomas Jefferson

The second office in the government is honorable and easy; the first is but a splendid misery.
Thomas Jefferson

The spirit of resistance to government is so valuable on certain occasions that I wish it to be always kept alive.
Thomas Jefferson

The spirit of this country is totally adverse to a large military force.
Thomas Jefferson

The strongest reason for the people to retain the right to keep and bear arms is, as a last resort, to protect themselves against tyranny in government.
Thomas Jefferson

The tree of liberty must be refreshed from time to time with the blood of patriots and tyrants.
Thomas Jefferson

The whole commerce between master and slave is a perpetual exercise of the most boisterous passions, the most unremitting despotism on the one part, and degrading submissions on the other. Our children see this, and learn to imitate it.
Thomas Jefferson

The world is indebted for all triumphs which have been gained by reason and humanity over error and oppression.
Thomas Jefferson

There is a natural aristocracy among men. The grounds of this are virtue and talents.
Thomas Jefferson

There is not a sprig of grass that shoots uninteresting to me.
Thomas Jefferson

There is not a truth existing which I fear... or would wish unknown to the whole world.
Thomas Jefferson

Timid men prefer the calm of despotism to the tempestuous sea of liberty.
Thomas Jefferson

To compel a man to subsidize with his taxes the propagation of ideas which he disbelieves and abhors is sinful and tyrannical.
Thomas Jefferson

To myself, personally, it brings nothing but increasing drudgery and daily loss of friends.
Thomas Jefferson

To preserve our independence... We must make our election between economy and liberty, or profusion and servitude.
Thomas Jefferson

Truth is certainly a branch of morality and a very important one to society.
Thomas Jefferson

Walking is the best possible exercise. Habituate yourself to walk very fast.
Thomas Jefferson

War is an instrument entirely inefficient toward redressing wrong; and multiplies, instead of indemnifying losses.
Thomas Jefferson

We are not to expect to be translated from despotism to liberty in a featherbed.
Thomas Jefferson

We confide in our strength, without boasting of it; we respect that of others, without fearing it.
Thomas Jefferson

We did not raise armies for glory or for conquest.
Thomas Jefferson

We hold these truths to be self-evident: that all men are created equal; that they are endowed by their Creator with certain unalienable rights; that among these are life, liberty, and the pursuit of happiness.
Thomas Jefferson

We may consider each generation as a distinct nation, with a right, by the will of its majority, to bind themselves, but none to bind the succeeding generation, more than the inhabitants of another country.
Thomas Jefferson

We never repent of having eaten too little.
Thomas Jefferson

Were it left to me to decide whether we should have a government without newspapers, or newspapers without a government, I should not hesitate a moment to prefer the latter.
Thomas Jefferson

What an augmentation of the field for jobbing, speculating, plundering, office-building and office-hunting would be produced by an assumption of all the state powers into the hands of the general government.
Thomas Jefferson

When a man assumes a public trust he should consider himself a public property.
Thomas Jefferson

When angry count to ten before you speak. If very angry, count to one hundred.
Thomas Jefferson

When the people fear their government, there is tyranny; when the government fears the people, there is liberty.
Thomas Jefferson

When we get piled upon one another in large cities, as in Europe, we shall become as corrupt as Europe.
Thomas Jefferson

When you reach the end of your rope, tie a knot in it and hang on.
Thomas Jefferson

Whenever a man has cast a longing eye on offices, a rottenness begins in his conduct.
Thomas Jefferson

Whenever the people are well-informed, they can be trusted with their own government.
Thomas Jefferson

Whenever you do a thing, act as if all the world were watching.
Thomas Jefferson

Where the press is free and every man able to read, all is safe.
Thomas Jefferson

A countryman between two lawyers is like a fish between two cats.
Benjamin Franklin

A good conscience is a continual Christmas.
Benjamin Franklin

A great empire, like a great cake, is most easily diminished at the edges.
Benjamin Franklin

A house is not a home unless it contains food and fire for the mind as well as the body.
Benjamin Franklin

A learned blockhead is a greater blockhead than an ignorant one.
Benjamin Franklin

A life of leisure and a life of laziness are two things. There will be sleeping enough in the grave.
Benjamin Franklin

A man wrapped up in himself makes a very small bundle.
Benjamin Franklin

A penny saved is a penny earned.
Benjamin Franklin

A place for everything, everything in its place.
Benjamin Franklin

A small leak can sink a great ship.
Benjamin Franklin

Absence sharpens love, presence strengthens it.
Benjamin Franklin

Admiration is the daughter of ignorance.
Benjamin Franklin

All mankind is divided into three classes: those that are immovable, those that are movable, and those that move.
Benjamin Franklin

All wars are follies, very expensive and very mischievous ones.
Benjamin Franklin

All who think cannot but see there is a sanction like that of religion which binds us in partnership in the serious work of the world.
Benjamin Franklin

An investment in knowledge pays the best interest.
Benjamin Franklin

And whether you're an honest man, or whether you're a thief, Depends on whose solicitor has given me my brief.
Benjamin Franklin

Any society that would give up a little liberty to gain a little security will deserve neither and lose both.
Benjamin Franklin

Applause waits on success.
Benjamin Franklin

As we must account for every idle word, so must we account for every idle silence.
Benjamin Franklin

At twenty years of age the will reigns; at thirty, the wit; and at forty, the judgment.
Benjamin Franklin

Be at war with your vices, at peace with your neighbors, and let every new year find you a better man.
Benjamin Franklin

Be civil to all; sociable to many; familiar with few; friend to one; enemy to none.
Benjamin Franklin

Be slow in choosing a friend, slower in changing.
Benjamin Franklin

Beauty and folly are old companions.
Benjamin Franklin

Beer is living proof that God loves us and wants us to be happy.
Benjamin Franklin

Beware of little expenses. A small leak will sink a great ship.
Benjamin Franklin

Beware the hobby that eats.
Benjamin Franklin

Buy what thou hast no need of and ere long thou shalt sell thy necessities.
Benjamin Franklin

By failing to prepare, you are preparing to fail.
Benjamin Franklin

Certainty? In this world nothing is certain but death and taxes.
Benjamin Franklin

Clean your finger before you point at my spots.
Benjamin Franklin

Creditors have better memories than debtors.
Benjamin Franklin

Diligence is the mother of good luck.
Benjamin Franklin

Distrust and caution are the parents of security.
Benjamin Franklin

Do not anticipate trouble, or worry about what may never happen. Keep in the sunlight.
Benjamin Franklin

Do not fear mistakes. You will know failure. Continue to reach out.
Benjamin Franklin

Dost thou love life? Then do not squander time, for that is the stuff life is made of.
Benjamin Franklin

Each year one vicious habit discarded, in time might make the worst of us good.
Benjamin Franklin

Eat to please thyself, but dress to please others.
Benjamin Franklin

Either write something worth reading or do something worth writing.
Benjamin Franklin

Employ thy time well, if thou meanest to gain leisure.
Benjamin Franklin

Even peace may be purchased at too high a price.
Benjamin Franklin

Experience is a dear teacher, but fools will learn at no other.
Benjamin Franklin

For having lived long, I have experienced many instances of being obliged, by better information or fuller consideration, to change opinions, even on

*important subjects, which I once thought right but
found to be otherwise.*
Benjamin Franklin

*Gain may be temporary and uncertain; but ever
while you live, expense is constant and certain: and
it is easier to build two chimneys than to keep one
in fuel.*
Benjamin Franklin

Games lubricate the body and the mind.
Benjamin Franklin

Genius without education is like silver in the mine.
Benjamin Franklin

*God works wonders now and then; Behold a
lawyer, an honest man.*
Benjamin Franklin

Guests, like fish, begin to smell after three days.
Benjamin Franklin

Half a truth is often a great lie.
Benjamin Franklin

*Having been poor is no shame, but being ashamed
of it, is.*
Benjamin Franklin

He does not possess wealth; it possesses him.
Benjamin Franklin

He that can have patience can have what he will.
Benjamin Franklin

He that composes himself is wiser than he that composes a book.
Benjamin Franklin

He that has done you a kindness will be more ready to do you another, than he whom you yourself have obliged.
Benjamin Franklin

He that is of the opinion money will do everything may well be suspected of doing everything for money.
Benjamin Franklin

He that lives upon hope will die fasting.
Benjamin Franklin

He that raises a large family does, indeed, while he lives to observe them, stand a broader mark for sorrow; but then he stands a broader mark for pleasure too.
Benjamin Franklin

He that rises late must trot all day.
Benjamin Franklin

He that waits upon fortune, is never sure of a dinner.
Benjamin Franklin

He that won't be counseled can't be helped.
Benjamin Franklin

He that would live in peace and at ease must not speak all he knows or all he sees.
Benjamin Franklin

He that's secure is not safe.
Benjamin Franklin

He who falls in love with himself will have no rivals.
Benjamin Franklin

Hear reason, or she'll make you feel her.
Benjamin Franklin

Honesty is the best policy.
Benjamin Franklin

Human felicity is produced not as much by great pieces of good fortune that seldom happen as by little advantages that occur every day.
Benjamin Franklin

Hunger is the best pickle.
Benjamin Franklin

I conceive that the great part of the miseries of mankind are brought upon them by false estimates they have made of the value of things.
Benjamin Franklin

I guess I don't so much mind being old, as I mind being fat and old.
Benjamin Franklin

I look upon death to be as necessary to our constitution as sleep. We shall rise refreshed in the morning.
Benjamin Franklin

I saw few die of hunger; of eating, a hundred thousand.
Benjamin Franklin

I should have no objection to go over the same life from its beginning to the end: requesting only the advantage authors have, of correcting in a second edition the faults of the first.
Benjamin Franklin

I wake up every morning at nine and grab for the morning paper. Then I look at the obituary page. If my name is not on it, I get up.
Benjamin Franklin

If a man could have half of his wishes, he would double his troubles.
Benjamin Franklin

If a man empties his purse into his head, no one can take it from him.
Benjamin Franklin

If all printers were determined not to print anything till they were sure it would offend nobody, there would be very little printed.
Benjamin Franklin

If passion drives you, let reason hold the reins.
Benjamin Franklin

If time be of all things the most precious, wasting time must be the greatest prodigality.
Benjamin Franklin

If you desire many things, many things will seem few.
Benjamin Franklin

If you know how to spend less than you get, you have the philosopher's stone.
Benjamin Franklin

If you would be loved, love and be lovable.
Benjamin Franklin

If you would have a faithful servant, and one that you like, serve yourself.
Benjamin Franklin

If you would know the value of money, go and try to borrow some.
Benjamin Franklin

If you would not be forgotten, as soon as you are dead and rotten, either write things worth reading, or do things worth the writing.
Benjamin Franklin

In general, mankind, since the improvement of cookery, eats twice as much as nature requires.
Benjamin Franklin

In the affairs of this world, men are saved not by faith, but by the want of it.
Benjamin Franklin

In this world nothing can be said to be certain, except death and taxes.
Benjamin Franklin

Industry need not wish.
Benjamin Franklin

It is a grand mistake to think of being great without goodness and I pronounce it as certain that there was never a truly great man that was not at the same time truly virtuous.
Benjamin Franklin

It is easier to prevent bad habits than to break them.
Benjamin Franklin

It is much easier to suppress a first desire than to satisfy those that follow.
Benjamin Franklin

It is only when the rich are sick that they fully feel the impotence of wealth.
Benjamin Franklin

It is the eye of other people that ruin us. If I were blind I would want, neither fine clothes, fine houses or fine furniture.
Benjamin Franklin

It is the working man who is the happy man. It is the idle man who is the miserable man.
Benjamin Franklin

Keep your eyes wide open before marriage, half shut afterwards.
Benjamin Franklin

Laws too gentle are seldom obeyed; too severe, seldom executed.
Benjamin Franklin

Leisure is the time for doing something useful. This leisure the diligent person will obtain the lazy one never.
Benjamin Franklin

Let thy discontents be thy secrets.
Benjamin Franklin

Life's Tragedy is that we get old to soon and wise too late.
Benjamin Franklin

Lost time is never found again.
Benjamin Franklin

Many a long dispute among divines may be thus abridged: It is so. It is not so. It is so. It is not so.
Benjamin Franklin

Many a man thinks he is buying pleasure, when he is really selling himself to it.
Benjamin Franklin

Many foxes grow gray but few grow good.
Benjamin Franklin

Many people die at twenty five and aren't buried until they are seventy five.
Benjamin Franklin

Marriage is the most natural state of man, and... the state in which you will find solid happiness.
Benjamin Franklin

Mine is better than ours.
Benjamin Franklin

Money never made a man happy yet, nor will it. The more a man has, the more he wants. Instead of filling a vacuum, it makes one.
Benjamin Franklin

Most people return small favors, acknowledge medium ones and repay greater ones - with ingratitude.
Benjamin Franklin

Necessity never made a good bargain.
Benjamin Franklin

Never confuse motion with action.
Benjamin Franklin

Never leave that till tomorrow which you can do today.
Benjamin Franklin

Never take a wife till thou hast a house (and a fire) to put her in.
Benjamin Franklin

Nine men in ten are would be suicides.
Benjamin Franklin

Observe all men, thyself most.
Benjamin Franklin

One today is worth two tomorrows.
Benjamin Franklin

Our necessities never equal our wants.
Benjamin Franklin

Rather go to bed without dinner than to rise in debt.
Benjamin Franklin

Rebellion against tyrants is obedience to God.
Benjamin Franklin

Remember not only to say the right thing in the right place, but far more difficult still, to leave unsaid the wrong thing at the tempting moment.
Benjamin Franklin

Remember that credit is money.
Benjamin Franklin

Savages we call them because their manners differ from ours.
Benjamin Franklin

She laughs at everything you say. Why? Because she has fine teeth.
Benjamin Franklin

Since thou are not sure of a minute, throw not away an hour.
Benjamin Franklin

So much for industry, my friends, and attention to one's own business; but to these we must add frugality if we would make our industry more certainly successful. A man may, if he knows not how to save as he gets, keep his nose all his life to the grindstone, and die not worth a grout at last.
Benjamin Franklin

Take time for all things: great haste makes great waste.
Benjamin Franklin

The absent are never without fault, nor the present without excuse.
Benjamin Franklin

The art of acting consists in keeping people from coughing.
Benjamin Franklin

The Constitution only gives people the right to pursue happiness. You have to catch it yourself.
Benjamin Franklin

The definition of insanity is doing the same thing over and over and expecting different results.
Benjamin Franklin

The discontented man finds no easy chair.
Benjamin Franklin

The doors of wisdom are never shut.
Benjamin Franklin

The doorstep to the temple of wisdom is a knowledge of our own ignorance.
Benjamin Franklin

The eye of the master will do more work than both his hands.
Benjamin Franklin

466

The first mistake in public business is the going into it.
Benjamin Franklin

The learned fool writes nonsense in better language that the unlearned - but it's still nonsense.
Benjamin Franklin

The man who trades freedom for security does not deserve nor will he ever receive either.
Benjamin Franklin

The strictest law sometimes becomes the severest injustice.
Benjamin Franklin

The use of money is all the advantage there is in having it.
Benjamin Franklin

The way to see by Faith is to shut the Eye of Reason.
Benjamin Franklin

There are three faithful friends - an old wife, an old dog, and ready money.
Benjamin Franklin

There are three things extremely hard: steel, a diamond, and to know one's self.
Benjamin Franklin

There is no kind of dishonesty into which otherwise good people more easily and frequently fall than that of defrauding the government.
Benjamin Franklin

There never was a truly great man that was not at the same time truly virtuous.
Benjamin Franklin

There was never a good war, or a bad peace.
Benjamin Franklin

They that can give up essential liberty to obtain a little temporary safety deserve neither liberty nor safety.
Benjamin Franklin

Those that won't be counseled can't be helped.
Benjamin Franklin

Those who govern, having much business on their hands, do not generally like to take the trouble of considering and carrying into execution new projects. The best public measures are therefore seldom adopted from previous wisdom, but forced by the occasion.
Benjamin Franklin

Three can keep a secret if two are dead.
Benjamin Franklin

Time is money.
Benjamin Franklin

To follow by faith alone is to follow blindly.
Benjamin Franklin

Tomorrow every fault is to be amended; but tomorrow never comes.
Benjamin Franklin

Tricks and treachery are the practice of fools, that don't have brains enough to be honest.
Benjamin Franklin

Trouble springs from idleness, and grievous toil from needless ease.
Benjamin Franklin

Wars are not paid for in wartime, the bill comes later.
Benjamin Franklin

We are more thoroughly an enlightened people, with respect to our political interests, than perhaps any other under heaven. Every man among us reads, and is so easy in his circumstances as to have leisure for conversations of improvement and for acquiring information.
Benjamin Franklin

We must, indeed, all hang together or, most assuredly, we shall all hang separately.
Benjamin Franklin

Wealth is not his that has it, but his that enjoys it.
Benjamin Franklin

Well done is better than well said.
Benjamin Franklin

What has become clear to you since we last met?
Benjamin Franklin

What's a Sun-Dial in the Shade?
Benjamin Franklin

Whatever is begun in anger ends in shame.
Benjamin Franklin

*When befriended, remember it; when you befriend,
forget it.*
Benjamin Franklin

When in doubt, don't.
Benjamin Franklin

*When men and woman die, as poets sung, his
heart's the last part moves, her last, the tongue.*
Benjamin Franklin

*When will mankind be convinced and agree to settle
their difficulties by arbitration?*
Benjamin Franklin

When you're finished changing, you're finished.
Benjamin Franklin

Where liberty is, there is my country.
Benjamin Franklin

470

Where sense is wanting, everything is wanting.
Benjamin Franklin

Where there's marriage without love, there will be love without marriage.
Benjamin Franklin

Who had deceived thee so often as thyself?
Benjamin Franklin

Who is rich? He that rejoices in his portion.
Benjamin Franklin

Who is wise? He that learns from everyone. Who is powerful? He that governs his passions. Who is rich? He that is content. Who is that? Nobody.
Benjamin Franklin

Wine is constant proof that God loves us and loves to see us happy.
Benjamin Franklin

Wise men don't need advice. Fools won't take it.
Benjamin Franklin

Words may show a man's wit but actions his meaning.
Benjamin Franklin

Work as if you were to live a hundred years. Pray as if you were to die tomorrow.
Benjamin Franklin

Write injuries in dust, benefits in marble.
Benjamin Franklin

You can bear your own faults, and why not a fault in your wife?
Benjamin Franklin

You may delay, but time will not.
Benjamin Franklin

Your net worth to the world is usually determined by what remains after your bad habits are subtracted from your good ones.
Benjamin Franklin

A desire to be observed, considered, esteemed, praised, beloved, and admired by his fellows is one of the earliest as well as the keenest dispositions discovered in the heart of man.
John Adams

Abuse of words has been the great instrument of sophistry and chicanery, of party, faction, and division of society.
John Adams

All the perplexities, confusion and distress in America arise, not from defects in their Constitution or Confederation, not from want of honor or virtue, so much as from the downright ignorance of the nature of coin, credit and circulation.
John Adams

Arms in the hands of citizens may be used at individual discretion... in private self-defense.
John Adams

As much as I converse with sages and heroes, they have very little of my love and admiration. I long for rural and domestic scene, for the warbling of birds and the prattling of my children.
John Adams

Democracy... while it lasts is more bloody than either aristocracy or monarchy. Remember, democracy never lasts long. It soon wastes, exhausts, and murders itself. There is never a democracy that did not commit suicide.
John Adams

Facts are stubborn things; and whatever may be our wishes, our inclinations, or the dictates of our passions, they cannot alter the state of facts and evidence.
John Adams

Fear is the foundation of most governments.
John Adams

Genius is sorrow's child.
John Adams

Great is the guilt of an unnecessary war.
John Adams

Here is everything which can lay hold of the eye, ear and imagination - everything which can charm and bewitch the simple and ignorant. I wonder how Luther ever broke the spell.
John Adams

I always consider the settlement of America with reverence and wonder, as the opening of a grand scene and design in providence, for the illumination of the ignorant and the emancipation of the slavish part of mankind all over the earth.
John Adams

I have accepted a seat in the House of Representatives, and thereby have consented to my own ruin, to your ruin, and to the ruin of our children. I give you this warning that you may prepare your mind for your fate.
John Adams

I must not write a word to you about politics, because you are a woman.
John Adams

I must study politics and war that my sons may have liberty to study mathematics and philosophy.
John Adams

If we do not lay out ourselves in the service of mankind whom should we serve?
John Adams

In politics the middle way is none at all.
John Adams

Liberty cannot be preserved without a general knowledge among the people.
John Adams

Liberty, according to my metaphysics is a self-determining power in an intellectual agent. It implies thought and choice and power.
John Adams

My country has contrived for me the most insignificant office that ever the invention of man contrived or his imagination conceived.
John Adams

Old minds are like old horses; you must exercise them if you wish to keep them in working order.
John Adams

Power always thinks it has a great soul and vast views beyond the comprehension of the weak.
John Adams

Power always thinks... that it is doing God's service when it is violating all his laws.
John Adams

Property is surely a right of mankind as real as liberty.
John Adams

Remember, democracy never lasts long. It soon wastes, exhausts, and murders itself. There never was a democracy yet that did not commit suicide.
John Adams

The Declaration of Independence I always considered as a theatrical show. Jefferson ran away with all the stage effect of that... and all the glory of it.
John Adams

The essence of a free government consists in an effectual control of rivalries.
John Adams

The happiness of society is the end of government.
John Adams

The Hebrews have done more to civilize men than any other nation. If I were an atheist, and believed blind eternal fate, I should still believe that fate had ordained the Jews to be the most essential instrument for civilizing the nations.
John Adams

The right of a nation to kill a tyrant in case of necessity can no more be doubted than to hang a robber, or kill a flea.
John Adams

There are two educations. One should teach us how to make a living and the other how to live.
John Adams

There is danger from all men. The only maxim of a free government ought to be to trust no man living with power to endanger the public liberty.
John Adams

Think of your forefathers! Think of your posterity.
John Adams

When people talk of the freedom of writing, speaking or thinking I cannot choose but laugh. No such thing ever existed. No such thing now exists; but I hope it will exist. But it must be hundreds of years after you and I shall write and speak no more.
John Adams

While all other sciences have advanced, that of government is at a standstill - little better understood, little better practiced now than three or four thousand years ago.
John Adams

Yesterday the greatest question was decided which ever was debated in America; and a greater perhaps never was, nor will be, decided among men. A resolution was passed without one dissenting colony, "that these United Colonies are, and of right ought to be, free and independent States."
John Adams

References

Chapter 1   Radio Free Europe/Radio Liberty
Official Government Archives Of
Belarus

Chapter 2   Wikipedia

Chapter 3   Wikipedia

Chapter 4   Driving Techniques For Escape And
Evasion by Ronald George

Chapter 5   Internet Sources Including:

http://www.angelfire.com/clone2/darkcorner/tailing.html
http://155.217.58.58/cgi-bin/atdl.dll/fm/19-20/Ch2.htm
http://www.abcinvestigators.com/Surveillance.htm
http://www.stangrist.com/surveillance.htm
http://www.episode00.com/leifpe.html
http://www.skrewdriver.org.uk/zogopp3.html

Chapters 6 –16 United States Military
Survival Manuals
Russian Military Survival Manuals

Chapter 17   KUBARK Counterintelligence
Interrogation Central Intelligence
Agency, United States

Chapter 18   United States methods of execution
provided by the Clark County
Indiana (United States) Office of the
Prosecuting Attorney